3-4-2022

Mary —
 I've still got the socks!
 And... I still remember you with a smile! (On my face *and* yours!) ☺

Work(s)
in
Progress

Enjoy these random thoughts, and let's make sure you let me know when you'll be in Maine. We've got 42 years to catch up on. I'm not sure I'll be able to remember anything additional.

Be happy, and help others be that way, too!

Work(s) in Progress

Andy Young

Illustrations
by Mary Couturier

Jackanapes Publishing
CUMBERLAND, MAINE

© 2022 Andy Young
Published by Jackanapes Publishing, Cumberland, Maine

All rights reserved. No part of this publication may be reproduced, distributed, or transmitted in any form or by any means without the written permission of the author. Inquiries to Andy can be directed to Harrybright13@gmail.com.

Mary Couturier's drawings appear on pages 5, 9, 10, 25, 43, 45, 100, 105, 106, 117 and 174.

Cover and book design by Lori Harley.

ISBN: 978-0-692-03760-7

This book is dedicated to...

my parents, William and Mary Young, who infused me with honesty, integrity, and work ethic;

my siblings, Russell and Carol, and also to my 13 living cousins, whose perpetual support and friendship continue to be energizing and invaluable;

and my children, Willie, Tommy, and Maddie (forever Young to me), whose individual and collective presence reminds me of the importance of continuing to do the right thing(s), every day.

Contents

Introduction	*ix*
Foreword	*xi*

PART 1: Things That Matter   1

CONTINUING EDUCATION	Education's Two Most Important Months	3
	Easier Isn't Always Better	5
	Important Advice	7
	Report Card Time for Teachers	9
	The Importance of Giving and of Paying Attention	11
	The True Value of High School Sports	13
	Why a Prom?	15
	Channeling Dad's Ten Rules for Living	17
	How (Not) to Name Your Son	19
	Proper Snow Removal Etiquette	21
MEMOIR	Scammed by Skimming Scum	23
	I Found a Quarter!	25
	The Credit Card is Missing!	27
	Red Cross	29
	Heat Wave? Nahhh!	31
	74 Inches Are Just Fine	33
	Designating Great Memories	35
	A Very Brief Comeback	37
	It's Just a Rock	39
	The Role(s) Parents Play	41
JUST FOR FUN	One, Two, Three…Happy Birthday!	43
	Tastes Like Water	45
	Misunderstood March	47
	Reasons to Believe in Reincarnation	49
	Andy	51
	I Won the Lottery…again!	53
	So Close to a Bingo	55
	Vowing Never to Say, "Never Say Never"	57
	A Heartbreaking Void for an Unfortunate Few	60
	Knowledgeable Historians Agree: February is Fabulous!	62

FAREWELLS	A Ful (But All Too Brief) Life	65
	Gone, But Only Physically	67
	He Made Sports Fans Think	69
	Sleeper Holds and Willingly Suspending Disbelief	71
	The Greatest	73
	Leaving Quietly? Howe Appropriate.	75
	Farewell to Three Athletic Legends	77
	Wanton Murderer or Bold Reformer?	79
	Making a Lasting Impact with Kindness and Decency	81
	Still a Certainty, Even for Childhood Heroes	83

PART 2: Things That Matter Less 85

MOSTLY BASEBALL	The Designated Hitter Rule Must Go!	87
	It's Been a Lifetime Since the Mets Were Relevant	89
	A Pronounced Change in Major League Baseball	91
	Changes in the All-Star Game, for Better *and* for Worse	93
	Careful What You Wish For, Cubs Fans	95
	On Reading and Aging	97
	How Far Has Baseball Receded?	99
	Happy Birthday Moe	101
	Will Bill Buckner Get the Legacy He Deserves?	103
AT/ON THE FIELD	Just Let Them Play	105
	Accurately Gauging How Victory Feels	107
	Delusions of Grandeur on the Pitch	109
	Seeing an All-Time Great Before He Was Famous	111
	How Others See Us	113
	September 23, 1967	115
	Falling In and Out of Love with the Mets	117
	One Thing Baseball Taught Me	119
	Opening Day 1984	121
OTHER SPORTS	The Teflon League	125
	A Sport in Need of Repair	127
	Random Thoughts on Soccer	129
	A Sports-related Epiphany	131
	Super Bowl 41	133
	Eagerly Anticipating My Yearly Football Game	135
	How Soon Will Society Evolve?	137
	Which Contemporary Athletes Merit Admiration?	139
	Finally Kicking the Habit	141

THE WAY IT IS	Gracias Edgar. Ahora, adiós!	143
	Business as Usual in the Sports Business	146
	Why Baseball Won't Punish Steroid Users	148
	On Setting (and Breaking) Records	150
	An Autumn Gift from the Red Sox: Time!	152
	What Makes People Angry?	154
	Baseball's Changing Status	156
	NBA Work Stoppage is an Opportunity to Learn	158
	The Legacies of Two Red Sox Outfielders	160

PART 3: Pungent Social Commentary   163

OUTSIDE THE BOX	Born in November? Don't Seek the Presidency!	165
	Why Not, Indeed?	168
	Getting Down to 24	170
	Continuing Litterology Research	172
	Time to Kiss Wednesdays Goodbye	174
	An Eminently Adjustable Number	176
	Learning about the Few and the Proud	183
	Why Everyone Should Love Loving Day	185
	Want Me to Return Your Call? Here's How!	187
UNVARNISHED OPINION	Applying a Mother's Wisdom	189
	Justice or Vengeance?	192
	Two Memorable American Impact Makers	194
	Best of the Also-rans	196
	Fired Up about Our Fearless Leader	198
	Why He Must Fail	200
	Issuing a Much-needed Apology	202
	Troubling Dreams, Both Bizarre *and* Plausible	204
THANKFULNESS	An Overdue Admission	206
	A Hull of a Trip	208
	Hooray! Another Storm!	210
	Appreciating (Not Dreading) a Milestone	212
	Time to Take Out the Trash	214
	What a Famous Celebrity and I Know for Sure	216
	'Tis the Season to Get Good Mail	218
	Trying to Accurately Count Blessings	220

SUMMING IT UP	The Breaks Really *Do* Even Up	223
	Holding a Grudge	225
	Graduation Speech, June 9, 2019	227
Acknowledgements		*231*

Introduction

There's been much talk lately about various and sundry forms of privilege. Some staunchly assert certain people have benefitted unfairly from them. Others maintain, with equal or greater stridency, that no such privilege(s) exist. Aided and abetted by opinionators who've achieved obscene wealth and power by doing their utmost to keep our nominally united nation divided, some have gone to the extent of attempting, through litigation, to prevent even the discussion of such matters in the public schools of their communities.

As a heterosexual white male who stands over six feet tall, speaks unaccented English, and doesn't dress flamboyantly, I'm not in the position of being able to deny the existence of certain privileges. I've benefited from nearly all of them, including the biggest one of all: through no fault of my own I began life in the United States of America.

Like other children who had the good fortune of being born here to parents who were caring, gainfully employed, and fluent in English, I grew up harboring certain hopes and dreams. And thanks to having access to (for starters) hot and cold running water, three meals a day, reliable shelter, and breathable air, I was free to pursue some of them once I matured. Which, after thirty or so years of practice, I sort of did.

Some of my early aspirations were, as it turned out, not wholly realistic. (This sounds better than admitting they were largely delusional.) A prime example of this occurred when I decided that I wanted to play centerfield for the New York Mets. At the time I settled on that particular ambition a fellow named Tommie Agee already had that job. Plus I was eleven years old, and subsequent research showed there hadn't (and to date still haven't) ever been any eleven-year-old major league baseball players.

Other ambitions which came and went as years went by: mailman, cross-country trucker, goalie for the Minnesota North Stars (I loved their green uniforms), and boy toy for actress Teri Garr. Those particular objectives were quashed by, in order: unsubtle parental disapproval, learning about loneliness and stratospheric road taxes, an inability to skate (and later by the demise of the Minnesota North Stars), and Ms. Garr either being unaware of my existence, or having an understandable reluctance to become involved with any prepubescent would-be centerfielders.

Even after my three-decade adolescence ended and I began aiming at more realistic aspirational targets, writing a second book wasn't anywhere on the radar, primarily because I hadn't yet begun to think of myself as a writer. However, even if my goal had been to become the next Art Buchwald, Carl Hiaasen, Dave Barry, Erma Bombeck, or some hybrid version of all of them, authoring a second book requires having composed and published a first one, something I had, until seven years ago, neglected to do.

But in the fall of 2014, with the help of a couple of friends (they probably know who they are), a couple of siblings (they **definitely** know who **they** are), and an incredibly patient proofreader/tech-savvy publishing specialist who left the industry immediately after laying out *Young Ideas* (an event which to this day I fervently hope was coincidental), I did indeed become a published author. This allowed me to consider myself the equal (in a very small way) of, among others, Charles Dickens, Jane Austen, William Shakespeare, and Maya Angelou, assuming that they too had to pay someone to first get themselves into print.

The cover of my first book, *Young Ideas,* accurately touted its contents as "Twelve extraordinarily thought-provoking essays (and 58 others) by an exceptionally ordinary human being." And although seven years have passed since that anthology's initial publication, I'm still a fervent believer in truth in advertising. That's why I can assure you, now that I've accumulated 84 additional months of writing (and life) experience, that the ratio of essays in this book that are *actually worth reading (*compared to those just there to fill otherwise blank pages) has leapt from the 17% touted in *Young Ideas* to what some (okay...me) estimate to being as high as 30% of the stories contained in these pages. It could even be as high as 35%, but I've always felt that it's better to err on the side of modesty than it is to overstate the gravity of one's self-proclaimed "accomplishments."

In addition, this collection contains 106 columns, a 51% increase over its predecessor. Not only that, but if you buy (or hopefully have already purchased) this book at the cover price, know that the written discourses you'll be reading (and hopefully enjoying) are costing you a mere 15 cents apiece, a bargain compared to the 18.5 cents per essay you'd have paid to read the contents of *Young Ideas.*

But enough about math. This slender volume is intended to provide pleasurable exercise for the mind's creative side. The author wishes to assert for the record that any activation of logical and/or scientific thoughts brought about by reading any of the selections contained in this book of this is unintended, and as such he hereby absolves himself from any liability should the reading of these essays precipitate any unfortunate or untimely left-brain stimulation, or overstimulation.

And now that that's been established, indulge yourself!

But please do so non-litigiously.

Andy Young
July 31, 2021

Foreword

Some twenty years ago, when I was serving as English Department chair at Kennebunk High School, several colleagues and I were tasked with interviewing candidates to replace a retiring fellow teacher. One of the applicants was a tall, affable, and enthusiastic fellow on the cusp of middle age who was as yet untested as a teacher. For the previous two decades he'd been affiliated with various baseball teams in a number of roles. He'd recently completed a teacher certification program and now was ready to take on a "grown up job," as he put it.

Though there were a number of younger and more experienced applicants, this tall, smiling, enthusiastic rookie made a deep impression on our small committee, and we recommended him to the administration as our choice. The past two decades have shown that our instinct was correct. Andy Young has become a superb teacher. He's an asset and collegial friend to his fellow staff members, a role model for younger educators, an enthusiastic supporter of his school, and most important of all, an excellent teacher, mentor, and friend to any student who crosses the threshold of his classroom.

If he or she is to have any effect on young lives, a good teacher must, above all else, be real. Kids can spot a fake in a matter of minutes. A successful teacher must also have a sense of humor, which Andy has in abundance. Kindness, humility, and empathy make a difference in the classroom. He makes it his business to set aside time if a student needs to talk, to share the load with a caring adult. His compassion and his decency as a person allow his students to develop trust in him as a teacher and as a friend. An experienced teacher has a sixth sense and can usually tell when a student is carrying more than he or she can handle. He (or she) should be above all a humanist, a close observer of those around them.

For most of the twenty years Andy has taught, he has lived some thirty-seven miles from his workplace, which has meant that he has to leave his home frightfully early in the morning five days a week. Still, he has managed to arrive at school and be in his classroom long before most of his colleagues. And after a full workday (and often endless afterschool meetings) he has driven home to coach whatever activities his children might have been involved with at the time, or to referee youth soccer or umpire Little League games in his hometown. To relax, he might then ride his bike five or six miles, stopping to pick up trash along the road, one of the small things he insists is the duty of all citizens. He is interested in town affairs, and though he eschews television, he remains on top of major issues and events that affect us all. He's not afraid to speak up or, more often, to write about an injustice when he sees it affecting the greater good.

Amazingly, through all of these responsibilities and obligations, he has written a weekly newspaper column for most of his teaching years. I rather think these regular reflections are Andy's time to react to the world around him. Because he is always the gracious, ever smiling, dependable shoulder on whom others may lean, writing is no doubt his time finally to relax, to let go and say his piece. He sees the tragic, the ridiculous, the outrageous, the touching, the shortcomings, the triumphs, and the failures of the world around him, and somehow manages to write about them in clear, sometimes frustrated, and usually amusing terms.

You are holding Andy's second collection of essays. Like the first, the topics are eclectic, but they are arranged in convenient groupings such as "Continuing Education," "Farewells," "Baseball," "Unvarnished Opinion," and "Thankfulness," among others. Thus, the reader may skip about by title and read a sampling, or by grouping to find commentary on a somewhat similar subject, or simply read them from the first to the last. As you become more familiar with his style, you will note some interesting peculiarities, such as his fascination with numbers, or dates, or birthdays. Always, however, these interests of his are used to make the reader consider some larger issue or question, to make one THINK.

The bottom line: these are ruminations from a man whose writing reflects all the qualities that make him an excellent teacher, coach, and parent. They may be humorous, and the topics may show some quirkiness. They are self-deprecating and the joke, if there is one, is always on the writer. Most of these are pieces that teach us something that is important. There are stories that gently urge readers to be better stewards of the world around us, whether the subject is the environment, our relationships with one another, or our democracy. Reading Andy is always fun. His is a voice here of kindness, of concern for the "other guy" first, and of respect for the society that we will pass on to the next generation.

He turned out to be a darn good teacher indeed.

Joe Foster
Kennebunk High School
English Department
1969–2007

PART 1

Things That Matter

The 40 essays in this section are included here because they were, at least at one time, of consequence to me, and also to a smattering of readers of the (now defunct) Falmouth *Community Leader,* the (now defunct) Yarmouth *Notes,* the (now defunct) Biddeford *Journal Tribune,* and/or the (still extant) *Portland Press Herald.* I hope that by the time my children reach my current age, the topics discussed in these essays will, in some small way, still matter, and that newspapers (and books like this one) will still exist.

SECTION 1

Continuing Education

Education's Two Most Important Months

June 20, 2015

When it comes to acquiring skills, knowledge, and the ability to use them, there are no unimportant days, weeks or months for adolescents. For every youthful "Work in Progress," learning is an ongoing process; there's no telling when something will take place inside or outside of a classroom that will spark a life-changing epiphany.

But while there truly isn't any unimportant time in any single school day, there *are* certain months of year some see as more educationally significant than others.

September is when students return from their extended summer break and get their first and only opportunity to make a favorable initial impression on their new peers, not to mention the teachers whose classes they'll attend for the next ten months.

Final exams are administered in June. These provide tangible evidence of how efficiently and well a young person is learning. Such end-of-year assessments can impact the immediate and long-term futures of every youthful individual. June is also when high school seniors graduate to the next chapter of their lives.

But identifying education's most impactful month(s) is best illustrated with an analogy. Imagine a 16-year-old distance runner who trains diligently for the entire school year. By the end of her spring track season, she's consistently running five-minute miles. But then, after winning every race she runs, she spends her summer lying on the couch, chatting on social media, playing mind-numbing video games, and washing down junk food with caffeine-and-sugar-laced "liquid refreshment."

Come September there's no chance she'll run a five-minute mile. In fact, if she follows the regimen described above, she'd be lucky to waddle one in twice that time. Anyone who has worked hard to achieve excellence in any field of endeavor would suffer a similar fate after taking two full months off from exercising their talent, be it athletic, artistic, or intellectual. No serious young athlete, musician, or artist would take a ten-week hiatus from practicing what he or she excels at and realistically expect to resume their chosen activity sixty days later at a high level of performance.

So why then do so many young people, often with the tacit approval of their parents, totally abstain from reading and writing every July and August?

Aspiring to play a solo at the school concert, help win a basketball championship, or earn top student honors in a vocational program are all admirable goals, not to mention impressive achievements. But there is nothing physical or artistic a high school student can achieve which matters nearly as much in the long run as continuing to hone their thinking skills without interruption.

As disappointing as it would be to watch a gifted athlete fritter away his or her summer indolently, allowing a young person to let his/her brain lie fallow every July and August is exponentially worse. Those who annually take two months off from mental exertion are not only squandering potentially valuable growth time, they're setting a dangerous precedent. Young people who habitually disengage their brain every summer often find that doing so for longer stretches gets easier as they age. And as far too many genial slackers find out too late, attractive opportunities for those who have willfully or involuntarily slowed or ceased their intellectual growth are few and far between.

Students who take July and August off from reading and writing arrive back at school in September with literacy skills similar to the physical capabilities of the athlete who spent the summer physically inert. The difference: in ten years, high school athletic trophies will be dust collectors, but the abilities to read, write, listen, speak, and think will go a long way toward determining how much fulfillment, satisfaction, success and happiness an individual will attain during his or her remaining time on Earth.

People who believe June and September are educationally essential are absolutely correct. But the two months in between them are potentially, for better or worse, far more impactful. ●

Easier Isn't Always Better

December 20, 2006

Not long ago a young man in a study hall I was supervising asked me what 24 times 6 was. I informed him it was 144. A moment later he raised his hand and asked me what the product of 57 and 12 was. Without hesitation I replied that it was 684. Not long after that he asked me to multiply 15 by 22. I told him that the answer was 330. The student looked at me in utter amazement. "How do you do that?" he asked.

"Do what?" I asked.

"Multiply numbers in your head like that," he said. "That's amazing. Are you some sort of genius, Mr. Young?"

I smiled, then informed him that not only was I not even remotely close to being a genius, but by merely asking that question he had likely caused several of my former elementary and secondary school teachers to start spontaneously spinning in their graves. I can multiply numbers relatively quickly in my head because I learned to do so at a young age. People born prior to the 1960s learned the addition, subtraction, multiplication, and division tables by rote. Later on we mastered algebra by doing all of the problems out on paper. There were no such things as electronic calculators.

As a high school English teacher who currently use words far more frequently than numbers, I'm finding the basic literacy skills of today's youth are disappearing at least as quickly as the math skills of their parents did a generation ago. Some blame television, video games, and similar electronic devices for the falloff in basic skills, and no doubt they are at least partially correct. However, in my experience the technological innovations which have done the most to hinder education in the United States aren't those which were designed to fill leisure time, but rather those which were produced with the stated purpose of aiding students with their learning.

Some of the brightest students I have today think that there are two O's in the word "lose." Relatively few of them can differentiate between the words "quiet" and "quite," and hardly any can spell the word "definitely." I cannot begin to give an accurate estimate of how many essays I get with the word "defiantly" where "definitely" definitely belongs.

Most contemporary students in these parts have had access to a personal computer since they were old enough to reach the keyboard. Almost all these devices are equipped with programs that automatically check the user's spelling and/or grammar, and in the short run that's great. However, in the long run it's considerably less than great, because today's students feel no more need to be adept spellers than they do to be able to multiply two-digit numbers in their heads. Another drawback of technology: as computer use increases, legible handwriting (and subsequently note taking) decreases. Thanks to the availability of the Internet, putting together a research paper is much easier and far less time-consuming today than it was a generation ago. It's also much easier to obtain unreliable information and/or plagiarize such assignments.

The current generation is not the first whose basic life skills seem, to some of their elders, significantly less than those of their predecessors. In his relatively brief life, my father rebuilt and installed several automobile engines. He helped put an addition onto our home, and after he finished doing the electrical wiring for it, he constructed a fireplace and chimney on the side of the house brick by brick. He fashioned radio-controlled model airplanes that really flew, and also did several home plumbing jobs that looked nearly as unattractive as they smelled. In short, he was, when necessary, a carpenter, a mason, an electrician, a plumber, and a mechanic. I possess none of those skills. If my life depended on it, I could probably change a tire, but when the need arises I prefer to call AAA. It's easier.

All four of my grandparents grew up without electricity, so I can only imagine how little they thought of the basic capabilities of their own offspring.

Things have changed a great deal between the late 19th century, when my parents' parents were born, and the early 21st, when my children began their lives. The only thing that has remained constant during that time span: the more one ages, the clearer it becomes that easier is not always better. ●

Important Advice

April 17, 2008

Everyone receives countless pieces of advice in his or her life. Some of it is even helpful.

It's hard to identify the most important bit of wisdom necessary for coping with one's everyday earthly existence. However, if self-preservation is your concern, consider this helpful hint: under no circumstances should you startle a person who has been formally trained in hand-to-hand combat.

Years ago when I was serving as a basketball coach at my old high school, our team had a midweek away game against a school that was a significant distance from ours. Since we wouldn't be returning until late in the evening, I decided to stay at school that night. The alternative was driving home over icy streets, getting four or five hours of sleep, and then motoring back over the same wintry roads the following morning. To me the more sensible course of action was to sleep on the floor of the boy's locker room. Another reason my decision seemed sound: I'd be saving the gas required to get me to and from my place of residence that night.

The morning of the game Coach Anderson, one of the gym teachers and a habitual early arriver to the athletic offices, expressed curiosity about why I had a sleeping bag, two lunches, and two sets of clean clothes with me. After I explained my rationale he furrowed his brow, nodded, and then without comment went back to whatever he was doing. Coach Anderson was universally known as the "nice" gym teacher; anyone who dressed appropriately for his class and gave even the slightest effort received an "A" in phys ed. However, away from the students the coach was an intense individual who got to school promptly at 5:30 each morning to prepare the speech he'd be making to the faithful at the house of worship he attended each week. In addition, on occasion he'd suffer from paralyzing migraine headaches, which were likely byproducts of the harrowing time he spent in Vietnam as a United States Marine. He rarely talked about his experiences there. However, he did on at least one occasion every year warn each of his colleagues on the coaching staff to NEVER sneak up on him, even as a joke. He never explained why he made that request, and none of us ever asked. Word on the street was that in the Marine Corps Coach Anderson had been taught how to jab his hand so hard into an enemy's stomach that he could actually grab the man's spine and snap it, all in one motion. No one wanted to know whether or not the rumor was true.

That night both the varsity and JV teams lost their games, so the bus ride home was a quiet one. When we arrived back at the school the players and the other coaches dispersed rapidly, as I had anticipated. Once the last person had left, I descended the stairs that led to the subterranean locker room, brushed my teeth, unrolled my sleeping bag, and shut off the light. It was so dark that when I held a hand up in front of my face and wiggled my fingers, I couldn't detect even the slightest motion. It had been a long day, and despite how hard the carpetless cement floor was, I quickly fell asleep.

About five hours (but what seemed like about 30 seconds) later, I groggily became aware of the sound of jingling keys, which was followed by the appearance of a bright and rapidly widening sliver of light. Coach Anderson was arriving promptly at 5:30, whistling a merry tune and preparing to start his morning routine. He obviously was not expecting to see a semiconscious human being in a sleeping bag lying in the middle of the floor in his office. The high-pitched sound that emerged from his throat was enough to wake the dead. As he let out his primal scream, he assumed a position that he had most likely learned during combat training. He then picked up the sleeping bag (with me inside it), pulled it to a point where my face was about a millimeter from his, and shouted, "DON'T EVER DO THAT!"

In retrospect it's remarkable that my sleeping bag didn't need laundering, or outright disposal. Suddenly wide awake, I indicated to Coach Anderson by nodding, vigorously and wide-eyed, that I would never do that again, whatever "that" was.

And I never have. ●

Report Card Time for Teachers

June 26, 2009

It's been two weeks since the last of this year's final exams were administered at the high school where I teach English. Grades were due the next day, and report cards were presumably mailed out shortly thereafter. The 850 or so students at the school have begun their summer vacation and/or jobs, as have the faculty and staff.

While the availability of student grades on the websites of individual schools has changed the gravity final report cards have in some homes, there is another unofficial evaluation that, if thoughtfully and correctly given, can weigh heavily on the future performances of both students and their instructors. Those are the ones given by reflective teachers to themselves.

Allowing a week or so to decompress is probably a good idea for an educator interested in doing a fair self-evaluation, and fortunately for teachers, most of whom are at least as demanding of themselves as they are of their students, theirs is a job that allows just such an opportunity.

At Kennebunk High, where I've taught for seven years, most students get between six and eight grades, depending on how heavy an academic load they've chosen to carry. Ideally only those who show outstanding progress and do superior work earn high marks; those who do nothing or don't absorb the required material are assigned failing ones.

Instructors who are honest should assign themselves as many grades as they have students. For me that would mean about 80 different grades, one for each young person who took a class I taught during the just-completed academic year. And while I didn't give myself a lot of flawless evaluations, I'm proud of the few I did earn.

I gave myself an A for a student I had in an elective class on Sports in Literature last semester. He was a self-described reluctant reader and considered himself sub-standard as a writer, but by the end of the course was much improved in both areas. He asked important questions during class discussions, read voraciously, produced thoughtful written work, and earned the respect of his classmates. More importantly though, he finished the course genuinely caring about the quality of his writing, speaking, and thinking.

Unfortunately not all the grades I earned this year were that high. Some young people in that particular class put little effort into their work, which was doubly disappointing since it was an elective (rather than required) course. Students presumably *want* to take such a class, so failing to motivate an individual to put forth his or her best efforts makes me look hard in the mirror and at least *consider* the possibility that not everything I did was effective. No one method is guaranteed to be productive for getting the most out of every student in every class, but that's no excuse for an instructor to stop trying to obtain each pupil's best efforts. A class consisting of 18 assorted members often requires 18 slightly different methods of presenting the material, not all of which always succeed.

My efforts clearly didn't pan out with the seven individuals who failed a course they took with me this year. Four of them have yet to pass any English course at our school, but that doesn't make me feel any better. A teacher's job is to help everyone, and when someone doesn't complete the minimum requirements necessary to earn credit for a certain class, both the student and the teacher involved have failed. The inability to connect with some youthful individuals is inevitable, but that doesn't make my failure to impact a young person entrusted to me any less disappointing.

Realistic teachers know the vast majority of grades we earn in a given academic year are incompletes. At this point it's hard for students to know for sure what (if any) effect a particular class (and the adult who teaches it) has had on them. The teachers I remember most vividly from my own time in school were the ones who treated me with kindness and respect; the content of what they taught was usually secondary. It took me until at least age 30 to appreciate what some of my teachers did (or tried to do) for me. It's likely today's teens are no more perceptive about the long-term significance of certain things than I was back in the late 1970s.

Bottom line: if in a decade or two I encounter a pair of former students who can't remember who Shylock, Holden Caulfield, or Atticus Finch were, I won't necessarily be crushed. But if at that point they still haven't figured out the importance of being kind, respecting everyone they encounter, and thinking independently, then I'd know that in at least a couple of cases I'd failed to do my job effectively ten or twenty years earlier. ●

The Importance of Giving and of Paying Attention

December 31, 2018

The challenge of being a high school English teacher is to bring out the latent creative abilities in young people. Moving adolescents to read, write, listen, speak, and think can be accomplished through a myriad of methods. Given a variety of literature and a bit of imagination there's no limit to what a motivated, enthusiastic individual can help students accomplish. Having the opportunity to be such an educator is both a privilege ***and*** a pleasure.

I've always pitied colleagues whose content areas are more concrete. Take boring old math, for example. Addition, subtraction, multiplication, and division never change. The same goes for algebra; 2x plus 2x has always been 4x, just as 2x *times* 2x will always be four times x squared. The angles of a triangle will forever add up to 180 degrees, the diameter of a circle is always twice the radius, and sines, cosines, and secants remain the same as they were back when I was in high school myself not paying attention, and thus failing to grasp their alleged significance.

None of that is secret, but here's something that is: we public educators are compensated far more equitably than many people suspect. I realized that at the tail end of last month when I reconciled my 2018 finances and found my checking account had a significant surplus!

Naturally there are some extenuating circumstances. There are no cable bills, since I've chosen to have a TV-free home. The two-thousand-dollars-per-column fee I get every week from every newspaper that publishes my essays makes an impact, as does the $500 monthly rent I charge each of my children. (I feed the thirteen-year-old for free, but the older ones pay extra for that.) Still, seeing a black, four-digit bottom line was nothing short of shocking. When I double-checked the accounting, everything was accurate. I'm square with the mortgage, power, phone, internet, and water companies. I made every car payment on time, and my taxes are paid in full.

Ecstatic over my unexpected windfall, I quickly returned to reality. While it was tempting to arrange a cruise down the Nile, a swim with turtles off the Galapagos Islands, or a flight to Australia to find out if the little whirlpool really does spin backward when the toilet's flushed there, I couldn't in good conscience spend the entire bonanza on myself.

But it took two famous philosophers to remind me you can't take it with you, either. Denzel Washington observed in his graduation speech to Dillard University's Class of 2015, "You'll never see a U-Haul behind a hearse." And Sir Thomas Browne, who to my knowledge never penned anything I've ever disagreed with, wrote (in 1642), "Charity begins at home." Thus inspired, I decided to spread my good fortune around locally.

The food bank received a donation; its very existence should remind those of us who aren't food insecure just how fortunate we are. And knowing the importance of encouraging reading (and the love of it) in the young, I lavished money on a quartet of libraries: two near where I live, and another pair located in the district where I teach.

I also made a donation to Maine Public Broadcasting, which may seem counterintuitive, given my TV-lessness. But given the crass self-interest of the commercial networks, MPBN provides an important service. They also produce and broadcast "Maine High School Bowl" every winter. Modeled after "College Bowl," a student quiz show that was nationally televised from 1959 to 1970, the MPBN version features teams comprised of six students from sixteen different Maine high schools in a single-elimination tournament that tests both the youthful contestants' ability to recall knowledge quickly and their coolness under fire. Because the episodes are filmed in advance, I had a chance to witness a taping of the program last month, and what goes on behind the scenes is fascinating.

Full disclosure (and to reassure readers I am not a creepy, middle-aged weirdo who goes to TV studios just to sit around looking at bunches of random juveniles): one of my offspring is on a team participating in this year's "Maine High School Bowl." I'm sworn to secrecy about what transpired on the show I saw pre-recorded, but… well, while I *still* won't purchase a television, I do plan on visiting someone who's got one once I find out exactly when the program airs.

Writing all those checks to deserving organizations reminded me it truly **is** better to give than to receive; nothing beats the feeling of helping others. The unadulterated gratification all that altruism gave me didn't wear off until last week, when I learned my checking account was overdrawn. By a lot.

Stupid decimal points. Maybe I *should* have paid better attention in those boring math classes. ●

The True Value of High School Sports

November 7, 2017

Only two of Maine's 259 high school varsity soccer teams finished 2017 undefeated and untied: the Yarmouth boys, who collected their 4th consecutive Class B title with a 2-1 victory over Winslow, and the Yarmouth girls, who won their 2nd straight Class B Gold Ball with a 9-0 crushing of Presque Isle.

The now four-time defending Class B boys state champion Clippers were dominant this season, scoring 76 goals while allowing only ten. But it probably wasn't coincidence they didn't reach double-digits in any of their 14 wins. Good coaches do all they can to avoid embarrassing an opponent, partly out of common decency but also because the smart ones know that in sports as in life, what goes around often comes around. The Clippers won one game 9-0 and scored seven goals in four others, but I know from experience it's sometimes difficult for a highly skilled team to avoid amassing high goal totals against an undermanned opponent.

Nearly thirty years ago a high school junior varsity soccer team I led walloped an outclassed opponent 11-0 despite my making every possible effort to keep the score down. The opposing coach understood the situation and wasn't upset, but I felt far worse after that game than I did several months later when the basketball team I assisted absorbed a 104-39 beating from a far superior opponent that was still applying a full-court press in the 4th quarter. The difference? When our side was getting slaughtered, I had no control over the opposing coach's tactics, but when my squad was superior, I felt at least partially responsible for a one-sided drubbing that didn't benefit either team. Nothing good comes from a strong team humiliating an inferior one (in any sport), and doing so does a disservice to all involved.

Interscholastic and youth sports are important, but just *how* impactful they are is a matter of opinion. Athletics are, like other extracurricular activities, a potentially valuable component of a well-balanced childhood, and participating in them should result in multiple positive (or at the very least non-negative) outcomes.

While the season ended triumphantly in Yarmouth, nine Maine varsity teams lost every soccer game they played this fall. Hopefully the players, coaches, and families of the 0-14 boys' high school teams at Skowhegan, Nokomis, Penquis Valley, Dirigo and Machias Memorial and the winless, draw-less female squads at Maine Girls Academy, Fryeburg Academy, Washington Academy, and Valley got something from their just-completed seasons. But getting outscored 137-3 and losing by scores of 12-0, 15-0 (twice) and 16-0, as Washington Academy's girls did, can make finding a silver lining challenging. It's difficult to understand how or why a coach would allow his or her team to humiliate any opponent, particularly one that's already absorbed multiple double-digit beatdowns.

Ideally every well-rounded young athlete would experience being a member of a championship team at some point, but also play for one that loses a championship game, or one that struggles to win any games at all. Everyone should get a chance to be a star or key contributor, but experience the disappointment and frustration of being a seldom-used spare part as well.

The most important takeaways from participating in competitive youth athletics should be, in no particular order: being a part of something bigger than one's self; understanding the value hard work and collaboration play in achieving a goal; realizing the importance of (and getting in the habit of) maintaining physical fitness; learning how to handle success and deal with defeat gracefully; and forging lifelong friendships.

Too much winning can be, in the long run, no better than too much losing.

Several years ago my sons and I witnessed our hometown Greely Rangers win Maine's Class B high school baseball championship. During the raucous on-field postgame celebration someone nearby commented, "This is the greatest day of their lives!" Perhaps, but it would be cause for regret rather than celebration if winning that one game still qualifies as their life's top achievement 20 years from now.

The folks in Yarmouth are no doubt looking forward to watching their two high school teams attempt to repeat as state soccer champions in 2018. But if they really want what's best for their players, perhaps Clipper fans should root for a gut-wrenching loss or two along the way.

Writer's Disclosure: I've coached youth soccer in a neighboring town for nearly a decade, and while we've rarely beaten Yarmouth, their coaches and players have always shown nothing but respect for their opponents.

***Full* disclosure**: Okay, I only remember a Cumberland team besting Yarmouth once. And that was, perhaps not coincidentally, when my son's head coach was someone other than his dad! ●

Why a Prom?

May 4, 2011

"The Lottery" is the late Shirley Jackson's fictional, horrific tale about a drawing that ultimately entitles the "winner" to death by stoning. Arguably the most significant of its several themes: the reluctance of most people to willingly give up established customs or traditions, even those that have become outdated and/or counterproductive.

As a high school teacher, I have come to dread opening up the newspaper on Sunday mornings in May. The great majority of students who attend high school proms have a good time and conduct themselves appropriately, but inevitably some make poor choices, or temporarily lose impulse control. And despite the passionate efforts of local police, school authorities, and independent groups like Mothers Against Drunk Driving, each year too many young people compound such errors in judgment by attempting to operate a motor vehicle. That, combined with the average teenager's inexperience as a driver, all too often results in tragedy.

The number of alcohol-related prom night deaths in relation to the number of attendees at such functions is statistically negligible, but even a single avoidable premature demise of a young person is one too many.

Besides, there are reasons beyond the annual vehicle-related tragedies to wonder why proms are still held. Elitism, whether social, academic, athletic or some combination of the three, is a significant problem at many American high schools. And what makes the social type even more insidious: it's generally unacknowledged, since often as not prom committees consist of students from families for which the annual spring fete is both traditional and affordable. In addition, adults who generously donate time and effort to plan and oversee such events are often (though not always) children of some privilege themselves.

Those claiming Maine lacks diversity are only correct if they're referencing the racial, religious, or ethnic varieties. But the Pine Tree State's socioeconomic diversity is alive and well, even if it's hiding in plain sight. The combination of continuing rises in the cost of living, a lack of available jobs and the increasing difficulty of obtaining a post-high-school degree are turning the gap between "haves" and "have-nots" into a chasm.

Where I teach, some students can't afford prom tickets, let alone the dresses, tuxedos, corsages, boutonnieres and other accoutrements expected of those attending the event. But others, some of whom are the same people who bitterly decry the local school board's proposed $50-per-year student parking fee for next year, are apparently willing to pay several times that amount for one lavish evening on the town.

Elitism would be a significant problem even if were limited to social events and academia, but in 21st-century America it's far more widespread. As long as professional sports, concerts, movies, reality TV, and the internet continue to generate obscene profits and serve as efficient marketing tools for corporations peddling fast food, beauty aids, expensive apparel, credit cards, beer, and other nonessential products, too many youthful Americans will continue unconsciously emphasizing superficiality in their everyday lives. For many today the lure of achieving fame and celebrity is nearly as irresistible as it is unlikely, yet the collective fascination with Charlie Sheen, Lindsay Lohan, Snooki, or similarly shallow, self-centered entertainers and athletes is at an all-time high. Admiration and imitation of such individuals is equal parts frustrating and challenging for responsible parents and educators who are working hard trying to perpetuate the quaint but rapidly disappearing idea that in the long run substance is far more meaningful than style.

As long as school policies are set by wealthy, influential citizens with knowledge of (and the ability to game) the system, it's unlikely academic elitism will disappear. And as long as scores are kept and universities give full scholarships for athletics (though few will go to children from suburban Maine), athletic elitism isn't going away either. But while inherently tilted playing fields in education and sports aren't easily overcome by average citizens, there are ways to combat social elitism, and making thoughtful decisions about how to utilize one's hard-earned money is one way of doing it.

Enthusiastic prom-goers and their parents maintain they're free to spend excessively on one decadent evening because it's traditional, and so it is. But slavery, male-only suffrage, institutionalized racism/sexism, capital punishment, fraternity hazing, brides automatically taking their husband's last name, and debutante balls are or were customary as well. Does anyone seriously believe society is somehow worse off today because many of these "traditions" have been (or are in the process of being) discontinued?

So, why *do* high schools continue to sponsor proms? ●

Channeling Dad's Ten Rules for Living

June 8, 2014

I stink at shopping for Father's Day gifts. But there's a tangible reason for that shortcoming: lack of practice.

My father has been gone since 1974. But now, forty years after his untimely departure, I've finally figured out what to get him for Father's Day: a voice! What follows is some of his lifetime's worth of wisdom, which I was able to collect with the help of a medium, her crystal ball, and a pre-owned Ouija Board. Here he is, from the great beyond:

The planet's getting warmer, yet every day people wait, engines running, at drive-up windows to grab artery-hardening "fast food" they'll eat on the go when they ought to be exercising.

And what's with "storage facilities?" Americans have too much stuff! A family's storage facility should be the closet. If there's enough space for everything there, great! If not, throw it out, or if it's still functional give it to someone who can use it.

But I digress. Here are some simple rules that, if followed faithfully, will contribute to living a more fulfilling life.

Rule Number One: *Treat people the way* **you** *want to be treated. Listen when others speak. Look them in the eye. Tell the truth. Smile at strangers. Help those in need. Pick up after yourself. If you're young and healthy, park as far as you can from the grocery store. You'll benefit from the extra distance you'll walk, plus you'll accumulate plenty of good Karma by leaving the closer spots for those who really need them.* **Everyone** *(with the possible exception of clinically identified masochists) should abide by The Golden Rule.*

Rule Number Two: *Think before you act. If it's a need, do everything morally, ethically, and legally in your power to take care of it. But for a want, think hard about how long you had to work to earn the money the item(s) in question will cost. Then think again. And again. Better impulse control and a little education about the dangers of addiction would virtually eliminate alcoholism, smoking-related illnesses, tooth decay, obesity, and diabetes. Casinos and lotteries wouldn't exist, and celebrated athletes and performers wouldn't command more money in a year than what the average nurse, firefighter, police officer, or teacher earn (combined) in their lifetimes.*

Rule Number Three: *Waste not, want not. Eat everything on your plate. Shut the lights off. Go easy on the heat during winter, and on artificial cooling in summer. Cut down on unnecessary car trips. Reduce. Re-use. Recycle.*

Rule Number Four: *Do nice things for others. You don't need a reason; just do them on general principles. Even better, do your good deed(s) when no one's watching. Shovel someone else's driveway. Pay a stranger's toll. Put your neighbor's trashcans back in her garage. No one knew I tithed for my entire adult life, but the satisfaction I got from helping others bought me far more than all the money I gave away ever could have.*

Rule Number Five: *Be patient. You won't master everything on the first, second, or even third attempt. It's okay to fail, especially if you've tried your hardest. And don't speed through yellow lights! What will you do with the ten seconds you save by putting yourself, those riding with you, and random strangers in other vehicles at risk?*

Rule Number Six: *Avoid video screens. Their misuse and overuse (particularly by the young) discourages initiative, impedes imagination, and devalues literacy skills while simultaneously encouraging and even glorifying laziness, greed, envy, and instant gratification. Had cable television and YouTube been around when the Bible was written, it's likely there would have been eight deadly sins.*

Rule Number Seven: *Be true to your spiritual beliefs (or non-belief). If Islam, Catholicism, Protestantism, Judaism, Buddhism, Atheism, or any other -ism(s) help you and those around you live by Rule Number One, then keep it up. But don't subscribe to theology that derides other faiths. And if you call yourself a "Fundamentalist" anything, calm down.*

Rule Number Eight: *Don't fear long-term independence. Sure, most people would love to be in a long-term relationship with an attractive, thoughtful, sensitive soul mate. But that doesn't always happen right away (or at all). Being independent and single is infinitely preferable to being with Mr. (or Ms.) Wrong.*

Rule Number Nine: *Do what you love and love what you do. Enjoying your job and your co-workers makes the pay a bonus; you'll learn to live within your means. If you toil solely for the money, you'll just have more expensive problems than your happier (and spiritually wealthier) peers.*

*There is no **Rule Number Ten**. I'm tithing in the afterlife as well, and there are less-fortunate spirits who might need an extra Rule to hand down to **their** descendants.* ●

How (Not) to Name Your Son

May 31, 2018

I got some thrilling news from Florida recently: my friend Fawna is going to be a mom.

She's going to be a great one too, since she's selfless, creative, responsible, kind, and above all, patient.

But before she and her husband embark upon the business of feeding, clothing, nurturing, socializing, educating, housing, bathing, and chauffeuring their impending progeny, who is currently negative four months old, they've got an even more daunting task: what to call their offspring.

Deciding what name(s) a child will bear for the rest of his or her life is no small responsibility. According to tireless research conducted by a group of eminent sociologists I've taken great pains to imagine, the job of parenting officially begins at a child's birth, and continues until said person reaches 80 years of age or the baby's parents expire, whichever comes first. That's just one reason why assigning an appropriate name is so vital. Eighty years is a long time under any circumstances, but it's even lengthier for someone who's resented their name (and by extension, the people responsible for it) for as long as he or she has been answering to it.

There is nothing prospective parents need *less* than to have to graciously feign gratitude to individuals who feel they have the right to suggest a name for someone else's not-yet-extant child. Moms- and Dads-to-be have enough on their minds without having to pretend they'll consider some well-meaning relative's earnest suggestion that they name their baby daughter after dear Aunt Bertha.

Not wanting to be the cause of such insincerity myself, I have no intention of offering any silly suggestions regarding a name for anyone's child. In fact, I'm giving my friends in the Sunshine State (as well as expectant couples everywhere) something far more valuable than advice on what to name their soon-to-be-born son: *practical* advice on what NOT to name him!

History has made certain names completely unpalatable. It's been at least two millennia since any sane parents have christened their son "Caligula," "Nero," or "Attila." "Judas" is another appellation that has, due to an unfortunate decision on the part of an individual who once went by that name, pretty much gone the way of the dodo bird.

Some names subtly convey great meaning. Take, for example, a product that succeeds despite an infamous sobriquet. You know darn well Adolph's Meat Tenderizer is the best product of its kind if it continues to sell despite sharing its name, albeit spelled differently, with a mass murderer who tried to ethnic cleanse his way to world domination.

Certain names popular in some cultures are strictly taboo in others. That's why sensible Americans refrain from naming their son "Osama" or "Saddam." While those names are acceptable or even enviable on certain parts of the globe, around here they are all but guaranteed to make their owners the target of all types of abuse. Why subject one's child to preventable persecution? Parents of kids named "Tom," "Dave," or "Mark" will always have the consolation of knowing that if their son is always the last one picked for kickball, well, at least it isn't *entirely* their fault.

With today's 24-hour-per-day, 7-day-per-week news cycle, some names can disappear in nanoseconds. Recent events have likely relegated "Roseanne" and "Harvey" to lengthy stays on the suspended names list. Unlike "Vlad the Impaler," "Harvey" isn't exactly extinct, but it may turn out to be the 21st-century equivalent of "Benito," which is to say it's probably going on an extended hiatus.

But all the Harveys out there shouldn't despair. Names can make comebacks. Two decades ago "Monica" was all but defunct after a young woman bearing that name became a national punch line due to her dalliance with a sitting president who could control neither his libido nor his ego, and who had no problem lying about it. But today Monica Lewinsky is a passionate social activist and eloquent speaker/writer whose efforts to raise awareness of (and hopefully eradicate) cyber-bullying are as admirable as they are inspiring. In fact, were I to become a father again (an unlikely though technically possible scenario), I'd consider naming my daughter "Monica." Not my son though, since doing so might end up making *him* the last pick for kickball.

To summarize, here's everything expectant parents need to know about selecting a name for their male child:

1. Profusely thank everyone who offers you a possible handle for your son.
2. Say no to "Adolf," "Osama," "Manson," and, for the foreseeable future, "Donald" and "Donald Jr."
3. Kindly but firmly ignore everyone else's free advice.
4. Except mine. It's worth every cent you paid for it. ●

Proper Snow Removal Etiquette

December 11, 2017

It was kind of Mother Nature to choose this past weekend to deliver Maine's first significant snowfall of the season. The bulk of the white stuff fell after dark on Saturday night into Sunday, which is far less inconvenient for individuals needing to get to their place of employment in a timely manner Mondays through Fridays.

Because it's dark by 4:15 in the afternoon these days one can imagine anything is going on outside, and until daylight the following morning there's no evidence to the contrary. Late Saturday afternoon I decided the predicted storm was going to blow out to sea and leave just a dusting, one I'd be able to clear off the driveway with a couple of leisurely pushes of a broom the next morning.

Unfortunately, my fantasy was just that. Sunday morning there were six inches of snow on the ground, just as local weather prognosticators had predicted and local weather predictors had prognosticated.

It's a good thing that's all there was. My supply of cheap labor (three children with my last name) was away for the weekend, and their absence reminded me that "Use it or lose it" is an apt expression for many things, including the muscles involved in clearing snow and ice. Since depositing my shovels in the shed last spring I've spent many enjoyable hours walking, hiking or riding a bike. I've also cut grass, raked leaves (and then hauled leaf-laden tarps), washed dishes, vacuumed floors, done laundry, and performed whatever other regular bits of drudgery my current reality requires. However, none of that prepared my body for the workout it got Sunday morning.

Shoveling the driveway and the front walk, raking the roof, clearing the back porch, carving a trail back to the compost pile, and clearing a pathway for the oil man took me nearly three hours, and by the time I finished even my right hip was groaning. I silently told it to pipe down, since the rest of my joints, all of which are original equipment and thus more than a dozen times as old as the titanium complainer, were equally sore.

The season's first snowfall is as good a time as ever to go over a few basic dos and don'ts regarding clearing one's domicile of snow and ice. As one of the foremost authorities on Snow Removal Etiquette, I consider sharing my vast knowledge on this subject a public service.

You're welcome.

Monday through Friday the preferred method of moving snow is quietly, with a broom or a shovel. However, at times this is not feasible. Some people need to leave their homes on weekdays to get to work, buy gas for their generator, refill their oxygen tank, or take care of other vital chores. In cases such as those it is permissible to use one's gas-powered snow blower before 6 AM on weekday mornings, although firing up such noisy devices should be avoided if at all possible. Of course, in a perfect world that would be unnecessary, since all frozen precipitation would be light and fluffy, and no overnight weather event would involve more than three inches of snowfall.

Correction: in a perfect world snow would fall only on Christmas Eve, except in ski areas, where they'd get eight inches of fresh powder every night between Halloween and Easter. But I digress.

One other little-known fact relating to snow removal: according to the Bible, the Koran, and the Torah, five types of people are going straight to Hell, without any chance of redemption. They are, in descending order: people who use the last of the copier paper at the Xerox machine without bothering to refill it; drivers who consistently fail to turn down their high beams; slobs who leave their spent chewing gum on the ground, where it inevitably attaches itself to the sneakers of some innocent passer-by (in my experience, usually someone about six-foot-one with size 14 shoes); people who exhaust the supply of toilet paper in the bathroom and fail to replace it (or in the case of public restrooms, notify someone who can); and finally, cretins who use loud, gas-powered snow blowers before 7 AM on a Sunday morning.

There are actually several places where using such equipment too early in the morning is a crime, and in one nation doing so is punishable by death. Fortunately Saudi Arabia rarely gets the sort of snowfall that requires its swift removal, sparing some of its more impulsive, less thoughtful residents a terrible (though possibly deserved) fate. ●

SECTION 2

Memoir

Scammed by Skimming Scum

July 27, 2017

My children and I took a brief trip to Ottawa, Ontario last month, and when we returned I thought I'd get on the computer and have a look at the balance in my bank account, just to see **how much** we had enjoyed ourselves.

It's a good thing I checked. In addition to the charges for our hotel and a couple of dinners, there was a $63.98 payment to Edible Arrangements and a $90.00 payout to Topman.com, which I subsequently learned is a British company that sells apparel.

I'm reasonably confident I'd remember making an order from Edible Arrangements. As for Topman.com, well, rabbis shop for pork more frequently than I buy clothing. And since I have never, ever purchased **anything** via the Internet, I decided to give my friends at the Credit Union a call.

Until recently I thought a skimmer was either a long-handled apparatus used to remove grass, leaves, and insects from the surface of swimming pools, or a small, flat rock that when flung skillfully skips multiple times off the surface of a lake or pond.

However, it seems 21st-century skimmers are devices used by criminals to grab data off a credit card's magnetic strip. Nearly undetectable, once this kind of skimmer is placed inside an ATM, gas pump or similar machine, it can harvest data from anyone unwittingly using their debit or credit card to buy groceries, purchase gas, or make an electronic withdrawal from their bank account.

Anyone who surreptitiously inserts this apparatus has to come back to the compromised machine to pick up the file containing all the stolen data, but with that information he or she can create cloned cards, or steal money directly from bank accounts.

The woman I spoke to at my financial institution was both patient and helpful. When I told her I didn't do any business with Edible Arrangements or Topman.com, she took me at my word. She instructed me to fill out a form contesting the bogus charges. She also mentioned there may have been some additional items charged to my card.

The folks at the local credit union office were prepared for me when I arrived to sign the appropriate papers the next day. However, I wasn't quite prepared for the list of charges the person(s) who hijacked my information had made before their deception was discovered.

There were eight purchases from DunkinDonuts.com, totaling $320.

Etsy.com, an online company I'd never heard of that specializes in handmade and vintage merchandise, received a trio of jewelry orders. Those came to a total of $680.25.

Fry's Electronics, a software retailer based in San Jose, CA, got a $267.09 order.

There was a $780 charge from Selfridges, a high-end department store based in England. And to top it off there was a combined $816.23 worth of clothing purchased from RalphLauren.com and MrPorter.com, an apparently chic clothier with offices in New York, London, and Hong Kong. The total damage, including Topman.com and Edible Arrangements, came to over $3000! (Full disclosure: it was a tiny bit higher, but the $24.63 charge from a the Subway in Intervale, New Hampshire was legitimate: the boys and I had lunch there en route home.)

The folks at the credit union and Visa were accommodating and understanding about my misfortune, but it was still a tough lesson. It seems using one's debit card to buy gasoline is a risky proposition, and particularly on weekends, since thieves who use skimmers know most people can't get through to their local banks to report a problem before Monday morning, even if they become aware their information has been compromised.

Even more ironic in my case: if my Fairy Godmother dropped $3000 mad money from the sky and ordered me to spend it, not one dime would go toward expensive clothing, jewelry, electronics, or donuts.

I now have a slightly better understanding of why credit card companies charge the interest they do, since at least part of those usurious rates undoubtedly go toward compensating for the tens of thousands of cases of fraud they absorb each month. According to ACI Worldwide, an electronics payment systems company, 46% of Americans have had their credit card information compromised in the past five years. It's also estimated that there's a new identity theft victim every two seconds.

What I've learned: I'll be gassing up my car with cash for a while. And if I happen to run into a nattily-attired, bejeweled individual with donut crumbs on his (or her) designer suit who's listening to an expensive electronic device, well, he (or she) is going to have some explaining to do. ●

I Found a Quarter!

June 18, 2005

Rational, mature people shouldn't let a little thing ruin their day.

However, it's okay to let a little thing *make* your day. My day was made today when I found a quarter.

As I am of a generation that was alive when coins were actually worth something, I usually pick up loose change when I see it. I always pick up nickels, and will pick up pennies that have Lincoln's head facing up. I rarely pick up dimes. It's not that I have anything against Franklin Delano Roosevelt. It's just that the combination of my vision not being what it used to and my eyes being located nearly six feet above where lost change generally lies makes it difficult for me to see any discarded ten-cent pieces.

Several years ago I was visiting family in faraway New Jersey. At dinnertime someone in charge decided ordering pizza would be a good idea. We called in our request and were told the cost of our order would be $19.80. A group of us piled into a van to go pick up supper, and our 17-year-old nephew was designated to go into the pizzeria and bring back our order. Armed with a twenty-dollar bill, he marched into the restaurant.

Moments later he marched back out carrying the pizza and, in full view of all of us, tossed the two dimes he had received as change for the twenty into the trash can.

His father was incensed, and let his son know just how he felt. Others in the car wanted to let the matter drop, and said so. Fortunately no one asked my opinion, because if they had I'd have suggested my nephew be sent head first into that refuse bin to recover the 20 cents that one (or both) of his parents had worked hard to earn.

I suppose people under the age of 30 can't be blamed for not thinking much of money made of metal, since it's been at least thirty years since any single coin had much actual use. But it's not just the value of coins that's changed. Their jingle is different now. I recalled this thanks to an incident at my neighborhood grocery store a few years back.

I was standing in the "Ten Items or Less" checkout line waiting to pay for my apples and skim milk. The man in front of me, a seedy-looking fellow who clearly wasn't a slave to hygiene, had a bag of potato chips and a bottle of soda he wished to buy. When the teenage checkout girl totaled the price of his purchases, he pulled out a handful of change, then confided, "These are silver quarters, y'know. You should keep them for yourself." She looked puzzled, since as someone likely born in the 1980s, she didn't have the foggiest notion of what he was talking about.

Wondering where exactly the chip-eating soda guzzler had found his money, I asked the girl at the register if I could have the coins as part of my change. She happily obliged. I wish I could adequately describe the clinking sound those quarters made when she dropped them into my hand, but the best I can do is say they sounded like what money used to sound like.

Forty years ago finding that quarter would have been like finding a gold mine. As kids, my siblings and I each received an allowance of a quarter a week. We were also charged three cents per half hour of TV we viewed. We hated that, but in retrospect, our parents knew exactly what they were doing. Not only were we afforded a valuable lesson in economics, but we found things to do other than sit inertly in front of a video screen. Maybe that's why I'm writing things like this in my spare time, rather than idly watching American Idol, like too many idle Americans do. ●

The Credit Card is Missing!

August 18, 2007

Last week my six-year-old and I were standing in the checkout line at the grocery store when I got a terrible feeling in the pit of my stomach. The discomfort wasn't caused by anything I had ingested. It began when I was removing money from my wallet to pay for my purchases and noticed my credit card was missing.

I struggled to maintain an outer calm while simultaneously tearing that wallet apart, not wanting my son, the cashier, or the people in line behind me thinking they were in the presence of a dangerous maniac. However, few things unnerve me as quickly as the thought of my only credit card in someone else's hands.

As a youngster I developed a profound respect for the value of money. I was taught by parents raised during the Depression that you toiled hard to earn it, then spent it judiciously on needs, not wants. When I saw an item I wished to own I either bought it with ready cash, worked until I had sufficient funds to purchase it, or considered the price and realized that perhaps I didn't need it so much after all.

Having instant credit didn't cross my mind until the spring I was scheduled to graduate from college. At that time banks located in places like Texas, South Dakota, and Delaware began sending me letters telling me I had been pre-approved for one of their credit cards. I did just enough research to discover the interest rates these financial institutions wanted to charge me for being able to instantly gratify myself were similar to those demanded by people who a generation earlier had been referred to as "loan sharks." Since curbside recycling didn't exist in the late 1970s, I simply tossed every credit card solicitation I received into the trash.

Some years later I was going on a business trip to the West Coast and thought I'd need an automobile while there. I contacted a car rental company, but when the person I was speaking with asked which credit card I'd be using, I replied I didn't have one. The five-second silence that followed was broken by incredulous laughter at the other end of the line. Having figured out at that point I'd need credit to rent a car, I filled out an application form at a local bank and waited to receive my shiny new plastic. A week later a letter arrived explaining my application had been rejected due to lack of any credit record. Shrugging, I went down to the bank where I had been depositing my modest savings since I was five years old and applied for a card there. They rejected me too, and for the same reason: no credit history. "Of course I don't have any credit record," I wailed.

"That's because I pay my bills on time!" Ultimately I was reduced to having my mother co-sign an application which allowed me to use a card in her name. I'm sure she was as proud of her 30-year-old son as a mom could be. Just to make sure the card worked I used it to buy lunch for a friend, paid the bill at the end of the month, and then, credit established, retired it for a significant period of time.

Today I am saddled with mortgage payments, car payments, and far too many other long-term fiscal commitments. I've acknowledged that a credit card is a necessity, but still use it rarely and reluctantly. A brief but ugly experience with identity theft not long ago has made me even more paranoid about knowing where my card is at all times, which is why that queasy feeling hit me when I discovered it was missing.

Fortunately I remembered the last time I had used it, called the local eatery where I had gone the previous weekend, and learned the missing card was indeed still there. I picked it up and in gratitude pledged to go back there soon, which I will. And when we return I'll tell my kids to order whatever they want, and when the check arrives I'll pay for it (including a 20% tip) right then and there…in cold, hard cash. ●

Red Cross

August 2, 2006

Like chameleons, most human beings on occasion display the desire to assimilate. Some who aim to remain unnoticed unconsciously take on the attitudes of those around them. That established, if one wishes to blend in, it makes sense to surround him or her self with the smartest, kindest, and most positive individuals possible.

Armed with the knowledge that it may truly be beyond my control to avoid acting like people I spend most of my time with, I'm going to do my utmost to place myself amid the healthiest, most cheerful folks I can find.

Just as anglers all have favorite fishing spots, there are certain places where high-energy folks tend to congregate. For years I found upbeat people while running in road races. Such events are teeming with positive individuals who are dedicated to challenging and/or bettering themselves. Finding a negative person at the starting line of a 10K road race is about as common as seeing a Kerry-Edwards bumper sticker on a Hummer.

Unfortunately, last summer my doctor told me that due to a deteriorating hip, I would immediately have to halt all physically stressful activities, which included running long distances. His sobering diagnosis meant the physical, mental, and emotional benefits I had been getting from running every day would no longer be available to me.

Some people would have gotten depressed, but fortunately I have a family and friends who won't tolerate self-pitying lumps for long. I had to find a new method of absorbing positive energy by positioning myself amidst motivated, happy, energetic individuals.

Fortunately, I have located a venue in Portland where such individuals are plentiful. It's called the Red Cross Blood Donation Center.

My dirty little secret, one I've guarded for years, is that I *hate* needles, or more specifically getting poked with them. Despite that I've been a semi-regular at the Red Cross for the past decade or so, and while I'd love to claim the reasons for my pint-sized donations have been solely humanitarian, that wouldn't be the whole truth.

Every time I enter the Red Cross Donation Center, I am treated like the most important person on the planet, and that treatment stays consistent until the moment I depart the premises. I am attended to by skilled professionals, and while I wait I'm invariably engaged in pleasant conversation by complete strangers who not only seem truly interested in whatever I have to say, but are always fascinating individuals themselves. I've interacted with hundreds of people there over the years. Some were at least three decades older than me; others undoubtedly 30 years my junior. I've met people half my size, and others who likely weigh twice what I do. The individuals I've met there have probably included members of many different races, ethnicities, and creeds, but generally I've been too busy enjoying the ambiance to make note of inconsequential things like that. There is one thing everyone I've encountered at the Red Cross over the years has had in common, though. Each one of them was genuinely beautiful. I have never left the Red Cross Donation Center feeling like less than a million dollars, before taxes.

There are a variety of reasons that disqualify potential donors from contributing bodily fluids, but just because one can't *actually* donate blood doesn't mean he or she is ineligible to soak up some of the good karma hovering in and around 524 Forest Avenue. The Red Cross is always looking for volunteers to assist in a variety of ways, and the only prerequisite is having a desire to help. Maybe that's what's so special about the people at the Red Cross. On any given day <u>everybody</u> on the premises is there to do something that will ultimately benefit someone else.

Which brings me to a second little-known secret: doing things for other people actually yields a natural high to the doer! It turns out whenever I do something for someone else, I'm actually helping myself at least as much.

I give blood at the Red Cross because it makes ***me*** feel better. There. I said it.

I last gave blood on June 20th, which means that I'm eligible to donate again on August 16th. If it seems like I'm counting the hours until I can get down there again, it's only because I am. Fifty-six days is a long time to spend between days when you feel like a million dollars. Before taxes. ●

Heat Wave? Nahhh!

July 30, 2006

Forget what the weatherman says. We are *not* experiencing a heat wave in Maine. I lived two consecutive summers in Florida. *That* was hot.

Even in the best of situations South Florida isn't the ideal place to reside, and during summer, conditions there are anything but optimal. The town where I lived had its own smell, and it wasn't Chanel No. 5. Every morning at 6 AM automatic sprinklers went on so that the sparse vegetation existing between the strip malls could live for another day. Signs next to sprinkler heads all over town said, "Notice: this grass irrigated with reclaimed water." That meant water which had been used previously, and the smell permeating the town's thick air suggested its prior use had involved flushing.

On most Florida days in July, both the temperature and humidity rise to the 90-degree mark by 10 AM at the latest. The atmosphere feels like a steam bath until approximately 3:30 in the afternoon. At that point the sky darkens and rain subsequently cascades down in buckets for about 20 minutes. Incurable optimists might think precipitation would bring a reduction in humidity, but more often than not the sun reappears shortly after the rain ceases, steam rises off the pavement, and the atmosphere becomes even more oppressive than it had been previously.

There are few reliable methods of escaping the 24-hour suffocating heat and sweltering humidity of Florida in July, but for those who possess the will, there's always a way. For me it took a walk of about ten minutes to savor an enjoyable if temporary respite from the cauldron that is South Florida during the summer.

It was three-quarters of a mile from my apartment to the grocery store. I quickly learned the extra effort required to walk with dispatch was well worth it, since ambling merely lengthened the time I had to spend outside actively dehydrating. I watched traffic closely as I walked, since I needed to cross a heavily traveled Route 1 to arrive at my destination. Some people would dutifully go to the corner and wait for the light to change, but not me. Every second counted, and when there was a break in the traffic I would stride (or if necessary, sprint) purposefully across the road.

My previously dry t-shirt would be stained by perspiration, but that didn't trouble me, for I knew the moment my front foot touched the black rubber mat in front of the store, the double doors would open and I'd step into sweet sanctuary.

Once inside I'd quickly inhale two lungs full of delicious, humidity-free, 65-degree air. Refreshed, I would pretend the town outside the store was located not in Florida, but rather someplace more temperate, like West Virginia, Montana, or New Brunswick. I'd fantasize while I was shopping that the supermarket was being moved by kindhearted aliens to a parallel universe, and that when I stepped back out into the parking lot I'd be somewhere cooler and infinitely more pleasant.

The only thing worse than walking back to my apartment in that heat was doing so carrying multiple heavy grocery bags, so whatever I bought had to fit in one sack. Some days I'd buy milk or apples, but the only item I'd purchase every morning without fail was bananas.

Bananas aged quickly in Florida's heat and humidity. I never bought more than four at a time, and each one had to be lime-green when I purchased it. That meant that by the time I got it back to the apartment it wouldn't *quite* be fully ripe, but odds were good it would still be consumable the following morning. Any bananas that were still around 48 hours after I obtained them were useful for science experiments only.

Once I paid for what I'd bought, I'd walk ever so slowly toward the store's exit. I'd look back wistfully at the air-conditioned splendor I was about to leave. Once outside it quickly became clear there had been no mysterious change of venue. It took less than a nanosecond to realize that I wasn't in Bluefield, Butte, or Fredericton. One whiff of the heavy, sulfurous air confirmed what I had both suspected and dreaded. I was still in Vero Beach.

I don't care for winter in Maine, but given the choice I'll take a season of bundling up and shoveling snow over six months of the shadeless, breezeless, flat-as-an-ironing board cauldron that exists south of Savannah every time.

Count your blessings, Mainers. This is *not* a heat wave. ●

74 Inches Are Just Fine

February 16, 2006

When I was ten years old, I decided I wanted to be six-feet-six inches tall when I grew up.

My reasoning at the time seemed perfectly sensible. Being 6'6" would allow me to star in the National Basketball Association for the St. Louis Hawks, but not be so tall as to attract undue attention from strangers. I didn't want to be someone who was pointed at in the supermarket by frightened children who would exclaim (in hushed tones), "Mommy, look at that *man*!"

The genetic possibility of my growing to a height of 78 inches was slim, as my own father stood a mere 5'7".

Currently I stand six feet, two inches tall, or, as I occasionally tell people who ask, 5'14". It turns out 74 inches are just fine, except on those occasions when I forget about the iron girder, the bottom of which is a mere 68 inches above the ground, that helps hold up my mother's garage. I realize now that height has as much to do with who I am as a person as race, gender, weight, and age do. None of these things by themselves are of much consequence, nor will they ever be unless I inexplicably decide they are. I feel bad for anyone who feels disadvantaged due to any of the above-mentioned traits. None can easily be changed. However, all can be celebrated, at least with the right attitude.

When I was in high school, I wanted girls to notice me as more than just a funny kid who liked sports. It seemed like all the really cool guys had girlfriends. I never did, and as a result often concluded I was *not* a cool guy. And like most un-cool teenage boys, I desperately wanted to be like the cool guys.

That was then.

Today I am a teacher at a public high school.

Not long ago I was having an afternoon chat with one of my colleagues when we were joined by one of her former pupils, a young woman who had graduated less than two years earlier. On the day of her visit, she was accompanied by two people. One was her beautiful six-week-old son, who slept through the entire chat. Her other companion was a very attractive young lady I did not recognize. It turned out I didn't know her because she had attended another high school. She was 16 years old, and pregnant.

I remembered the older of our two visitors as a young lady who had taken great pains to make herself eye-catching in high school. Heads turned when she sashayed down the hall. When she was 17 years old she could easily have passed for 24, which was probably her aim at the time.

Now, at age 20, she could easily be mistaken for a tired 40. During her conversation with my colleague and me, she conceded that if she could somehow be a high school student again, she'd do a few things differently. She spoke less than charitably about the child's father, whose whereabouts she was currently unaware of. Neither my colleague nor I responded verbally to that, even though the young fellow of whom she spoke, a former student at our school, was, like most American males his age, not an ideal candidate for teenage fatherhood. (Which begs the question, "Is *anyone* in this day and age a good candidate for teenage fatherhood?")

I left that room feeling many things, not the least of which was a sense of relief. Had there been a desirable girl in as big a hurry as I was to become an "adult" when we were both 17, the absent father being muttered about in a similar conversation some years ago could have been me.

To all those females I liked, admired, and secretly coveted 30 years ago, thank you for recognizing (and appreciating) me for what I was at the time: an agreeable, immature late-bloomer with a sports obsession.

And more importantly, thank you for leaving me that way. ●

Designating Great Memories

May 31, 2015

In spite of official attendance figures compiled through increasingly creative counting methods, it's obvious the percentage of Americans who follow Major League Baseball with any passion is far smaller than it was four or five decades ago. Never mind the game's often torturously slow pace; it's hard for the average person to care about the doings of young men whose annual salaries *average* $4.25 million.

But exploring the history of the sport that long before there was any such thing as a DH (designated hitter) was unquestionably the nation's favorite is different. That's why I was looking forward to our family's visit to the National Baseball Hall of Fame in Cooperstown, New York, at least as much as my 14-year-old and 9-year-old sons/traveling companions were.

Getting to Cooperstown from these parts takes six hours by car, or longer if the driver doesn't want to chance picking up a speeding ticket in Maine, New Hampshire, Massachusetts, and/or New York en route.

All risks aside: if the trip took six *days* it would still be worth it.

The Hall of Fame is a vibrant, busy place between Memorial Day and mid-October. However, those visiting the bucolic village in the middle of April can easily pretend they have it to themselves, particularly when, as was the case when we arrived, the skies are grey, intermittent snow is falling, the temperature is hovering in the low 30s, and most of the town's 1800 or so inhabitants are either indoors or invisible.

But forget the cold, the snow, and the fact that half the Main Street stores were still closed for the winter. Cooperstown in general and the Hall of Fame in particular is Heaven on Earth for baseball fans of all ages.

After checking into our DM (designated motel), the boys and I walked all of 400 yards or so to the Hall, where we took a cursory look around the first floor and bought tickets giving us admission to the entire museum for both the remainder of the afternoon and all of the following day. When the place closed at five o'clock, we walked around town, took a few pictures, had some wonton soup and fried rice at a restaurant intriguingly named Foo Kin John's, and went to bed at a reasonable hour.

The next day we arrived when the Hall's doors opened at 9 AM. It would have required far more time than we had to take in all that the shrine contains. There are numerous displays highlighting the history of storied teams like the New York Yankees and Boston Red Sox, lots of artifacts celebrating the careers of famous players like Babe Ruth and Hank Aaron, and several attics worth of other National Pastime–related ephemera. Want to see the hat Ken Johnson of the Houston Colt 45's wore on April 23, 1964, the night he lost to the Cincinnati Reds despite pitching a no-hitter against them? It's there. For more casual fans there are fascinating exhibits concerning women in baseball, the Latin-American influence on the game, the promotional trip around the world a group of major league players took during the winter of 1888/89, and the "Negro Leagues" that existed not just until the Brooklyn Dodgers were integrated in 1947, but for more than a decade afterward.

On the way back to our lodgings we stopped at one of the many Cooperstown shops which peddle baseball memorabilia, and while neither I nor my boys had any interest in parting with over $100 to purchase a replica jersey of any current major league player, we did invest in some reprinted 1953 baseball cards, which were selling at an eminently reasonable 50 cents per 12-card pack. We opened them back at the hotel, and the kids liked them so much I went back the next morning right before leaving town and bought the few they had left. Later that day for a few fleeting moments my sons and I went back in time together, eagerly tearing open ten packages of baseball cards to see who we'd be adding to our collection. The intangible feelings I got were the same ones I did when I was their age: elation when a Willie Mays, Yogi Berra, or Bob Feller was revealed, but disappointment when, hoping for a Jackie Robinson or Mickey Mantle, we pulled yet another duplicate Don Kolloway, Hal Brown, or Billy Johnson.

Each of us bought one small memento, but the most precious things we took home from our trip were unique memories each of us will treasure for the remainder of our earthly days. Which, with any luck, will last longer than the 1969 Seattle Pilots, a one-year major league team whose hat I purchased as my DS (designated souvenir). ●

A Very Brief Comeback

July 13, 2010

When I was in my mid-20's I modestly considered my athletic abilities to be just shy of an Olympic Decathlete's.

In retrospect, they weren't. Those familiar with my sport of choice at the time know any slow-pitch softball player with a pulse should hit at least twice his weight, or three times it if he weighs under 175 pounds.

My organized softball career began in 1983, when an old college chum asked me to join his team, one which was sponsored by Electrolux Vacuum Cleaners. Flattered but concerned because I hadn't played in a league before, I wondered aloud if my inexperience might hurt the squad. My friend allayed my fears by informing me they had gone 2-24 the previous season. Learning that Electrolux sucked in more ways than one convinced me that any real or imagined incompetence on my part couldn't cost my new teammates any more than two victories, so I eagerly joined up.

It turned out that I could indeed play softball, or at least the slow-pitch variety. I hit .500, led the team in home runs, and caught every fly ball that stayed in the park. Better yet, we finished at 13-13 and made the playoffs, which was the equivalent of today's Pittsburgh Pirates qualifying for post-season play.

The following season began even more promisingly, but on a Monday about a third of the way through our schedule, I got a phone call from someone offering me a terrific summer job. The problem: it was in Fairbanks, Alaska, and I had to be there that Friday. Later that same night I banged out three hits in my final game, a victory that raised our record to 7-3. In my impromptu postgame retirement speech, I wished the team well while silently pitying them for having to finish such a potentially great season without their leadoff-hitting sparkplug and defensive ace. But I had a professional opportunity I couldn't afford to pass up, so off I went. I wouldn't swing a bat in earnest for another quarter of a century.

Fast-forward to 2010. I have a wife, a job, and some children, none of which I possessed in 1984. Some guys I coach Little League baseball with asked if I'd like to join them for some Sunday morning softball, assuring me the games are fun, the players low-key, and there is absolutely no stress involved. Since my coaching colleagues are good guys themselves, I figured they must know other such people when they see them, so I agreed to give it a try.

I arrived the following Sunday morning wearing 20-year-old soccer cleats and my wife's softball mitt, a glove large enough to double as a jai-alai cesta. There were enough players for two teams, so we chose up sides and started playing. When my turn to hit arrived in the top of the first inning, I grabbed the nearest bat, took a practice swing, got in the batter's box, and hacked at the first pitch. The result: a solid line drive to left-center field. I cruised into second base with a stand-up double. Time had stood still; 26 years had elapsed and I hadn't aged a second!

In the bottom of the inning my impressed teammates sent me out to play shortstop, a position I wasn't allowed near back when I was in my prime. The first batter hit a one-hopper to me; I snagged it cleanly and threw him out. We retired the other team with no runs scoring, but more importantly (at least from my perspective) did so without my being exposed as an aging fraud.

On my next at-bat I crushed a ball out to left field that one-hopped the fence! I tore out of the batter's box, determined to impress a bunch of guys I'd just met by hustling out a three-base hit. Then, as I turned first base, something happened behind my right hamstring that felt like what I imagine a nuclear explosion does. I dragged myself into second, planning my re-retirement speech with each excruciating hop.

A week later there was a bruise behind my knee which made it appear as though I had been a loser in a paintball game where the ammunition had been the size of cannonballs.

My abortive softball comeback was the second-most humbling athletic-related event I have ever experienced. The first occurred in September of 1984 when our team captain called me after I returned from Alaska, wondering when I could come by and pick up my trophy. Electrolux had won the league championship that summer, winning 21 of the 22 games they played *after* their leadoff-hitting sparkplug and defensive ace had deserted them for summer employment in the Land of the Midnight Sun! ●

It's Just a Rock

August 14, 2018

Last month I visited Plymouth Rock.

It's a rock.

My opportunity to see that famous bit of Americana came about when I was invited to spend a weekend-long celebration with a friend's family in Plymouth, Massachusetts.

Such summer holiday gatherings were truly special when I was growing up. On virtually every Memorial Day, July 4th, and Labor Day our entire family, which included my two siblings and our parents, 14 cousins, seven aunts and uncles, and three living grandparents, would gather for a day chock full of fun and (for the most part) wholesome activities. There was never any shortage of outdoor games. Wiffle ball, football, hide 'n seek, badminton, tag, and horseshoes were all options. Perhaps it's just selective childhood memory, but I honestly cannot remember even one rainy family holiday get-together.

In those casually sexist days, someone's dad was always at the grill. Moms manned the kitchen, prepping hot dogs and hamburgers, tossing salads, slicing fruit, and facilitating peace talks between children with the colossal temerity to do their bickering indoors. (Adult males settled outdoor disputes, but their method of negotiation generally began and ended with, "Knock it off, or else!") Perhaps most special for my brother, my sister, and me on these occasions: a large ice chest filled with ten-cent, 12-ounce cans of soda, a much-desired beverage that was totally unavailable to us on non-holidays.

On January 1, 1971, the Uniform Monday Holiday Act (UMHA), which created numerous three-day national holiday weekends, went into effect. Until then America's only national Monday holiday was Labor Day. Memorial Day had always been May 30th, and Independence Day, which back then was universally referred to as the Fourth of July, always fell, oddly enough, on July 4th. In those days nothing was more frustrating for kids than years when Memorial Day or Washington's Birthday (February 22nd) fell on a Saturday or Sunday, depriving America's youth of a day off from school we saw as rightfully ours. Historical note: prior to the UMHA, which also created President's Day, Lincoln's Birthday (February 12th) was a national holiday, but it generally fell during a scheduled school vacation, so there wasn't any outrage when *it* occurred on a weekend.

Another feature of those magical summer holidays that has all but disappeared: seed-spitting. Nothing was more gratifying to an immature pre-teenage boy (a redundancy if there ever was one) than seeing a sibling or cousin walking around all afternoon, unaware of the watermelon seed clinging to his or her face or neck. And that delight multiplied exponentially if the enjoyer knew for certain it was he himself who had ptui-ed that particular seed into place. But sadly, seed fights have gone the way of the pay telephone. Nowadays the only thing rarer than a parent willing to allow his or her offspring to engage in such unsanitary rituals is the availability of watermelons with seeds in them.

Those long-ago, carefree days came to mind again last month in Plymouth. The similarities between my friend's family and my own extended clan were abundant: their celebration was a multi-generational gathering of enthusiastic game players and venerable, garrulous types skilled at the art of relating various bits of family lore. The only difference between this gathering and the ones of my childhood were the ages of the attendees (all were younger than me, save for the grandparents), and the absence of seeded watermelon and ten-cent cans of soda.

The raucous activities went on well into Saturday night, but I was up early Sunday for my customary morning stroll. As I approached downtown Plymouth, I began seeing signs trumpeting the nearness of the famous stone marking the place where the Pilgrims allegedly disembarked from the Mayflower in 1620. Imagine my exultation when, after a lengthy, sweaty hike of four miles or so, I approached a granite gazebo, looked inside, and saw...a rock.

And not even a big rock! If I sat on it (which I could not, as it is surrounded by sturdy-looking metal bars), not only would my feet have touched the ground, I'd have had to bend my knees. I expected at the very least a boulder the size of a Winnebago, but this thing could probably fit in the back of a Jeep Wagoneer. However, while Plymouth Rock is at least as underwhelming as some more notorious tourist traps, arriving there on foot at 8 AM on a Sunday to glance at it is significantly more economical (*and* far less stressful) than finding parking, overpaying for it, and subsequently forking over the inflated price of admission to Graceland, Niagara Falls, or any wax museum you can name.

But be forewarned about Plymouth Rock.

It's still just a rock. ●

The Role(s) Parents Play

April 28, 2019

I've long believed keeping company with positive, high-energy people is the best way to live life to its fullest, which is why I try to surround myself with friendly, proactively gracious types. But on the theory that it never hurts having another cheerful, kind individual around, I am always delighted when another upbeat person enters my immediate orbit. And with the right attitude these sorts of opportunities, though utterly random, occur more frequently than one might suspect.

Last Saturday was rainy, raw, and dreary, but despite those conditions the Little League Baseball season opener I had committed to umpire started right on time, at noon. I was shivering, soaked to the skin, and devoid of all feeling in any of my fingers when the game was mercifully called after two sloppy, miserable innings. But every rain cloud has a silver lining; I went home, changed into dry clothing, and found myself with an unanticipated block of leisure time on my hands. But before I could figure out how to use it, the phone rang. My daughter, who had spent the previous evening at a birthday party/sleepover with three of her friends, needed to be picked up. The family hosting the event lived in another town, and I had never been to their house. But after getting directions I headed on over.

When I arrived and got out of my car I was greeted by a large, black Labrador Retriever which, after the required barking and a few perfunctory sniffs, led me to the front door. I knocked and a few seconds later was greeted by a woman I correctly assumed was the birthday girl's mom. Smiling, though clearly in the midst of making lunch for the four female teenagers at the kitchen counter, she said, "I'll be right with you." Quickly taking something off the stove, she said, "Follow me," as she headed into a small mud room off the kitchen. There she put on a pair of boots and bade me to follow her out through a side door.

Once we got outside she began leading me on an impromptu tour of her family's impressive homestead. She showed me where their strawberries come up every year; last summer the modest-looking little plants yielded two separate crops of small but exceptionally sweet berries. Then she pointed out some scraggly-looking blueberry bushes, ruefully admitting they weren't yet yielding much fruit. She showed me the swimming pool they had added a couple of years previously, and the sauna her husband had built. There was a scruffy-looking, weedy area further out in the back yard, which, she confided, really needed clearing out. She critiqued their sizable lawn, much of which was under water that day, and then showed me a few more bits of landscaping she and her family had done. It was all very impressive, and I found myself charmed not only by the house and its physical surroundings, but the over-the-top courtesy and generosity of spirit I was getting from a fellow parent who ten minutes earlier hadn't known of my existence.

After walking nearly all the way around the yard we approached the front door. I was preparing to tell her how much I had enjoyed her hospitality, specifically my impromptu stroll around the grounds, when a small white van with a green logo on the side turned into the driveway. Looking puzzled, my hostess murmured, "I wonder who that is?"

I assumed it was just the parent of another one of the girls, but a second glance made me reconsider, as the man getting out of the truck looked a lot closer to my daughter's age than he did to mine. My hostess's uncertainty seemed to elicit some confusion from the truck's operator. She looked at me, then at him. Not wanting to be the cause of any awkward post-sleepover driveway congestion, I volunteered that I should probably get my daughter and depart. That's when the woman who had given me the marvelous tour of her yard said, "You're not the landscaper?"

Nope. The man in the truck was. I just happened to show up at the precise moment he was due at their home to give an estimate for some yardwork that needed doing. We all had a good laugh over the case of mistaken identity; she couldn't wait to tell her husband.

In the car on the way home my daughter remarked, "Daddy, you *do* sort of look like a landscaper."

Some people might not know how to interpret that comment, but I took it exactly the way it was intended: as a sincere compliment to landscapers in general and me in particular! ●

SECTION 3

Just for Fun

One, Two, Three... Happy Birthday!

February 10, 2009

A very important member of our family turned 81 years old last week. Her big day took place less than three weeks after she watched the inauguration of our nation's 44th president. I'm not sure how many other chief executives she's witnessed take the oath of office, but she definitely didn't see the installation of all 15 who've served during her lifetime, since both of Calvin Coolidge's swearings-in had taken place by the time she was born on February 8, 1928. How many numerologists would love to have been born on 2-8-28?

Every birthday ought to be special, but some are more unusual than others. Last week Bob Griese, the pro football Hall of Famer who led the Miami Dolphins to victory in Super Bowls VII and VIII, turned 64. What's so special about that? It means that the former Purdue quarterback was born on February 3, 1945, or to use familiar numerical shorthand, 2-3-45.

Painstaking research reveals Griese isn't the only accomplished person whose birth date, when spelled out numerically, contains four consecutive numbers. John Abraham, a defensive end for the NFL's Atlanta Falcons, was born May 6, 1978 (5-6-78). Lacrosse superstars Gary and Paul Gait were born April 5, 1967, and Kermit Driscoll, a well-known jazz bassist, was born March 4, 1956. (A challenge to any and all nitpickers who want to dispute the use of the term "well-known jazz bassist" here: name a jazz bassist who is better known than Mr. Driscoll.)

For those who prefer four consecutive numbers in descending order, Willie Randolph, for years a player and coach for the New York Yankees and until last summer the manager of the New York Mets, was born on July 6, 1954. The late Robert Karvelas, who played Larrabee, the lunkheaded assistant to the chief of CONTROL on the 1960s TV series *Get Smart*, was born on April 3, 1921. Bill Walker, who played college basketball for Kansas State and on rare occasions these days gets off the bench for the Boston Celtics, was born October 9, 1987 (10-9-87).

Canadian politician Mike Harris was the only person I could find with six consecutive numbers in his birthday. The man who was premier of the province of Ontario from 1995 to 2002 was born on January 23, 1945 (01-23-45). I've tried desperately to find even one other person whose birthday can be abbreviated with six consecutive numbers, but thus far I've been unable to locate a record of anyone born on December 34, 1956.

Some birth dates are geometric rather than sequential in progression. Two examples are former president George Herbert Walker Bush, who was born on June 12, 1924 (6-12-24), and Robert Pinsky, the Poet Laureate of the United States from 1997 to 2000, whose birth date was October 20, 1940 (10-20-40).

Other examples of well-known people with numerically significant birth dates include 95-year-old Herman Franks, who managed the San Francisco Giants in the 1960s and the Chicago Cubs in the 1970s. The eighth-oldest living former major league baseball player was born January 4, 1914 (1-4-14). Singer Barbara McNair was born March 4, 1934 (3-4-34); Marion Barry, Jr., the former mayor of Washington, DC, on March 6, 1936 (3-6-36); hockey Hall-of-Fame defenseman Paul Coffey on June 1, 1961 (6-1-61); and basketball superstar Clyde Drexler a year and a day later, on June 2, 1962 (6-2-62). Sidney Crosby, the Pittsburgh Penguin forward who some consider the best player in professional hockey today, was born on August 7, 1987 (8-7-87).

Finding birth dates that are numerical palindromes can provide hours of fun for anyone with too much time on his or her hands. Famed aviator Charles Lindbergh was born on February 4, 1902 (2-04-02). Other noted individuals with similar status: Maureen Reagan, the eldest of former president Ronald Reagan's four children (1-4-41); Axl Rose, lead vocalist for Guns N' Roses (2-6-62); English anthropologist Jane Goodall (4-3-34); King Farouk I of Egypt (02-11-20); and baseball Hall-of-Fame slugger Hank Greenberg (1-1-11).

Ignoring or downplaying the importance of birthdays is a mistake. Not only are they a good excuse for a celebration, but no one has the luxury of having them forever. To paraphrase Casey Stengel, the loquacious Hall-of-Fame baseball manager whose rambling pronouncements occasionally made sense, "A lot of people who don't celebrate their birthday are dead at the present time." ●

Tastes Like Water

October 11, 2011

I may be a high school English teacher with a bachelor's degree from an accredited university, but I'm extraordinarily ignorant about human behavior. For instance, I can't fathom why anyone who's not already hooked would ever try smoking. It's incomprehensible to me why someone living at or below the poverty line would vehemently oppose slightly higher tax rates for America's wealthiest citizens. And I cannot begin to perceive why anyone would waste even a second of his or her time watching "reality" TV shows. To list all the things that I don't fully or even partially understand would take exponentially more space than I've been allotted here.

Here's a typical example: the other day a student in one of my classes asked if she could get a drink. I indicated that would be fine, since the water fountain is just a short walk from my classroom.

Some minutes later she returned holding a small, transparent bottle with a blue label and a white cap. "I thought you were just going to get some water," I chided, though not unkindly.

"I did," she replied. I took a closer look at the plastic container in her hand. The label said, "Pure Water. Perfect Taste." It also sported a logo indicating the bottle it surrounded contained the official water of Major League Baseball. When I asked how much her 20-ounce mini-jug had cost, she informed me she had paid a dollar for it.

That seemed a bit steep, particularly for something obtainable for free from the fountain down the hall. Curious, I took a cup out of my desk and asked if I might have a taste of her cold libation. She cheerfully poured me about a nickel's worth, then watched as I chugged it. It tasted just like water. The label had been accurate.

When the bell rang at the end of class I headed straight for the drinking fountain. Leaning over, I took a long, satisfying swig. The flavor was identical to what had been inside the bottle with the blue label. It tasted like water.

Later that day another student arrived for class carrying a plastic container of H2O, but the familiar-looking green label indicated the contents had been bottled right here in Maine. Curious, I asked him for a sample, which he gave me along with a slightly puzzled look. I poured myself the equivalent of a snifter, then took a slug. It was eminently watery.

Before I went home I cadged a sip of yet another brand of one-dollar purified water from a slightly bewildered-looking student whose bottle had a green cap. Its blue label proclaimed, "Enhanced with minerals for a pure, fresh taste." I took a swallow and sure enough, it too was reminiscent of water. And like its competitors, it contained 0 calories, 0 grams of fat, 0 grams of protein, 0 grams of total carbohydrates, and 0 milligrams of sodium.

When I got home from school I proceeded directly to the kitchen sink, turned the right-hand faucet in a clockwise direction, and watched a stream of clear liquid flow into my glass. I took a sip. It was cold and tasted exactly like water. I toyed with the idea of putting ice in it, but decided against it for fear of watering it down and diluting its natural absence of taste.

There are plenty of commodities available for Americans to purchase in unlimited quantities. These include judgment-impairing alcohol-based beverages which cause permanent damage to the imbiber when used improperly or too frequently; premium cable television channels which, when viewed too often, can do to the mind what excess alcohol does to the liver; and tobacco, a product poisonous to its consumer even when used as directed. If one absolutely *must* buy something and the choices are alcohol, cable TV, cigarettes, or bottled water, I wholeheartedly endorse the last of these four options.

I don't know exactly how much my water bill was last month, but I'm fairly confident that whatever I pay works out to significantly less than five cents per ounce.

There's no question drinking water is vital. But the last time I checked, the fluid coming out of my home's faucets was clear, cold, odorless, colorless, and had nothing floating in it. And until such time as that changes, I do not intend to spend one penny of my hard-earned salary to obtain a product which I can obtain as much of as I want with a mere turn of a wrist! ●

Misunderstood March

March 5, 2018

If the late comedian Rodney Dangerfield were a month, he'd have been March.

March gets no respect. No respect at all. It is cold, dreary, and endless.

Winter-lovers inhabiting the northern hemisphere hate March. Seeing the third page of the calendar means the impending end of the skiing, snowboarding, snowmobiling, and ice fishing seasons. Not only that, but as winter recedes, larval forms of scourges like ticks and mosquitoes begin stirring, readying for their annual assault upon any and all vulnerable warm-blooded animals, including outdoor-activity-loving human beings.

March shouldn't have an inferiority complex. Every other month is only a proper noun, but March can be a regular one (e.g., funeral march) as well. *And* it's the only month that can function as a full-fledged verb, although May claims auxiliary status in that area. March could have been an adjective, too…if it had been willing to subjugate itself by accepting a lower case first letter and pretentious alternative pronunciation, like August/august did.

For centuries the proud third month of the Gregorian calendar looked down haughtily on its immediate predecessor, since over the course of a decade March can contain as many as 28 more days than February. But the diminutive second month towers over March in American historical significance. George Washington, the father of his country, and Abraham Lincoln, the Great Emancipator, were both born in February. Presidents born in March include the eminently forgettable John Tyler, an obscure, unelected chief executive who at the end of his life was serving in the Confederate Congress, and Grover Cleveland, who fathered a child out of wedlock twelve years before marrying a woman 27 years his junior in the White House.

March's only "holiday" honors the saint who allegedly chased the snakes out of Ireland, but it's also responsible for an appalling number of March 18th hangovers. And anyone connected with education, be they student, teacher, or other staff member, loathes the year's third month, since there are no school holidays, vacations, teacher workshops, half-days, three-day weekends, or anything remotely resembling time off during the entire 31-day stretch. (Note: while March is agonizing for all who attend school on a daily basis, educators and students should exercise judiciousness regarding who, if anyone, they complain to about this state of affairs. Iron workers, nurses, poultry farmers, retail clerks, chefs, truck drivers, and police officers are just some of the professionals notorious for having a hard time empathizing with those whose annual work schedule consists of approximately 180 days.)

The month's few distinctions are sour ones. Osama bin Laden was born in March, as were Nazi holocaust architects Adolf Eichmann and Josef Mengele. The Boston Massacre happened in March, as did the My Lai Massacre and the Three Mile Island nuclear reactor disaster. William Shakespeare wrote, "Beware the Ides of March" in his play about Julius Caesar because the title character was literally and figuratively backstabbed on that date in 44 B.C. (For those—like myself—who didn't know, the Ides was the date on the Roman calendar marking the approximate middle of the month. There are a dozen of them every year, but the only one anyone remembers is March's.)

It would seem only fair that a reputable historian or two should recommend commemorating President Lyndon Johnson's passionately advocating for the Voting Rights Act in 1965, the first-ever collegiate women's boat race (between Oxford and Cambridge) in 1927, or Maine's becoming America's 23rd state in 1820. All those great events occurred on the Ides of March as well.

And why doesn't anyone mention the tragic Ides of July 1888, when nearly 500 people were killed by a volcanic eruption in Japan? Or the dreadful Ides of October 1793, when Queen Marie Antoinette of France was sentenced to death in a hastily arranged sham trial? Or the horrible Ides of May 1718, when London attorney James Puckle patented the world's first machine gun?

And then eleven years ago some Washington bureaucrats added insult to injury by deciding Daylight Savings Time would henceforth commence annually on the third month's second Sunday. As a result of clocks "springing forward," March loses an hour, and thus is actually a full 60 minutes *shorter* than its 31-day brethren January, May, July, August, October, and December. In fact, it's only 22 hours longer than 30-day November, which gets a bonus hour on its first Sunday each year. That Arizona, Hawaii, Guam, Puerto Rico, and the US Virgin Islands don't use DST is small consolation to March's few remaining advocates.

To paraphrase Shakespeare, the third month was born under an unpropitious star.

My sainted mother urged me to say nothing at all if I couldn't say anything good about someone or something. The good thing I can say about March: it's my *second*-favorite month.

My favorite?

The other eleven are all tied for that distinction. ●

Reasons to Believe in Reincarnation

August 16, 2011

Skeptics dismiss reincarnation as superstitious poppycock, but believing that upon the death of a human body its soul comes back to Earth in another body or form is a central tenet of Sikhism and Hinduism, and the idea of rebirth is central to Buddhism as well.

People of those and other faiths believe in (and in some cases look forward to) a next life, hoping it will be happier and/or more fulfilling than their current one. And while not everyone adheres to a theology encouraging belief in reincarnation's legitimacy, certain groups unaffiliated with any particular faith, like manufacturers of pay telephones, Pittsburgh Pirate fans, and moderate Republicans have good reason to hope that earthly life after death is indeed fact rather than fancy.

There's plenty of anecdotal evidence suggesting the possibility that reincarnation exists. Renowned American poet Amy Lowell passed away on May 12, 1925, the very same day Yogi Berra was born in St. Louis, Missouri. Could the chunky, cigar-smoking, Pulitzer Prize–winning imagist who wrote several memorable poems about drinking ("Vintage" and "Absence," to name just two) have been reborn as the stocky, cigarette-smoking, Yoo-Hoo chugging catcher who, while compiling a Baseball Hall of Fame career with the New York Yankees, was also known to wax philosophical from time to time? The ideas of both are widely known, although hers were generally written down, while his were primarily spoken.

Jesse Owens was undoubtedly considered America's greatest athlete in 1936, when he won four gold medals at the Berlin Olympics and in the process debunked Adolf Hitler's "Master Race" theory. Owens died on March 31, 1980, the same day that saw the birth of major league baseball pitcher Chien-Ming Wang in Tainan City, Taiwan. A quarter of a century later Wang was recognized by many as *his* nation's best athlete. Reincarnation doubters take note: is this too mere happenstance?

Superstar entertainer Marilyn Monroe died on August 5, 1962, the same day basketball superstar Patrick Ewing made his earthly debut. Canadian writer Lucy Maud Montgomery, whose *Anne of Green Gables* stories entertained millions, died on April 24, 1942, the day Barbra Streisand, whose voice entertained millions, was born. Comedienne Janeane Garofalo was born the same day comedian Harpo Marx died, September 28, 1964. Can these *all* be eerie coincidences?

Those truly wanting to believe in reincarnation might be tempted to cite two nominally independent events which occurred 63 years ago today. George Herman "Babe" Ruth, who prior to the introduction of night games, non-Caucasian players, performance-enhancing drugs and ESPN was by acclimation the greatest player in American professional baseball history, died on August 16, 1948, after 53 very memorable years on the planet. The birth of Michael Jorgensen in Passaic, New Jersey, that day was greeted with considerably less fanfare than the Bambino's death was. But the Garden State native turned out to be quite an athlete in his own right, and just 20 years later debuted as a major league player for the New York Mets. Could Jorgensen have been the reincarnation of Ruth?

Both men spent time with New York–based teams. Each batted and threw left-handed, played some outfield, and was taller than average (Ruth 6'2", Jorgensen 6'0"). Both had long major league careers. Hair splitters might point out the Babe hit .342 with 714 homers over 22 major league seasons while Jorgensen managed just 95 round trippers and a .243 average during his 17 big league campaigns. But consider this: each man once hit 11 home runs in a season, and Jorgensen did it in just 287 at-bats in 1974, while it took the Babe 317 at-bats to accomplish the same thing in 1918.

Baseball-Reference.com not only provides complete statistics for anyone who ever played major league baseball, it even lists the ten players to whom any hitter was statistically most comparable to at various stages of his career. How good was Babe Ruth? The ten major league players whose offensive numbers are most similar to his are Barry Bonds, Ted Williams, Lou Gehrig, Jimmie Foxx, Willie Mays, Hank Aaron, Mel Ott, Frank Robinson, Ken Griffey Jr., and Manny Ramirez. Seven of those men are in the Hall of Fame, Griffey will be in five years, and the other two will make it if and when Major League Baseball officially admits that virtually every outstanding hitter who played during the ten years beginning in the mid-1990s was pharmaceutically enhanced.

Baseball-Reference.com lists the most statistically comparable players to Mike Jorgensen as Mike Lum, Dave May, Tom McCraw, Greg Brock, John Milner, Randy Bush, John Lowenstein, Lee Thomas, Dan Meyer, and Ed Kirkpatrick, all solid, left-handed hitting journeymen. Like Mike Jorgensen.

So maybe there's no such thing as reincarnation. But it's probably worth mentioning that Ichiro Suzuki, a true artist with a baseball bat and arguably his sport's most skilled hitter of the last decade, was born October 22, 1973, the day another world-renowned virtuoso, cellist Pablo Casals, breathed his last. ●

Andy

December 5, 2005

As is the case with height, skin color, and sex, an individual has absolutely no choice in what his or her name is, at least initially. There's a reason that what's typed on your birth certificate is called your "given" name.

If someone wants to get your attention, more often than not they'll address you by your first name. It would be a shame for anyone to dislike hearing their own name, especially if that's the way the rest of the world constantly refers to you.

Fortunately, I like my name. If I didn't I'd have to come up with some contrived nickname and hope I could convince the folks around me to identify me by that chosen moniker. I've had a couple of short-lived nicknames, but neither of them stuck. One was "Stork," which came about some years ago after I had intercepted my third pass of a gym class football game. When the intended receiver of those passes yelled at his teammate who kept throwing the ball in my direction, the frustrated quarterback shouted back, "What do you want from me? I can't throw the ball around that %@!*%! stork!" As many 15-year-olds would, I thought having a nickname was pretty cool. "Stork" didn't stick, though, and neither did another nickname, one which I attempted to hang on myself in an effort to seem more macho. However, despite my efforts no one would call me "Killer." Maybe it had something to do with the fact that I was packing about 110 pounds on a 5'8" frame back then. It's just as well, though. My perspective on a great many things has changed since my freshman year of high school. I doubt any girl would have ever agreed to go out with a guy called Killer Young. Unless it was, in the immortal words of Rick James, "the kind you don't take home to mother."

With the exception of several horrifying driver's license photos, I've never carried a picture of myself. However, for years I carried a likeness of Andy Young in my wallet. Andrew Jackson Young was elected to Congress from Georgia three times, served as our country's ambassador to the United Nations under President Carter, and later served two terms as the mayor of Atlanta. He also worked for non-violent change alongside Martin Luther King with the Southern Christian Leadership Conference in the 1960s. While I'd like to think of myself as the original Andy Young, the fact is Ambassador Young was born a quarter of a century before I was. In short, he was here first. However, I have no problem taking a back seat to the man whose father once told him, "Racism is a sickness. You don't get *angry* with people who are sick; you just find a way to get them well."

I recommend naming your son Andrew if you want him to go on to great things. Andrew Carnegie and Andrew Mellon were both self-made millionaires whose many philanthropic contributions helped make Pittsburgh the major city that it is today.

Andy Warhol made the Campbell's Tomato Soup can a work of art. Andy Griffith was just as likeable and convincing as an aging country lawyer as he was an endearing young small-town sheriff. Andy Rooney is one of the greatest social commentators of our time.

Andy Robustelli is in the Professional Football Hall of Fame. Andy Bathgate is in the Professional Hockey Hall of Fame. The late Andy Phillip is enshrined in the Basketball Hall of Fame. Andy Summers, the guitarist for The Police, is in the Rock and Roll Hall of Fame. No one named Andy is yet in the baseball Hall of Fame, but if Andy Pettitte can string together another four or five good seasons, that unfortunate situation could be remedied.

At least one high profile woman has adopted my name as well. Rosalie Anderson McDowell has appeared in 35 feature films since 1984, billing herself as "Andie" in each of them. And while we have neither gender nor the spelling of our first name in common, there's one thing that Ms. McDowell and I share.

Neither of us cares to be called "Rosalie." ●

I Won the Lottery...again!

August 24, 2006

My friend Hank was none too cheerful when he read this week's Powerball winning numbers. Hank started buying Powerball tickets when the multi-state lottery game began in 1988, when it was called Lotto America. Although he didn't win anything for the first eight years despite buying five tickets each week, Hank felt that his luck was about to change on June 8, 1996, when Lotto America switched its name to Powerball. He was so sure that he was due for a big win that he began buying ten tickets per week.

Ten years later Hank still hasn't won the big prize, or even any one of the somewhat smaller prizes, which in Powerball can run to six figures before taxes.

While Hank is my good friend, I have to smile at his naïveté. Five years ago I told him that he'd never win the big prize by buying just ten tickets per week. You've got to think big if you're going to beat odds that Wikipedia, the Internet Encyclopedia, lists as one in 146,107,962. That's why he ought to be buying 20 tickets a week, I told him. I'm feeling a little guilty about that, since now Hank is out $5200 over the past five years. I later found out that by upping his weekly investment to $20 Hank wasn't increasing his odds of hitting the jackpot to 20 in 146,107,962. He was merely buying 20 chances (each at 1 in 146,107,962 odds) at hitting it. If he had stuck with his old methods, he'd have only blown $2600 on losing Powerball tickets since mid-2001.

However, this story isn't about poor (literally and figuratively) Hank. It's about me emerging triumphant in the Powerball lottery yet again last week. Defying my own philosophy about what it takes to win, I didn't buy 20 tickets last week. Instead I summoned up the will power to buy none. Again.

I lived in a state that participated in Lotto America when it began, so I've had the opportunity to buy tickets for nearly 20 years now. Although I wasn't a math prodigy, I knew that by buying 20 tickets a week rather than 10 I'd double my chance of collecting an eight- or nine-figure windfall. However, despite being in possession of that valuable knowledge I have yet to buy a single Powerball ticket.

By choosing not to buy my complement of 20 Powerball tickets last week, I saved another $20. That brought my total Powerball winnings (since 1988) to $18,720. I've also won by never having driven to New Hampshire to buy tickets during the years when Maine wasn't one of the states participating in Powerball. Add that to the money I didn't spend during those weeks when the jackpot got so high that everyone was buying more than their usual number of tickets and I would conservatively estimate that I've accumulated well over $20,000 by not buying Powerball tickets since the game came into existence.

There's another reason I don't buy lottery tickets. As a teacher and a parent, I spend every day of my life trying to convince young people there aren't any substitutes for hard work. If people worked half as hard in school or at their jobs as they do at looking for nonexistent shortcuts to success, they'd be a lot better off. If I ever won a pile of money with a winning lottery ticket, I couldn't ever look one of my children in the face again. How could I in good conscience spend what I hadn't done anything to earn?

Much of what many Americans desire today is based upon their want (not need) of instant gratification. Achieving something that you've worked long and hard to attain is far more gratifying than being handed something you did little or nothing to merit. Maybe, as Hank points out, it's not 146,107,962 times as rewarding, but it's gratifying nonetheless.

Despite all of this, I have to give the folks who run Powerball their due. The enticements they use to convince people to buy tickets usually include a line which urges people to play responsibly.

There are two things I have yet to figure out. One is how one responsibly spends money trying to win a lottery when the odds against him or her winning the big prize are 146,107,962 to one.

The other is how I'm going to use the 20 dollars that I'm guaranteed not to lose on Powerball next week. ●

So Close to a Bingo!

October 2, 2019

I've always enjoyed playing games that require keeping score, but as my days on the basketball court, baseball field, and soccer pitch are long past, I've had to find other, less physical forms of competition.

Fortunately, on Thursday evenings some friends and I gather at our favorite local watering hole to take part in Trivia Night. And one of these weeks when the Trivia Master asks, "What do Warren, Alfred, Raymond, and Troy have in common?" I'll be ready for him.

Lesser teams will recognize these as four reasonably common male first names, but then they'll have to figure out exactly which four guys they are and/or were. The quartet of understudies to the Beatles, perhaps? The defensive linemen who comprised the original "Fearsome Foursome" of the late 1960s Los Angeles Rams? The first four losing United States presidential candidates of the 20th Century? Or, for out-of-the-box thinkers, maybe the official military secret code for the word "wart."

Wrong, wrong, wrong, and wrong.

Any thoughtful person from these parts knows Warren, Alfred, Raymond, and Troy are all Maine municipalities. I know this because I have recently received calls on my cell phone originating from each of those places. I've also gotten calls from Acton, Augusta, Bangor, Bar Harbor, Biddeford, Brunswick, Calais, Freeport, Gardiner, Gray, Harrington, Hermon, Island Falls, Kittery, Lewiston, Lincolnville Center, Portland, Rockland, Rumford, Scarborough, Skowhegan, Smyrna Mills, Stacyville, Sullivan, Waterville, Wells, and Windham.

Unfortunately, none of the callers from any of these far-flung, exotic Pine Tree State locales has left a message, leading me to conclude I am either an unusually intimidating fellow or I am being besieged by telecommunication robots.

Getting junk calls at all hours can be upsetting even when it's not an election year. Some people get pretty bent out of shape about it, but not me. First of all, I never answer the phone if the number on the screen isn't one I know, although I will respond to those who leave me a message, assuming I am interested in the contents of their recorded information.

Besides, why get upset over something unimportant when you can have fun with it? In fact, as I write this I am in the midst of a fierce competition with several friends that's every bit as intense as Thursday Night Trivia.

In order to win at Robocall Bingo you have to receive calls from five numerically consecutive area codes. The beauty of the game: anyone can play, and the more bogus calls from far-off locations you get, the better your chances to emerge triumphant.

Like several other deceptively easy-sounding games of chance, Robocall Bingo is tough! Luckily I have a great many Robofriends in some far-flung places, so I'm a serious contender. Within the last month I've gotten Robocalls from 26 different states and seven of the ten Canadian provinces. I've even gotten a few messages. "Jamie" called from toll-free area code 833 to offer me help with my crushing tax debt. "Emma" tried twice with the car insurance rates she said I had asked about, once from Elmhurst, Illinois (area code 630), and the other time from another toll-free (844) number, although she left me a 949 (Orange County, CA) callback number. Although both young-sounding women had friendly, melodious voices, I didn't follow up with either of them because despite Jamie's overture I don't have any crushing tax debt, and I hadn't requested any auto insurance figures from Emma (or anyone else, either).

No one I know has achieved Robocall Bingo yet, but I've been agonizingly close for some time now. I've got a 201 (New Jersey), a 202 (Washington, DC), a 203 (Connecticut), a 204 (Manitoba) and a 206 (Washington state). I have never wanted a phone call from Birmingham, Alabama (area code 205) more than I do right now.

One friend of mine thinks he's on the verge of victory, since he's got a 559 (Fresno, CA), a 561 (south Florida), a 562 (Long Beach, CA, area), a 563 (northeast Iowa), and a 564 (western Washington). I'm not worried, though, since at the moment there is no area code 560, or 565.

Another intense competitor tells me she's within one of winning, since she's got 769 (Jackson, Mississippi), 770 (a newer Atlanta area code), 772 (Port St. Lucie, FL), 773 (Chicago vicinity) and 774 (multiple communities outside of Boston). I just don't have the heart to tell her that area code 771 is currently unassigned.

I have to admit, though: sometimes getting upwards of ten phantom calls per day can get mighty irritating. If anyone reading this is a genuine telemarketer (or even worse, someone who controls all of those infernal dialing robots), please leave me alone!

Unless you're from Birmingham, Alabama. Then by all means give me a ring. ●

Vowing Never to Say, "Never Say Never"

December 5, 2018

In his 1837 novel, *The Pickwick Papers,* Charles Dickens became the first-ever author to use the now-familiar axiom, "Never say never."

Dickens may have been a great writer, but he clearly wasn't a genius.

Never say never? Really? How dumb is that? Literally millions of situations cry out for those very words.

For example, I am 100 percent certain that…

I will *never* skinny dip inside a sewage treatment plant.

I will *never* dunk over LeBron James.

I will *never* eat ghost pepper ice cream.

I will *never* throw a small animal into a rotating airplane propeller.

I will *never* dive into a vat of sulfuric acid to see how long I can hold my breath.

I will *never* try to put out a fire with premium gasoline.

I will *never* let a donkey sit on my living room couch.

I will *never* use an electric toaster while taking a bath.

I will *never* chew tobacco.

I will *never* smoke a cigarette.

I will *never* wrestle an alligator.

I will *never* wrestle an alligator that smokes cigarettes.

I will *never* have an Afro like Julius Erving's in the '70s.

Julius "Dr. J" Erving operates on the Spirits of St. Louis on November 6, 1974.

I will *never* sprinkle rat poison on a friend's Corn Flakes.

I will *never* drink anything containing automatic transmission fluid.

I will *never* keep a camel for a house pet.

I will *never* put a female porcupine in someone's bed.

I will *never* eat, touch, or imagine haggis.

I will *never* ask Jennifer Aniston to play horseshoes. (However, if *she* challenges *me*, it's on!)

I will *never* shoot one of my friends in the face on a hunting trip.

I will *never* roll around naked in a pit of pink fiberglass insulation.

I will *never* lick a white line on any interstate highway.

I will *never* buy a basement apartment in New Orleans.

I will *never* undergo butt enhancement surgery.

I will *never* star in a remake of "Hairspray."

I will *never* staple a full box of Cap'n Crunch cereal to anyone's clavicle.

I will *never* chant, "Yankees suck," "Boston sucks," or any similarly vulgar sentiments. (However, I will, if the time is right, chant "Vacuum cleaners suck.")

I will *never* jump in front of a car at Indianapolis Motor Speedway.

I will *never* wear any article of clothing bearing the image of a televangelist.

I will *never* run over a perfectly good watermelon with a steamroller.

I will *never* display a stuffed platypus head over my fireplace.

I will *never* go to a Halloween party dressed as Willie Nelson, Oprah Winfrey, or Yoda.

I will *never* hide poison ivy leaves inside a stranger's hat.

I will *never* give an exploding cigar to a nun.

I will *never* drive a Prius to victory at a NASCAR event.

I will *never* cut off someone's feet with a chain saw while he (or she) is playing a guitar solo.

I will *never* push an electric lawn mower through Mexico City barefoot while eating a kale-flavored popsicle.

I will *never* pay an adult film star for her silence regarding our affair.

I will *never* tattoo an image of Dora the Explorer on a friend while he is asleep.

I will *never* tattoo an image of Bill Cosby on a friend while *she* is asleep.

I will *never* sprinkle itching powder on the driver's seat of a police car.

I will *never* take a date I want to see again to a Mixed Martial Arts event.

I will *never* take *anyone* to a Justin Bieber concert, whether I want to see them again or not.

I will *never* buy a piano at Wal-Mart.

I will *never* attempt to eliminate my (or anyone else's) post-nasal drip with a blow torch.

I will *never* wipe a child's nose with coarse sandpaper.

I will *never* take a course on Uruguayan architecture.

I will *never* try *any* recipes from the Hannibal Lechter cookbook.

I will *never* send money to a Nigerian prince, no matter how nicely he asks.

I will *never* buy a raffle ticket for a chance to win a bottle of drinking water that's been imported from Flint, Michigan.

I will *never* eat a pizza topped with Brussels Sprouts, anchovies and lug nuts.

I will *never* send anthrax or explosive devices through the mail to my enemies. (However, if the enemies are nasty enough, I *would* consider sending them anonymous chain letters, postage due.)

I will *never* try selling rainbow flags outside a Ku Klux Klan rally.

I will *never* stop to give money to a panhandler who, between swigs from his Jim Beam bottle, is muttering curses in Urdu while brandishing a bloody machete.

And I will *never* write or publish an essay so silly and totally lacking in redeeming qualities that it can never benefit anyone or anything.

After this one, that is. ●

A Heartbreaking Void for an Unfortunate Few

October 8, 2018

On the second-to-last day of last month two people I know observed their half-birthday. Jane, a colleague I very much like, turned thirty and a half on September 30th, while Dave, an accomplished fellow who lives three time zones away, became 80.5 years young.

Naturally I sent both of them hearty congratulatory notes on their achievement, as any decent friend would. But in the midst of contemplating all the gala events each was undoubtedly attending that day to commemorate their respective milestones, a somber thought came over me. Suppose each had been born one day later, and thus didn't have the opportunity to celebrate?

Sadly, that nightmarish scenario is all too real for 1.7% of the world's current population. As there is no September 31st on the Gregorian Calendar, people born on the last day of March are doomed to go through life without the opportunity to commemorate their half-birthday.

Famed jazz trumpeter, composer, songwriter, and Tijuana Brass headliner Herb Alpert was born March 31, 1935, and as such has never known the unbridled joy of celebrating the date that falls precisely six months after his most recent birthday and six months before his next one. The same lamentable fate has befallen actress/singer Shirley Jones (born 3-31-1934), who would undoubtedly trade her starring role in the film adaptation of *Oklahoma* **and** her title as Miss Pittsburgh 1952 in exchange for the half-birthday all but a very few unfortunates (like her and Mr. Alpert, to name two) have the option of celebrating every year.

The too-often-overlooked psychological issues associated with being born on the 31st of March are undoubtedly daunting. But sometimes being dealt a bad hand produces character and strength which might have otherwise lain dormant. One inspiring local example is Angus King, who despite being born on March's last day in 1944 attained Maine's governorship for two terms, and currently represents our fair state in the United States Senate. Vermont Senator Patrick Leahy (1940), former Massachusetts representative Barney Frank (1940), and former vice president Al Gore (1948) were also born on

Senator Angus King (I-Maine)

March 31st, and the heights to which that trio has risen politically bolsters the argument that having no half-birthday provides valuable fuel for those already equipped with healthy amounts of determination and ambition. Others born on the third month's final day include accomplished actors Richard Chamberlain (1934), Christopher Walken (1943), Gabe Kaplan (1945), and Rhea Perlman (1948).

Life is similarly unfair to people born May 31st, or on the last two days of August. Actor Clint Eastwood (5-31-1930), Super Bowl-winning quarterback Joe Namath (5-31-1943), actress Brooke Shields (5-31-1965), philanthropist Warren Buffett (8-30-1930), comedian Lewis Black (8-30-1948), basketball great Robert Parish (8-30-1953), actress Cameron Diaz (8-30-1972), baseball Hall-of-Fame member Frank Robinson (8-31-1935), actor Richard Gere (8-31-1949), hurdler Edwin Moses (8-31-1955), football star Larry Fitzgerald (8-31-1983), and Portland-born Olympic swimmer Ian Crocker (8-31-1992) all must deal with the ongoing anguish caused by perpetual half-birthdaylessness.

Being born on Halloween is scary enough, but October 31st babies are further burdened with the heartache of knowing they'll never formally observe their half-birthday. Among those afflicted: newsman Dan Rather (10-31-1931), football coach Nick Saban (10-31-1951) and rapper Vanilla Ice (10-31-1967). And while New Year's Eve may be a great night to party, those born December 31st, including actors Ben Kingsley (1943), Bebe Neuwirth (1958), and Val Kilmer (1959), will never be able to live it up on their half-birthday, as there is no June 31st on which to celebrate.

Those born on August 29th, like baseball Hall-of-Famer Eddie Murray (8-29-1956) and Supreme Court justice Neil Gorsuch (8-29-1967), get a half-birthday every four years. It may not seem like much, but at least they get the opportunity to kick up their half-heels once every 1,461 days.

But there's no reason to let being born on a seemingly inopportune date have any long-term adverse effects. Never celebrating a half-birthday didn't prevent now-departed people of substance like artist Henri Matisse (12-31-1869), educator Maria Montessori (8-31-1870), General Chiang Kai-shek (10-31-1887), baseball star Ted Williams (8-30-1918), clothiers Geoffrey Beene (8-30-1927) and Liz Claiborne (3-31-1929); comedians Buddy Hackett (8-31-1924) and John Candy (10-31-1950); and hockey greats Gordie Howe (3-31-1928) and Jean Beliveau (8-31-1931) from achieving greatness in their chosen fields of endeavor.

Sure, it's possible to compensate for an unfortunate birthday, assuming one has enough imagination. For example, French skier Jean-Claude Killy (born 8-30-1943), who won three gold medals at the 1968 winter Olympics, will turn 40 million minutes old next September 18th. But really, who honestly thinks an arbitrary, haphazard excuse for a holiday like that has even a fraction of the significance a truly meaningful occasion like a half-birthday does? ●

Knowledgeable Historians Agree: February is Fabulous!

February 4, 2019

Those of us fortunate enough to have been born in February have long known ours is the most significant of the twelve sections of the Gregorian calendar.

Doubt it? Check out this tiny sampling of notable human beings who began life during the year's second month.

A mere quartet of America's 45 presidents were born in February. But look at which ones! Knowledgeable historians consider George Washington and Abraham Lincoln the two greatest United States commanders-in-chief ever. A third February native, Ronald Reagan is rated somewhere between "Best president of all time" and "God's other son" by Conservatives. As for the fourth, well, William Henry Harrison never got the chance to display his presidential mettle, as he was struck down by pneumonia just 31 days after his inauguration. Nevertheless, in 1979 he was named "**Potentially** greatest president ever" by the knowledgeable historians at William Henry Harrison High School in West Lafayette, Indiana, during their monthly after-school faculty meeting in—when else?—February.

As impressive as that roster is, what's equally striking is its utter lack of mediocre or bad presidents. Go ahead; check the list again. There's nary a Harding, Nixon, Buchanan, or p***y-grabbing hamberder-eater in the bunch.

Distinguished literary scholars everywhere, even those who always assiduously avoid alliteration, fervently fancy fantastic February. Henry Wadsworth Longfellow, Langston Hughes, Gertrude Stein, Charles Dickens, John Grisham, Laura Ingalls Wilder, John Steinbeck and Jules Verne were all born in the second month.

Giants of the science world like Charles Darwin, Thomas Edison, Nicolaus Copernicus, Steve Jobs, and Galileo Galilei are February natives. And Februarians more impressed by physical feats than mental ones would happily point out that Hank Aaron and Babe Ruth, baseball's two greatest non-steroid-aided home run sluggers, were born this month, as were fellow elite athletes Michael Jordan, Bill Russell, Cristiano Ronaldo, Neymar, Jaromir Jagr, Phil Esposito, Jim Brown, Roger Staubach and Mark Spitz, to name just a few.

Bravery is a long suit for February natives. Frederick Douglass, Rosa Parks, Susan B. Anthony, Charles Lindbergh, and Ralph Nader all provide proof of that.

Singers including Johnny Cash, Dr. Dre, Garth Brooks, Ja Rule, Sheryl Crow, Smokey

Rosa Parks and UPI journalist Nicholas Chriss in the front seats of a Montgomery bus on December 21, 1956, the day the buses were integrated; posed shot of Jack Benny preparing to open the vault at his home—a long-running joke which included a supposed 24-hour guard—circa 1950s; Christie Brinkley, model, actor, and Board Member of the UN's Global Security Institute (GSI), speaks during a panel discussion entitled "Progressive Initiatives" in 2009; Hank Aaron swinging for the Atlanta Braves, circa 1966.

Robinson, Jason Aldean, Ice T, Travis Tritt, Roberta Flack, and Clint Black were all born in February, as were distinguished actors Sidney Poitier, Elizabeth Taylor, John Travolta, Clark Gable, Joe Pesci, and Burt Reynolds. Funnymen Jack Benny, Chris Rock, and Tom Smothers started life in February, as did trusted newscasters Tom Brokaw and Ted Koppel. Artist Norman Rockwell, clothier L.L.Bean, model Christie Brinkley, and Wild West showman Buffalo Bill Cody all began breathing independently between the 32nd and 59th days of their respective birth years.

Nearly as impressive as the lengthy listing of distinguished February births is the month's total lack of misguided, cruel, or evil natives. Adolf Hitler, Osama bin Laden, Saddam Hussein, Muammar Khadafy, Ayatollah Ruhollah Khomeini, Charles Manson, Ivan the Terrible, Pol Pot, Josef Stalin, Heinrich Himmler, Josef Mengele, Adolf Eichmann, Mao Zedong, Mohamed Atta, Idi Amin, Benito Mussolini, Jeffrey Dahmer, Attila the Hun, Nero, Caligula, Whitey Bulger, and Benedict Arnold were all born in other months. One possible exception is the late North Korean dictator Kim Jong-il, who began life on February 16, 1941. But recent research by an elite team of knowledgeable historians indicate he was born 15 days prematurely, which officially consigns him to March.

Some February natives harbor a tinge of justifiable resentment over our month's having been allotted a mere 7.73 percent of a non-leap year, while 31-day months like big, bad January and March each encompass 8.77 percent. What right do these neighboring months have to 744 hours each, when February has been unfairly limited to 672? January is darker, with weather no better than February's, and gloomy, endless March was considered so insignificant it was limited by the Gregorian calendar's designers to a mere single syllable.

Knowledgeable historians concur: in a more just world each of the year's first three months would have exactly 30 days, which could easily be accomplished by ceding January's last day and March's first one to February. Do that and February would cheerfully donate the piddling extra day it gets once every four years to some poor, less-significant month that can use it, like April, September, or November. A 30-day February wouldn't need it.

Were this simple adjustment made, February could claim Jackie Robinson, Zane Grey, and Ernie Banks (all born on January 31st) as natives, not to mention March 1st babies like Justin Bieber, Lizzie Borden, and Khalid Sheikh Mohammed.

Hmmm. After careful consideration, February elects to annex January's last day, but passes on March 1st. Knowledgeable historians born in February (like me) concur: 29 days are quite sufficient for what clearly is already the calendar's most impressive month. ●

SECTION 4
Farewells

Will Fulford, 1987 – 2016

A Ful (But All Too Brief) Life

January 1, 2017

Now expired itself, the year 2016 saw the death of Muhammad Ali, arguably the most recognizable human face on Earth a few decades ago. Astronaut and U.S. Senator John Glenn died last year, as did literary giants Harper Lee, Elie Wiesel, W. P. Kinsella, and Pat Conroy; sports legends Gordie Howe, Pat Summitt, and Arnold Palmer; journalists Morley Safer and Gwen Ifill; and noted entertainers David Bowie, Prince, Florence Henderson, Debbie Reynolds, Carrie Fisher and Merle Haggard.

Baseball-obsessed folks of a certain age (okay; *my* age) took wistful note of the 2016 losses of less widely known baseball players, childhood and/or early adulthood heroes including Dick McAuliffe, Walt "No-neck" Williams, Monte Irvin, Choo-Choo Coleman, Jim Davenport, Jim Ray Hart, Sammy Ellis, Chico Fernandez, Jim Hickman, Phil Hennigan, Phil Gagliano, Steve Arlin, Steve Kraly, Russ Nixon, John Orsino, Milt Pappas, Clyde Mashore, Vern Handrahan, Kevin Collins, Doug Griffin, Jay Ritchie, and Charlie Sands. Another athlete whose passing shouldn't go unnoticed: basketball's Nate Thurmond, the best NBA center of his era not named Bill Russell or Wilt Chamberlain.

But annually noting the passing of famed individuals is nothing compared to the sort of painful and personal loss everyone, save for those destined to die young themselves, will experience as their own lifetimes extend.

Will Fulford began his Kennebunk High School career in September 2002 inside the now-demolished Room 17 of what had previously been part of the town's middle school. He was one of just three freshman members of an advisory assigned to a first-year teacher precisely three times the slender, quiet 9th grader's age. Advisory ("Homeroom" in earlier generations) meets four times per week at KHS. Students have the same advisor for four years, an arrangement designed to give them an opportunity to build a relationship with one somewhat random adult who, with luck, can have a positive impact down the road.

Will's advisor was by utter coincidence fortunate enough to have the earnest and hardworking young man as a freshman English student. Two years later Fulford took an 11th grade writing course, one that his advisor was teaching for the first time. The dogged determination that made him one of the top harriers on Coach Mike Dinehart's KHS cross-country team helped make Will a success in the classroom as well. Unlike others who would show up for "extra help" in a less-than-subtle effort to boost their grade, Fulford sought assistance from his teacher because he truly wanted to get better at writing. As a senior he took a speech course taught by that same advisor. It was a major challenge; public oration *wasn't* Will's thing. But to no one's surprise (save for possibly his own), Fulford conquered that challenge as well.

Will Fulford's post-high school career involved more hard work, more success, and more leadership by example. That the soft-spoken but dynamic young man became a successful college athlete and subsequently a highly esteemed coach and educator merely confirmed the legitimacy of all he valued and modeled. Listen, watch, learn, apply that learning, and give the absolute best you have to give, every day, every time. Do all that and you'd ultimately reach whatever goal(s) you'd set. Once he'd learned those lessons Will Fulford didn't just preach them; he lived them.

Will and his soulmate, Ashley Potvin, a fellow educator/coach possessed of limitless energy and dedication, were married this past July 9th. Their charmed life together was just beginning. Then on December 11th Will Fulford died after working out on a treadmill at the University of New England. The seemingly tireless, universally cherished coach, teacher, husband, brother, son and friend was just 29 years old. Newspaper and TV news accounts of his life and all-too-early death accurately portrayed him as beloved, respected and admired by all who knew him, a quiet, determined, dedicated leader and role model who had given much to many, but had a great deal more to give. In his all-too-brief time coaching at Kennebunk High School, Biddeford High School and the University of New England, he impacted countless young people in ways that will undoubtedly reverberate for generations.

Will's KHS advisor still teaches at Kennebunk High. He had his classes read Will Fulford's obituary the day it came out, and asked them to try to write what lesson(s) they could learn from it.

"Always do your best," was a common theme. Ditto, "Live for today." But sadly, so was, "Life isn't always fair."

There's abundant evidence that whoever decided to assign students to the same advisor for four years at KHS knew what they were doing. A teacher really *can* have a life-changing impact on a student. But it can work the other way around as well. ●

Gone, But Only Physically

May 4, 2019

Jeff Huot was the loyal, patient, true friend everyone wishes he or she had.

Jeff and I had a lot in common back in 1982, when we took a two-week, 4000-mile camping/driving vacation together. He was tall and slender; *I* was tall and slender. He graduated from the University of Connecticut, where he ran a residence hall; *I* graduated from UConn and ran a residence hall. He was athletic, studious, and attractive to the ladies; I was tall and slender.

We took Jeff's Buick Regal. I had never driven anything that big, but Jeff said not to worry about it, so I didn't.

Jeff Huot in Madison, Wisconsin (July, 1982)

Four hours into Day One of the trip Jeff said, "I need a break. Can you drive?" Shortly afterward, nearing our exit off the New York State Thruway, I magnanimously volunteered to pay the toll. But since my shorts lacked pockets, my wallet was between my feet on the car's floor. Approaching the toll booth I slowed, manipulating the steering wheel one-handed while looking down and trying to secure the proper change with the other. I thought I was headed straight… until a shower of sparks flew by the left side of the car.

I had sideswiped the guard rail at 50 MPH. Jeff got out and grimly inspected the damage. But seeing me looking despondent, he took a deep breath, smiled *almost* cheerfully and said, "You know, I've always wanted a car with a racing stripe!"

The next day he got his revenge. Back at the wheel, he stopped for something crossing the road *at the precise moment* I tipped an open container of grape juice toward my mouth, intent on taking a cool, refreshing swig. When he braked I ended up wearing the bottle's contents on what *had* been a white shirt. But even then he didn't chuckle until he saw me laugh first.

Following brief sojourns to Niagara Falls and Toronto we picked up a mutual friend in Wisconsin and headed for the woods. I prepared our delicious dinner over a roaring campfire: a nutritious fresh vegetable stew. Everyone ate heartily, but only Jeff woke up the next morning with a roaring case of Montezuma's revenge.

When we went to historic Wrigley Field to see a Chicago Cubs game, I was the one who urged Jeff to grab the parking space a guy offered us in his driveway for the relatively low cost of five dollars. That was one-eighth of the price of the parking ticket we found on our windshield after the game.

Returning from the Midwest late on a rainy night an exhausted, sleepy Jeff asked for the second time on the trip if I could get behind the wheel. About a half-hour later and confused by the wet road's glare and some construction lights, I drove up an exit ramp attempting to get onto the eastbound Pennsylvania Turnpike. Maybe it was the headlights in our faces that woke him up, or perhaps it was all the honking horns. But whatever the reason, Jeff took over the driving at that point. Permanently.

A female colleague from Jeff's residence hall staff at school lived outside of Washington, DC, and he'd promised to visit her on our way home. That friend was smart, thoughtful, funny, and attractive, **plus** she had a great family. We stayed with them for a couple of days, and before leaving I asked for (and got) that young woman's phone number. After we got home I called her; one thing led to another, and that fall when she went back to UConn to finish her Master's degree, we began seeing one another. That never would have happened without Jeff. And today, more than three decades later, she's got her PhD, two beautiful kids, and she's been happily married for almost 30 years.

Not to me…but that's not the point of this story.

Naturally Jeff distinguished himself professionally and personally; he was a success in business, and as a father and husband. But he hadn't counted on contracting primary lateral sclerosis (PLS), an incurable motor neuron disease he fought for a decade with determination, courage, and dignity. Last month his battle ended.

Jeff's funeral was infinitely less somber than his life was festive and productive, which undoubtedly would have pleased him. His work ethic, inclusiveness, sense of humor, and common decency were inspiring. He improved my life, and by extension the lives of those around me.

Being Jeff's friend was a privilege and a pleasure, and while he's no longer here physically, as long as those who knew him emulate the kindness, integrity, and everyday courtesies he shared during his memorable but all-too-brief earthly time allotment, his influence will remain present indefinitely. ●

He Made Sports Fans Think

January 20, 2013

Pulitzer Prize-winning reporter David Halberstam wrote more than a score of outstanding books on a variety of subjects which included Vietnam, where he served as a correspondent for the *New York Times*; the Civil Rights movement, which he covered for two daily newspapers in the south when he was in his 20s; and America in the 1950s.

But in the latter part of his five-decade journalistic career, Halberstam shifted his considerable energies and writing talents toward a different subject: athletics. He wrote *The Amateurs*, a critically-acclaimed account of four young oarsmen vying for spots on the 1984 United States Olympic Rowing team. The prolific author's other sports-related work included books on National Basketball Association superstar Michael Jordan, New England Patriots coach Bill Belichick, and the 1949 American League pennant race between the New York Yankees and the Boston Red Sox. All were widely praised, and justifiably so; everything Halberstam ever wrote was insightful, impeccably researched, encyclopedic in detail, and eminently readable.

This month's sports headlines have been distressing ones for nominal fans of games and of certain athletes who play them. For the first time since 1996, no eligible candidate was admitted to the Baseball Hall of Fame, most likely because of an ongoing controversy involving which of the best-known nominees did or didn't use performance-altering substances during his career. One of the top two players eligible for admission—a record-setting home-run-hitting outfielder—loudly, self-righteously, and arrogantly lied about his use of pharmaceutical enhancements for years. Another elite candidate, a much-decorated pitcher who played for both the Red Sox and Yankees during his stellar 24-year big league tenure, continues to self-righteously and stridently deny his use of illegal substances despite overwhelming evidence to the contrary and a dwindling audience which increasingly thinks of him as yesterday's news, if they think about him at all.

Amidst much ballyhoo last week, a seven-time "winner" of cycling's Tour de France admitted what had been evident to all but the most willfully naïve for some time: he pharmaceutically augmented himself in order to attain and then perpetuate domination of his chosen sport. He made his confession to a national cable TV audience after years of angrily, effectively, and on occasion litigiously denying wide-spread allegations of his cheating with a shrill audacity that should have made Barry Bonds, Roger Clemens and their legions of enabling defenders green with envy.

Then the story of Notre Dame University football standout Manti Te'o's nonexistent girlfriend came to light. At this writing it's uncertain whether or not the star linebacker invented the tale of the imaginary lady friend who succumbed to a disease she never had shortly after being seriously injured in a car wreck which never occurred, but this much is clear: he continued to earnestly answer media questions about her even *after* the hoax had been privately revealed to him by Notre Dame officials.

David Halberstam undoubtedly saw all this coming.

In February of 1995 Major League Baseball was in the midst of a labor impasse which had caused the cancellation of the previous season's final three months, including the playoffs and World Series. At the time, Halberstam was putting the finishing touches on *October 1964*, his nostalgic, detail-rich look back at the two teams (the Yankees and the St. Louis Cardinals) contesting that autumn's Fall Classic. The eloquent introduction he penned that winter chided those responsible for the sport's ongoing state of affairs. Of Major League Baseball's plutocracy he wrote, "The owners have seemed from the outset, despite their claims to the contrary, determined to break the powerful players' union, even though it is the owners themselves who have handed out what often seem like demented salaries to their stars and semi-stars." Similarly, he noted that the players had exhibited "…a palpable me-first arrogance in recent years in terms of their treatment of both their fans and the media. They may be bigger, stronger, faster, and more talented, but they are not necessarily more likeable." Then he added this gem: "Regrettably, nothing unlocks the ego lurking within the young more than early, premature financial independence."

Those words seem prescient in light of current events. He might have added this coda: "And nothing can change the honesty, ethical standards, morality, and sense of fair play amongst young athletes and their sycophantic followers like the prospect of *achieving* that premature financial independence, not to mention the entitlements and celebrity that often accompany it."

But we'll never know for sure. Six years ago Halberstam died in a real car crash, unlike the contrived one that injured Manti Te'o's fictitious, leukemia-doomed girlfriend.

Halberstam's actual tragic accident not only snuffed out the remaining natural life of a still-active and reasonably healthy 73-year-old man, it deprived America of one of its fiercest, most dedicated and insightful journalists. ●

Sleeper Holds and Willingly Suspending Disbelief

April 10, 2012

Reality is a powerful thing. Sooner or later even those who for whatever reason(s) suspend their disbelief in the unlikely or the impossible will get jarred back to it.

Last week brought the news that much-beloved professional wrestler Chief Jay Strongbow had died at age 83. But his obituary bore some information which had to be shocking to some: the headdress-wearing, war-whooping Native American who for decades was billed as the pride of Pawhuska, Oklahoma, was in reality a Philadelphian named Joe Scarpa.

Anyone surprised the "Chief" was more Italian-American than American Indian shouldn't have been; one of his two most famous tag team partners was a faux Native American as well. "Billy White Wolf," who paired with Strongbow to win the World tag-team championship in 1976, was actually Adnan Al-Kaissy, a native of Baghdad, Iraq. However, "Jules Strongbow," Chief Jay's purported brother, was an actual native American named Francis Huntington.

Professional wrestling wasn't always peopled by steroid-addled behemoths and run by aspiring U.S. senators. But its business plan hasn't changed since the days it aired Saturday mornings on black and white TVs. Its success requires its avid fan base to individually and collectively suspend all rational thought processes week after week. In the 1960s and 1970s cauliflower-eared grapplers like Gorilla Monsoon (real name: Robert Marella), George "The Animal" Steele (William Myers), Greg "The Hammer" Valentine (John Wisniski, Jr.), Professor Tanaka (Charles Kalani, Jr.), and Bruno Sammartino (actual name: Bruno Sammartino!) put on choreographed weekly performances during which they twisted one another into pretzels when they weren't pounding each other with fists and/or whatever foreign objects they could get their hands on. Then as now, true believers ate it up.

The willing suspension of disbelief is nothing new. British poet/philosopher Samuel Taylor Coleridge suggested that if an author could somehow infuse "human interest and a semblance of truth" into an otherwise less-than-plausible story, eager-to-believe readers would consciously or subconsciously choose to ignore certain dubious aspects of the tale.

Early American folklorists relied on that sort of cognitive estrangement when concocting embellished tales of real-life men like Daniel Boone, or of fictional ones like Paul Bunyan.

Most rational thinkers realize no real person (or strange visitor from another planet) can stop speeding bullets or leap over skyscrapers, any more than such an individual would be able to hide his identity by simply donning a pair of glasses. Yet the timeless popularity of Superman in comic books—on television and in the movies—indicates there are occasions when readers and viewers willingly send reality on a holiday. Moe Howard's continual eye-poking, face-slapping, and stomach-punching of Larry and Curly was no more realistic than a talking prairie wolf running off a cliff, plunging deep into a canyon, and emerging seconds later none the worse for wear save for a bandage or two, yet generations of children of all ages laughed as hard at the absurd mayhem of the Three Stooges as they did at the animated violence of Wile E. Coyote and his Looney Tune cohorts.

Contemporary society abounds with examples of humanity's willingness to collectively ignore reality. Witness the wide appeal of stories with vampires as central characters, the Harry Potter books and movies, and certain politicians and infotainers whose fiercely loyal followers willingly and inexplicably take anything which comes out of a demonstrated liar's mouth as gospel.

Reading of Joe Scarpa's demise undoubtedly saddened some. Subsequently learning of the deceptions rife in professional wrestling—even before the proliferation of steroids, sellout crowds at gigantic arenas, and glitzy, overhyped, pay-per-view specials ruined the "sport" for thousands of otherwise rational individuals—was likely depressing to many as well. Introspective types still capable of independent thought may wonder which other "facts" in their lives are actually no more than products of their decision(s) to ignore what to others is readily apparent.

But optional escapes from inconvenient truths are never far away. This past Sunday morning marked, in many homes, a visit from another character whose authenticity has been questioned by non-believers, the Easter Bunny. His annual "appearance" can, at least temporarily, quell any creeping skepticism (or cynicism) threatening those preferring to exist in more selective realities.

And for bereaved wrestling fans mourning Chief Jay Strongbow's passing, consider this: can someone who never truly existed ever really die? ●

The Greatest

June 6, 2016

Few words written about Muhammad Ali, who died last week at age 74, will reveal anything more about the man than those he himself wrote and/or spoke.

> *"The best way to make your dreams come true is to wake up."*
> — **Muhammad Ali**

In the mid-1960s the reigning world heavyweight boxing champion was unquestionably white America's most disliked (and feared) athlete.

Three decades later he was by acclamation its most beloved one.

A walking contradiction, Ali was a supremely skilled self-promoter, capable of both insufferable arrogance and genuine humility. Devoutly religious, he was also unfaithful to at least three of his wives. Paradoxically he was a man of peace, but one who also was capable of inflicting harsh mental and physical cruelty on opponents; his business was, in his words, "beating people up." An indifferent high school student (he graduated 376th in a class of 391), he ultimately became an insatiable seeker of knowledge and wisdom.

Ali, then known by his birth name of Cassius Clay, first came into the American public's consciousness in 1960 as an endearing, loquacious boxer who at age 18 won the gold medal as a light heavyweight at the Rome Olympics. Two months after that he launched his professional career with an unremarkable six-round victory over an opponent whose day job was police chief of Fayetteville, West Virginia.

He became world heavyweight champion in February 1964 with a shocking victory over the universally despised yet seemingly invincible Sonny Liston. But the combination of Ali's braggadocio and his bold public embrace of the unapologetically racially divisive Nation of Islam brought about something even more unlikely than his winning the title; it made Liston, a crude, intimidating, perpetually-glowering bully with a lengthy criminal past, into a sympathetic figure. But Ali's two-minute knockout victory in their Lewiston, Maine, rematch—one which ended with a mysterious and controversial "phantom punch"—consigned the former champion to permanent obscurity while simultaneously propelling Ali to even further prominence.

> *"Service to others is the rent you pay for your room here on Earth."*
> — **Muhammad Ali**

In 1967 the still-undefeated Ali was stripped of his title for claiming conscientious objector status and refusing to submit to the military draft. Summarily convicted of draft evasion, he was sentenced to five years in prison and a $10,000 fine. His reaction at the time: "I ain't got no quarrel with them Viet Cong. My conscience won't let me go shoot my brother, or some darker people, or some poor hungry people in the mud for big powerful America. And shoot them for what? They never called me nigger, they never lynched me, they didn't put no dogs on me, they didn't rob me of my nationality… How can I shoot them poor people? Just take me to jail."

> *"Don't count the days, make the days count."*
> — **Muhammad Ali**

In retrospect his refusal to submit to military service was as correct as it was principled, courageous, and sincere, though it wasn't generally viewed that way at the time. "Draft dodger" and "traitor" were two of the milder terms applied to him by a vast majority of Americans whose opinions were shaped largely by hawkish government propagandists and a reliably compliant media.

Ali immediately appealed his conviction, but during the ensuing three years of litigation he was unable to obtain a license to box, effectively robbing him of his athletic prime and unquestionably costing him millions of dollars. But opposition to the Vietnam War increased, public opinion inexorably shifted, and Ali never wavered. Years later he recalled, "Some people thought I was a hero. Some people said that what I did was wrong. But everything I did was according to my conscience. I wasn't trying to be a leader. I just wanted to be free."

Ultimately vindicated when the United States Supreme Court unanimously overturned his conviction in 1971, Ali never did jail time. But ironically he spent his last three decades imprisoned, quivering and virtually mute, inside a body crippled by a condition quite likely caused by the savage profession he pursued until age 39, long after time had robbed him of his once-incomparable skills.

> *"Silence is golden when you can't think of a good answer."*
> — **Muhammad Ali**

While he was arguably one of history's greatest boxers, Ali's numerous athletic achievements constitute just a tiny part of his legacy. Cited as a significant source of inspiration by accomplished individuals like Nelson Mandela, Martin Luther King, Jr., Paul McCartney, a veritable who's who of world leaders, and countless everyday people, Ali's influence and historical significance will likely endure for generations. He was the rare (and perhaps only) athlete who truly transcended his sport.

> *"Live every day as if it were your last, because someday you're going to be right."*
> — **Muhammad Ali** ●

Leaving Quietly? Howe Appropriate.

June 12, 2016

Few universally beloved individuals make the kind of impact on a major city (Detroit) and/or an entire nation (Canada) as significant as Gordie Howe did. The National Hockey League's greatest player was as fierce and merciless a competitor as the game has ever known on the ice, but away from the rink he was an admirable and endearing blend of modesty, kindness, wholesomeness, and patience.

Who says "Mr. Hockey" (a name actually trademarked by Howe's business-savvy late wife Colleen) was the best ever? Certainly not the man himself; for Howe to even suggest such a thing would have been at odds with his genuine humility. But when all-time great players like Wayne Gretzky, Bobby Orr, and the late Maurice Richard—each of whom has a significant following that thinks *he* is the greatest ever—unanimously testify that the man who led his sport in virtually every meaningful statistical category when he retired for good in 1980 is their superior, well, it's worth taking heed.

Howe's off-ice affability was every bit as genuine as his reputation for toughness on it. I know.

In December 1978 the editor of my college's student newspaper wanted a feature story on Howe, who was playing three-quarters of an hour or so down the road for the New England Whalers of the World Hockey Association. Fifty years old at the time, Howe was in the midst of what would turn out to be the penultimate season of his unprecedented 32-year playing career.

I was the natural choice for the assignment; I knew a bit about hockey, and outwardly emitted confidence and competence. It was a false front. The reality was I was a mediocre, directionless student who was obsessed with sports. Even *I* knew I wasn't anywhere near athletic enough to make a living competing, and while I was 21 chronologically I was about 14 socially. Any woman I liked seemed unaware of my existence, and the few who actually did discern I was alive were universally immune to my charms. Lacking any confidence whatsoever, I felt pretty insignificant at the time. And as I have since learned, feeling worthless all too often puts one on the fast road to *actual* worthlessness.

I spent a sleepless night before my scheduled trip to Hartford preparing deep and meaningful questions for my intended subject. I prayed the Whalers would win, terrified that if they didn't, hockey's grand old man would be far too distraught over the defeat to talk to some wannabe reporter representing a very minor publication.

Naturally the Whalers got thrashed, and after the game I headed with great trepidation to the locker room, fearing The Great Man wouldn't want to talk to anyone, let alone some sweater-clad nerd from a college newspaper. I just hoped he'd reject my interview request quietly, rather than increase my inevitable humiliation tenfold by loudly dismissing me in front of others.

Feeling equal parts invisible and irrelevant, I waited for all the real reporters camped in front of Number Nine's locker to finish their work. When the last one finally departed, I reluctantly slithered in his direction.

"Uh…Mr. Howe?" I meekly squeaked in a high, nervous voice that came out sounding like a cross between Porky Pig and Alvin the Chipmunk. The weary gladiator glanced up, curious to see who was stammering in his space.

Determined to try again, I mumbled, "MynameisAndyYoungfromtheConnecticutDaily CampusandIwaswonderingifyoucouldmaybe…"

At that point the seemingly ageless hockey legend mercifully interrupted. "Where'd you say you were from, son?"

"The University of Connecticut," I gasped.

He gave me a big smile, heartily slapped me on the back, and said, "That's okay. I won't hold that against you!"

For the next few minutes Gordie Howe patiently and thoughtfully answered questions he had undoubtedly heard hundreds of times before, but did so in a manner suggesting *he* felt privileged to be talking with me, rather than the other way around. I left the Civic Center that night feeling ten feet tall. More importantly, I never, ever felt completely insignificant again, no matter who I was interacting with.

Perhaps if Gordie Howe hadn't cheerfully given me his time and attention nearly four decades ago I'd still be the same productive, happy, and reasonably successful fellow I am today.

Or maybe not.

It's a shame that between Muhammad Ali's passing earlier this month and the horrific events over the weekend in Orlando, Florida, the death of professional hockey's greatest player is likely to get lost in the shuffle. But it's also appropriate. Leaving quietly and without fanfare was most likely exactly how the unassuming, inherently decent Gordie Howe would have wanted to end his ordinary, extraordinary 88-year earthly existence. ●

Farewell to Three Athletic Legends

October 3, 2015

Three titans of 20th-century American sports history passed away last month.

Moses Malone, whose heart gave out on September 13th, was huge in more ways than one. Literally a behemoth at 6'10" tall, the first player in modern basketball history to sign a professional basketball contract directly out of high school was also a figurative giant in his game. A 12-time all-star who topped the National Basketball Association in rebounding six different seasons, he led the Philadelphia 76ers to the NBA championship in 1983, and retired as the league's all-time leader in offensive rebounds. A three-time NBA Most Valuable Player, Malone was deservedly elected to the Basketball Hall of Fame in 2001, the first year he was eligible for the honor.

Lawrence Peter Berra died of natural causes on September 22nd. The much-quoted "Yogi," who may have actually mouthed a few of the many memorable quips attributed to him over the years, was a beloved American icon whose fame transcended his sport. His was truly a Horatio Alger story: born to impoverished immigrant parents, he dropped out of school after the 8th grade, but later earned a Purple Heart during the D-day invasion and ultimately became a rich man in every sense of the word. One of the most unlikely looking professional athletes ever, the squat, swarthy Berra played for the nation's most glamorous professional team in an era when baseball wasn't just America's national pastime, it was unquestionably the nation's favorite sport as well. A legitimate superstar who played for 14 pennant winners and 10 World Series championship teams in 17 seasons with the New York Yankees, Berra was a three-time American League Most Valuable Player, a solid defensive catcher and clutch performer with a deserved reputation for swinging at any pitch he could reach. Later on he managed two different teams to the 7th game of the World Series, and lived out the remainder of his remarkable 90 years as both an innately decent goodwill ambassador for baseball and a dispenser of quirky, plainspoken common sense.

A third athletic impact-maker died of pancreatic cancer on September 16th. His passing didn't generate national headlines, but it should have.

Joe Morrone grew up playing baseball, football, hockey, and basketball in Worcester, Massachusetts. He first tried soccer and lacrosse at the University of Massachusetts, excelling at them to the point that he was hired to coach both sports at Middlebury (VT) College after graduating from UMass. Eleven seasons later he was hired to take over the soccer program at the University of Connecticut. To say soccer was flying under the radar both nationally and at UConn in 1969 is a massive understatement. The few in Storrs, CT, who were aware the game even existed viewed it with a sort of casual bemusement and/or disinterest, assuming they concerned themselves with it at all.

Joe Morrone's passion and dedication helped transform soccer into a major sport all over America.

But as with everything else he did in his life, Joe Morrone threw his heart and soul into changing that perception. He built a perennial powerhouse, winning over 350 games in 28 years at UConn's helm. His teams finished 16th or higher in the NCAA rankings 14 times between 1975 and 1996, going to three Final Fours and winning the national title in 1981. Connecticut remains the only New England school to have won a Division I national soccer championship. Morrone was deservedly elected to the National Soccer Coaches Association of America Hall of Fame in 2002.

But Morrone didn't just coach dominant teams; he began building the foundation necessary to make soccer a true major sport. Sellout crowds at UConn's Sunday home games became routine, and as time went on Husky fans became nearly as knowledgeable as they were rabid. Morrone personally set up widespread youth soccer programs in Connecticut, establishing a model widely imitated throughout the nation. He also ran a successful summer soccer school for a quarter of a century. Most importantly though, Morrone, often at his own peril, butted heads with and ruffled the feathers of disdainful old-school college athletic administrators who were unwilling or unable to put significant resources or effort into any sport other than football or men's basketball. His work ethic and determination to promote soccer as a major sport knew no boundaries; even detractors acknowledged his fervent, brave and tireless efforts to build the game. No one ever outworked Joe Morrone, on or off the field.

It is neither inaccurate nor disrespectful to say Joe Morrone impacted his game more than Moses Malone and Yogi Berra did theirs. Malone and Berra were both giants in their respective fields of endeavor, but the pioneering, innovative Morrone was a colossus in his. ●

Wanton Murderer or Bold Reformer?

June 7, 2011

Not many individuals were demonized as vociferously and consistently during their lifetime as Jack Kevorkian. However, the Michigan pathologist who died last week at age 83 believed far too strongly in his cause to be discouraged by hidebound, vicious critics who hysterically compared him to every murderer from Adolf Hitler to Charles Manson to Vlad the Impaler.

But if few people were publicly raked over the coals as ferociously and unrelentingly as Kevorkian was, even fewer enthusiastically embraced being slandered like he did. Although his dogged efforts to legitimatize and legalize the right to choose how and when to die resulted in his being labeled "Dr. Death" and far worse by opponents of the nascent "Death with Dignity" movement, Kevorkian never backed away from his beliefs.

In retrospect, Kevorkian's harshest and most persistent critics unwittingly aided his efforts to gain acceptance for assisted suicide; their relentless attacks on him kept his cause in the public eye. He undoubtedly knew part of the price he'd pay for his views was shrill, endless, and nearly universal vilification from a large and intractable segment of the population equally as ardent about their point of view as Kevorkian was about his. But his uncompromising commitment and dedication to his cause required far more courage than heaping abuse upon him did from his detractors. Kevorkian risked (and ultimately welcomed) imprisonment for the actions he took in order to further his beliefs; how many of his antagonists were willing to pay that price?

The reaction Kevorkian received in response to his determined and deliberately provocative challenges to social taboos was consistent with treatment past social reformers have gotten. People have resisted change for as long as human beings have banded together to form societies, even on those occasions when the proposed modification(s) would benefit nearly everyone involved. Throughout history, those suggesting alterations to accepted sociological, technological, biological and religious norms have been laughed off, dismissed, derided, undermined, demonized, assaulted, and in extreme cases, eliminated by those who, for whatever reason(s), were unable or unwilling to let go of what they took to be right because, well, they just *knew* it was right, damn it!

Some of Dr. Kevorkian's more rabid critics compared him to John Brown, the wild-eyed abolitionist whose fanatical opposition to the evil of human bondage led him to armed insurrection and murder. But Brown's hatred of slavery led him to kill innocent people; Kevorkian merely assisted able-minded individuals wishing to end their own suffering to terminate their own lives.

Elizabeth Cady Stanton and Susan B. Anthony were initially ignored when they formed the American Equal Rights Association in 1866 in order to promote universal suffrage. But later, when it began to appear their efforts might indeed bear fruit, they and their allies were vilified by the establishment of their day with a ferocity similar to that which Dr. Kevorkian was treated to more than a century later.

The Wright Brothers were dismissed as crackpots when they suggested man could fly; early proponents of automobiles got the same derision, which grew more intense as the possibility of their vision becoming reality became more likely. And much of the resistance to their proposed innovations came from horse breeders, wagon builders, and others who stood to lose out financially if the inventors looking to change society were successful.

For similar reasons, those proposing sociological changes have always faced the same obstacles technological groundbreakers have, and from the same kinds of sources. Many religious leaders denounced Charles Darwin's evolutionary theories as heresy in the mid-19th century. Their successors just as predictably vilified Margaret Sanger and other proponents of reproductive rights nearly 100 years later when the birth control pill was introduced.

But as Darwin pointed out, human beings evolve, and so do societies. Few presidents were as bitterly criticized while in office as Abraham Lincoln was; today he is nearly universally considered one of American history's few deities. Half a century ago Martin Luther King, Jr., was seen by much of America as a disrespectful, uppity rabble-rouser; today America rightly marks the anniversary of his birth with a national holiday.

Jack Kevorkian's courage resulted in the growth of hospice care in the United States, and in an increased willingness by society in general, and doctors in particular, to reconsider their thoughts about palliative care.

If America continues to progress there's little doubt history will view Jack Kevorkian as a courageous reformer sooner rather than later. Two decades after he became the only U.S. president to resign in disgrace, Richard Nixon was memorialized on a postage stamp. If the United States Postal Service still exists 20 years from now, America's boldest pioneer in the field of end-of-life protocol ought to be on one as well. ●

Making a Lasting Impact with Kindness and Decency

May 3, 2018

I learned of Lee Cheney's passing in a card that arrived in my mailbox late last month. He died in the small community just outside Albany, New York, where he and his wife Pat had been residing for the past decade or so.

When I moved north from Raleigh, North Carolina, in 1996, the Cheneys were my first Maine neighbors. I thoroughly enjoyed residing in Saco, but it wasn't solely the house, the first for which I made monthly mortgage (rather than rent) payments, that elicits such fond memories. It was the people who occupied the place next door.

Veteran homeowners whose children were already grown, Lee and Pat were probably half a generation older than me, but half a generation younger than my parents. They knew a lot of local lore, but shared it discreetly, and only when it was appropriate. Any and all relevant background or details about local happenings and the people involved with them were shared in a matter-of-fact, informative way, rather than a gossipy one.

The houses in our neighborhood were close together. Most of the lots on the dead-end street were sized similarly; ours was, according to the deed, .17 acres. It was, at the time, the perfect place to live. I could cut every blade of grass in the yard (and rake it up if I were so inclined, though I rarely was) in less than a half-hour.

Lee and Pat were the ideal next-door neighbors: friendly, helpful, and fun without being ubiquitous, prying, or judgmental. When the sorts of questions new homeowners inevitably have arose, whether they concerned ice jams, flooded basements, or how best to fertilize tomato plants, Lee and Pat were happy to help. They also weren't afraid to request assistance themselves when it was necessary. Nothing made (or makes) me feel more vital than being asked for aid I am capable of providing, like helping to lift something requiring two pairs of reasonably strong hands, or retrieving an object located on a shelf too high for most people to reach without a stepladder. Of all the reasons for me to appreciate my neighbors, the most significant was that they accepted and celebrated me for who I was and what I was good at, rather than fixating on or getting irritated over the many useful skills I quite apparently didn't possess.

Lee and Pat made me feel like I was part of the neighborhood from the very first day I moved in, which was no small feat. Virtually everyone is a nominal stranger at some point(s) in life, and at those times smooth assimilation cannot be taken for granted. Unqualified acceptance isn't fully appreciated until the time arrives when it isn't forthcoming. When all an individual desires is to fit into a new situation professionally, culturally, or personally, timely kindness can be the difference between a smooth transition and a painful, traumatic setback.

As a taller-than-average white male with no discernible accent and a non-remarkable mode of dress, I've undoubtedly been guilty more than once of taking my relatively stress-free, heartache-free, doubt-free existence for granted. I know now people like Lee, Pat, and countless other similarly generous, compassionate, and tolerant people were a big reason for that. Every professional, personal, and physical uprooting and subsequent rebirth I've experienced has concluded with a soft landing thanks to kindhearted people like the Cheneys, who invariably provided timely and often much-needed support. It's because of people like them I have, at least so far, precious little experience with long-term loneliness or disconnection, a state of affairs for which I am profoundly grateful.

At around midnight on an early January night in 2001 my pregnant wife's water broke unexpectedly. With barely enough time to collect anything beyond our thoughts we hurried to the hospital in Portland, where our son was born the next day. That night York County got hit with a significant storm, meaning I had to make a challenging drive home the next morning, clear a path to the house, and collect the necessities we had, in our haste, neglected to bring to the hospital. Sleep-deprived and anticipating backbreaking labor, as I turned onto our street I was treated to the sight of Lee, Pat, and another neighbor, all significantly older and smaller than I was, tossing the last shovelfuls of snow from our driveway.

If you believe, as I do, the words of Jackie Robinson, who famously said, "A life is not important except in the impact it has on other lives," then Lee Cheney's recently completed time on Earth was exceptionally well spent. ●

Still a Certainty, Even for Childhood Heroes

January 13, 2019

Two hundred thirty years ago, 83-year-old Benjamin Franklin confided in a letter to his friend Jean-Baptiste Leroy, "In this world nothing can be said to be certain, except death and taxes."

Today as in 1789, death is a part of life. Last year saw the departures of, among others, George and Barbara Bush, Senator John McCain, Stephen Hawking, and Aretha Franklin.

But while these luminaries and untold legions of others made significant impacts with their earthly deeds, no demise impacted me personally more than one which occurred in Springfield, Missouri, on the second day of 2019.

Jerry Buchek batted .220 in five partial seasons with St. Louis, but hit a comparatively lusty .236 with the Mets in 1967, when he hit 14 of his 22 career home runs.

Jerry Buchek spent ten years playing professional baseball, including parts of seven seasons in the major leagues with the St. Louis Cardinals and the New York Mets. His career statistics were, to be kind, pedestrian; the infielder compiled a lifetime batting average of just .220. He was a member of the National League pennant-winning 1964 Cardinals, but even that came with an asterisk; he made just 33 plate appearances while participating, however briefly, in just 35 of his team's 162 games that season. He earned immortality, sort of, by compiling (and later retiring with) a World Series batting average of 1.000. His one-out single in the bottom of the 9th inning of the sixth game knocked New York Yankees pitcher Jim Bouton out of the box, although its effect was minimal, since a double play two batters later finished off an 8-3 Yankees victory. That extended the series to a winner-take-all finale the next day, a contest Buchek witnessed from his familiar seat on the bench.

But nearly three years after that 7th game, a Cardinal victory that gave the team its first championship in 18 years, Buchek did something that was, to at least four young fans, far more important than anything he had done (or as it turned out, would do) in his entire athletic career.

On September 23, 1967, my father and my uncle took my nine-year-old brother, our cousins (ages ten and eleven), and ten-year-old me to our first-ever major league baseball game. Going to Shea Stadium, then a three-year-old palace located a mere 75-minute drive from our home in southern Connecticut, was our holy grail; who cared if the game that Saturday night featured the National League's two worst teams, the last-place Mets and their slightly-less-incompetent guests, the 9th-place Houston Astros?

The playing surface was the greenest I'd ever seen, which in retrospect made perfect sense, as every game I'd witnessed previously had been televised in glorious black and white.

Neither Dad nor Uncle Eddie was particularly enthralled by baseball, but each recognized his sons' passion for it, which justified spending a combined fifteen dollars for six tickets. Numerous 25-cent hot dogs, 50-cent hamburgers, and 15-cent sodas made it a fairly pricey night on the town, but to my youthful peers and me it was simply Heaven. We were seeing an entire major league baseball game, live, from start to finish.

Or maybe not. A rookie Met pitcher named Tom Seaver was mowing down the Astros with seeming ease, but his Houston mound opponents were doing the same to the home team. With the game still scoreless in the top of the 8th inning, our chaperones began murmuring about "beating the traffic." Looking back, that excuse was laughable. The modest official attendance count (just over 11,000) was probably double the number of actual fans present that night. We boys unanimously wanted to stay for the finish, but after a brief conference the adults decreed we would be going home at the conclusion of the 9th inning, regardless of whether the game was over or not.

Neither team managed even a baserunner in the 8th inning, and when the Astros went down in order in the top of the 9th, it was clear: if the Mets didn't score in the bottom of the inning our first-ever trip to a major league baseball game would be an incomplete one.

But lo and behold: a leadoff double, an intentional walk, and a bunt single loaded the bases with no one out.

That brought up New York's shortstop, who had been hitless in his first three trips to the plate that night. But with the game on the line, Jerry Buchek belted a ball over the leftfielder's head that sent everyone home happy.

Thanks to Buchek's timely hit I slept soundly the whole way home. Which, in retrospect, seems far preferable to enduring the decades of psychological therapy a premature exit from an uncompleted game would undoubtedly have necessitated.

I don't wish to downplay the value of anyone else's life, but Jerry Buchek's passing was more challenging for me to process than were the departures of any past president, first lady, U.S. senator, theoretical physicist, or Queen of Soul. ●

PART 2

Things That Matter Less

The fervor with which Americans follow professional athletics (a category which includes the major college revenue-producing ones) is nearly as troubling as the youth sports industry's encouragement of youthful athletes (and their parents) to pursue, at significant expense, unrealistic goals. But old habits die hard, and despite my contempt for those who care more about profits than they do about sports, I (and others like me) still can't help paying attention.

SECTION 5

Mostly Baseball

The Designated Hitter Rule Must Go!

February 15, 2007

Pitchers and catchers checked in to Major League Baseball spring training camps in Florida and Arizona this past weekend, and position players are required to do the same later this week. It's not clear, however, when (or even if) designated hitters are scheduled to report.

In the early 1970s baseball in general was suffering from a perceived lack of runs, and the American League in particular was experiencing a noticeable dearth of fans. The designated hitter rule was put into effect in 1973 in an effort to address both concerns. Today there is more than enough offense in the game and fans are streaming into AL parks, particularly those in Boston and New York. The DH rule has long since served its purpose, yet it remains on the books today, and by doing so continues to make a mockery of many of baseball's most time-honored records.

How many home runs might Babe Ruth have hit had there been a designated hitter rule in the 1930s as his career was winding down? Would Jimmie Foxx, Mel Ott, and Ted Williams be higher on the all-time home run list? Would more recent sluggers like Jim Rice, Reggie Jackson, Juan Gonzalez, Jose Canseco, and Frank Thomas have compiled the same lusty offensive statistics were there not a designated hitter rule for them to take advantage of?

Pitching statistics have similarly become less meaningful since the dawn of the DH. Striking out 300 batters for an American League team is a far more impressive feat than accomplishing the same thing in the National League, where a significant number of those whiff victims are likely to be weak-hitting pitchers. Had there been a DH rule 40 years ago, how many more games might Hall of Famers like Sandy Koufax, Bob Gibson, or Juan Marichal have won? Each would have had many more complete games (and opportunities to win those tilts) if they didn't have to leave for a pinch-hitter in the late innings of close contests when their team was trailing. The DH rule is rendering many of baseball's most important career statistics meaningless.

Countless potential fans have turned away from baseball because they see the game as too slow, or too long. Contributing to this problem is the fact a DH usually takes far more pitches to complete his turn at the plate than a bat-wielding pitcher normally does, which adds more time to contests already perceived by many as too lengthy. In addition, contemporary American League hurlers who don't have to appear at the plate themselves often feel little or no hesitation about throwing at skilled batters on opposing teams, since with the DH rule no opportunity for direct retribution exists. If pitchers knew they had to appear at the plate at least once every three innings like everyone else in the lineup, they might think twice about firing a delivery that could injure another team's star player(s).

Perhaps the worst thing about the designated hitter rule: it perpetuates the mistaken idea that pitchers are inherently poor hitters. In Little League, Babe Ruth League, high school baseball, and American Legion ball, the best athlete is often the pitcher, who usually occupies a spot somewhere in the middle of the batting order. Many times when a team's top hurler is not on the mound he is playing shortstop, catcher, or some other important position on the diamond. So why is it that pitchers can't hit in pro ball? Because *nobody* can hit if the bat gets taken out of his hands! It's not surprising most American League pitchers look helpless during their infrequent trips to the plate. Barry Bonds wouldn't be much of a hitter if he never took batting practice and got only ten or so at-bats per season. Without the DH rule good hitting pitchers would get to the plate more regularly. Wes Ferrell, Warren Spahn, Don Newcombe, Earl Wilson and Don Drysdale are just a few examples of pitchers whose skill at the plate helped make them even more valuable to their teams during their careers. However, thanks to the DH rule most of today's big league hurlers look forward to a trip to the batter's box with the same sort of anticipation the rest of us feel immediately prior to visiting the dentist.

While baseball is at least nominally still the National Pastime, the reality is the Grand Old Game has been losing fans at an alarming rate for several decades. Many of the reasons for the decline in the game's popularity are beyond the control of the people running Major League Baseball. However, there are *some* problems the lords of the game *can* do something about, and repealing the DH rule is one of them. Doing so would shorten the time required to play, make the sport safer for the participants, bring some uniformity back to the game's records, and give the best athletes the opportunity to excel in all aspects of the game, not just one. The time for baseball's designated hitter rule has come…and gone! ●

It's Been a Lifetime Since the Mets Were Relevant

March 19, 2020

The start of the Major League Baseball season marks an annual rebirth of sorts that stirs the feelings of countless New Yorkers. And while prior to the pandemic-related delay of this season's launching many Yankee fans were no doubt eagerly anticipating this year's edition of the team making another run at winning the storied franchise's 28th World Series, even cautiously optimistic Met fans like me were (and will continue to be, when and if the games begin anew) consumed by a sort of fatalistic trepidation, wondering exactly when and where our team's figurative ship is going to spring a leak this year, and what event(s) will ultimately cause it to sink.

It wasn't always this way. A half-century or so ago during my (and the team's) formative years, the Mets were fun, and on the rise. They owned New York, or so it seemed to me. The Bronx Bombers of Babe Ruth, Joe DiMaggio, and Mickey Mantle were long gone; from the mid-60s through the early 70s the pinstriped frauds the Yankees annually rolled out were mediocre at best, but more often dreadful, boring, or both.

But that was then.

Some say that things began changing on April 2, 1972. That was the day that Gil Hodges, the beloved Brooklyn Dodger first baseman who had skippered the Miracle 1969 Mets to their implausible World Series victory over the vaunted Baltimore Orioles, dropped dead of a heart attack after playing a round of golf in West Palm Beach, Florida, with three members of his coaching staff. Hodges was two days short of his 48th birthday when he died; his life had lasted exactly 17,531 days.

March 31, 2020, is precisely 17,531 days after that tragic event. Today Gil Hodges has been dead for *exactly* as long as he was alive. And if it seems like a lifetime ago that the Mets were New York's team and the Yankees were struggling for relevance, well, that's because, at least in the case of Gil Hodges, it has been. Literally.

Hodges is the first member of the 1962 Mets to have been deceased as long as he lived. He won't have company in that department until September 13, 2029, when one of the team's original coaches, Rogers Hornsby, will have been dead for the length of his lifespan, which in his case was 24,358 days. There won't be another *player* from the 1962 edition of the squad to reach "dead as long as alive" (DALAA) status until Bob Moorhead, a relief pitcher who died at 42 in 1986, reaches the dubious milestone on October 13, 2035. And for those who need to know, Hodges isn't the first Met *player* to have been dead for as long as he lived. That unfortunate distinction belongs to the ill-fated Danny Frisella, a relief pitcher for the team between 1967 and 1972, who reached DALAA status on November 1, 2007, precisely 11,261 days after a dune buggy accident ended his life on New Year's Day, 1977.

Obviously the length of one's life span has a direct bearing on when an individual has been expired for a period of time equal to when he or she existed. That explains how the inventor of the telephone, Alexander Graham Bell (born 1847) and singer/songwriter Janis Joplin (born 1943) could both become DALAA in the same calendar year (1998). There are other examples: in 2024 singer Aaliyah, who died at age 22 in a 2001 plane crash, will achieve DALAA status three months before Orville Wright, the co-inventor of the airplane who was born more than a century before she was. Harry Truman and basketball superstar Kobe Bryant will both have been dead as long as they lived in the year 2061, an even more stark incongruity given that basketball didn't exist when America's 33rd president was born in 1884, and Truman had been dead for over half a decade by the time Bryant was born in 1978.

Next year Tupac Shakur, Biggie Smalls, and Kurt Cobain will all become dead for as long as they were alive. With that in mind, enjoy the 2020 baseball season—if there is one—for all it's worth. Because as Kobe Bryant, Janis Joplin, and Gil Hodges (if they were able) would no doubt remind us, our days are no less numbered than theirs were.

A Pronounced Change in Major League Baseball

July 5, 2009

July is the only remaining month during which Major League Baseball has America's undivided attention. No one living outside the Sun Belt plays or watches the game until mid-March, which is just about when everyone becomes fixated on college basketball tournaments. That madness subsides right when the National Basketball Association and the National Hockey League begin staging their respective playoffs. It's only from mid-June, when the NBA and NHL finally get around to crowning their champions, until the opening of National Football League training camps in late July that baseball occupies center stage for most of the nation's sports fans.

As far as youth participation goes, baseball has long since been surpassed by both basketball and soccer.

When I was a boy America's sporting landscape was far simpler. There was baseball, and then there was everything else. There was no debate over the identity of America's number-one spectator sport. The National Pastime truly **was** the national pastime. Time stood still in early October, when the World Series between the pennant winners of the American and National Leagues would be contested. Each spine-tingling contest of that best-of-seven series was played in the afternoon, when everyone (or at least everyone who played hooky from school and/or work) could see every pitch.

Today professional football is unquestionably the king of revenue-producing spectator sports. It's estimated over a billion people watched the Super Bowl earlier this year. In contrast, no one knows how many hundreds witnessed the end of the five World Series games that were played between Philadelphia and Tampa Bay last fall; exact figures are tough to come by since no gainfully employed person who lives in the Eastern Time Zone has any idea when late October World Series night games actually conclude.

One positive byproduct of the game's waning dominance in North America has been its remarkable growth overseas. Baseball is now being played at reasonably competitive levels on virtually every populated continent, and that's reflected by the diversity of the people now playing the sport at the major league level.

Forty years ago baseball cards bore the likenesses of guys whose names were generally easily pronounced. Bob Miller, Nelson Mathews, Bill Bryan, Willie Smith, Fred Newman, and Gene Oliver are just a few of the ones I remember from my own boyhood. There were a few exceptions: for example, the exotically named Pedro Gonzalez came from a mysterious place called the Dominican Republic, which wasn't one of the 50 states or one of the two Canadian provinces (Ontario and Quebec) I had heard of.

Last month at the end of my son's just-completed season in the Cumberland-North Yarmouth Farm League, his appreciative and thoughtful coach presented each player on their team with a blue ribbon and a pack of seven baseball cards.

Excitedly opening the pack and seeing the first card, my boy excitedly shouted, "Look, Daddy! I got AINGE-jill Suh-LOAM." I politely corrected him, informing him that Angel Salome's name was pronounced AHN-hell Sah-LOW-may.

The next card pictured Jarrod Saltalamacchia, whose last name my son haltingly sounded out as SALT-uh-luh-MAH-chee-uh. (Apparently the correct pronunciation of the Texas Ranger catcher's last name is SALT-uh-la-MOCK-ee-uh, but give the lad some credit for trying; he is, after all, only eight years old!)

But at least Jarrod's consonants outnumber his vowels; the third card was one of Matt Tuiasosopo (TOO-ee-ah-so-SO-poe), an aspiring third baseman for the Seattle Mariners. Thankfully the next cardboard photo was one of Cincinnati Reds outfielder Jay Bruce, but then came a Baltimore Orioles catcher named Guillermo Quiroz. My son looked at me quizzically. "Ghee-YAIR-moe KEY-roce," I said, unsteadily.

I was grateful the following card was one of Mike Cameron, not only because his was an easy name to pronounce, but because it was one I was familiar with. I actually remember him playing for the Chicago White Sox back when I was still paying attention, and thus glumly figured he must be about 50 years old. Happily, a cursory glance at his statistics indicated the outfielder who currently plays for the Milwaukee Brewers is only 36.

Read it, but not out loud: Kosuke Fukudome.

Then my son pulled out the last card in the pack. The player depicted on it was an outfielder for the Chicago Cubs. "Daddy, how do you say this man's name?" he said, handing me the two-inch by three-inch cardboard rectangle. I took one look, affected my best concerned and preoccupied expression, and told him that I needed to go check up on his mother and sister. Then I quickly hurried off to investigate some imaginary problem.

There are some things that should *never* be done in front of impressionable children, and trying for the first time to pronounce Kosuke Fukudome's name correctly is definitely one of them. ●

Changes in the All-Star Game, for Better *and* for Worse

July 5, 2016

Half a century ago baseball really *was* the nation's favorite sport. But in retrospect Americans took much of what they loved about the National Pastime for granted.

Back then great players generally stayed with one club for virtually their entire career. The game's superstars rarely changed teams during their prime.

Until Game 4 of the 1971 Fall Classic, every World Series game was played during the afternoon, meaning young people could actually see the end of the weekday contests. They could even follow them from the beginning if they were resourceful enough to stick a radio in their pocket, tape the earphone cord up their arm, and lean into the hand with the earpiece in it for the last hour or so of school.

There was one other sure thing: the National League was going to win the annual All-Star Game each summer. In the 1960s, 1970s, and early 1980s they toyed with their American League opponents. At one point the NL won 19 out of 20 midsummer classics, including 11 in a row from 1972 to 1982. Even the Capistrano Swallows weren't that reliable.

But there were reasons for all that.

Players didn't switch teams because they *couldn't.* Contractually bound until such time as their employer deemed them to be of no further use, a player's choice was to perform for the team owning exclusive title to his services and do so for whatever money they felt like paying him, or do something else for a living.

Afternoon World Series games ended once those same baseball team owners who kept their employees in perpetual servitude for the first seven or so decades of the 20th century learned how much television networks would pay to air the sport's signature tilts during prime time.

The cause of the National League's All-Star Game domination was even more insidious.

During the years from 1949 to 1964, all but one of the National League's eight non-expansion teams appeared in at least one World Series. Given such competitive balance, signing the best available talent (regardless of skin tone) was imperative. It's unlikely the Brooklyn Dodgers would have won four pennants between 1952 and 1956 without Jackie Robinson, Roy Campanella, Don Newcombe, Joe Black, and Jim Gilliam—African Americans all. From 1951 on *every* National League pennant winner featured key players who were black and/or Latino.

During that same 16-season stretch the New York Yankees, an organization known for its reluctance to sign or promote players of color, won 14 American League pennants, doing so with little to no minority presence. But the foolish and often haughty attitude of their competition was, "If the Yankees can win without minority players every year, why can't we?" A pattern had been established, and it took nearly two decades for the junior circuit to catch up.

The All-Star Game played 50 years ago, won by the National Leaguers 2-1 in ten innings, is instructive. The first four hitters in the NL lineup that day were African-American: future Hall of Fame members Willie Mays, Roberto Clemente, Hank Aaron, and Willie McCovey. (Joe Morgan would have been a fifth, but he missed the game due to an injury.) The NL had seven other future Hall of Fame members on the team that day: Sandy Koufax, Jim Bunning, Juan Marichal, Gaylord Perry, Willie Stargell, Joe Torre, and Ron Santo. Future Cooperstown inductees Lou Brock, Billy Williams, Ernie Banks and Orlando Cepeda didn't even make the NL's team that summer, nor did league batting champion Matty Alou or future batting champ Pete Rose. By contrast only six future Hall of Famers were 1966 American League all-stars. Five were white English-speaking Americans: Brooks Robinson, Harmon Killebrew, Carl Yastrzemski, Catfish Hunter, and Al Kaline. Only one was black: Frank Robinson, who had been dealt to the Baltimore Orioles the previous winter by the National League's Cincinnati Reds. Somehow it's fitting the best pitcher in the American League during much of the period from 1949 to 1964 was New York Yankee ace "Whitey" Ford!

Every player appearing in the 2016 Major League Baseball All-Star game will make more money this season than the *total* Jackie Robinson earned in his ten-year career, but since that's based primarily on talent and improved bargaining power rather than race and/or ethnicity, it's probably a good thing.

However, I won't watch this year's annual baseball all-star game for the same two reasons I've missed the last 25 or so.

One is utter disinterest in sitting inertly for three hours to view youthful, uber-rich, athletically gifted millionaires generate a significant revenue stream for a bunch of corporations and billionaires that need additional wealth even less than the players themselves do.

The other?

I can't stay up that late. ●

Careful What You Wish For, Cubs Fans

October 23, 2016

Major League Baseball's World Series begins tonight, and it could very well be one for the ages. This best-of-seven clash between the American and National League champions has the potential to make fans in the two involved cities ignore, at least temporarily, an exceptionally ugly presidential campaign many Americans would prefer to tune out entirely.

The Cleveland Indians haven't been their sport's champion since 1948, when they conquered Boston's two big-league teams (the Red Sox in a one-game playoff for the American League pennant and the Braves in the World Series) five times in an eight-day span. One sign that times have changed radically since then: Cleveland's quintet of October victories that year took an average of two hours to complete. That's about as long it takes to televise five ad-saturated, pitching-change-fraught innings these days.

But even though Cleveland's team hasn't won the World Series in 68 years (and have only participated in it once since 1954), the general public hasn't embraced the Tribe as lovable, long-overdue underdogs. That's because their opponents, the Chicago Cubs, last played in the World Series in 1945, a year that began with Franklin Roosevelt in the White House, and last won it in 1908, when the president was *Theodore* Roosevelt.

Even the terminally hard-hearted have to concede 108 years between championships is a long drought, so it's no wonder much of America has embraced Wrigley Field's suddenly formidable team. But giddy Cubs followers should be advised to proceed with caution.

Not long ago another large group of avid baseball fans was starved for a championship. The Boston Red Sox hadn't won the World Series since the last year of World War I. Agonizing post-season defeats in 1946, 1967, 1978, and 1986 only made their suffering worse, but even more galling was the success of their team's arch-rivals. The perennially arrogant New York Yankees had won 26 titles since Boston's last World Series triumph. The only emotion even close to the limitless devotion Red Sox fans had for their team was antipathy for the haughty, perennially successful Bronx Bombers and their entitled followers. Not only were the contemptible New Yorkers perpetually obnoxious winners, but the despicable manner in which they obtained their titles, outbidding every other team for the game's top talent simply because they could, truly stuck in Boston's collective craw.

But with the possible exception of the North Pond Hermit, everyone in northern New England vividly remembers the magic autumn of 2004. After being humiliated by the hated Yankees in the first three games of the American League Championship Series, the Sox became the first team in Major League Baseball history to storm back from such a deficit to win a best-of-seven matchup. And before that joy subsided, they swept the St. Louis Cardinals in four straight World Series contests, ending their 86-year title drought.

Demons exorcised, the team rapidly won two more titles, in 2007 and 2013, and contended for several others.

But not everything was ideal after the "Curse of the Bambino" was broken. Buoyed by new and deep-pocketed ownership, the Red Sox bought (and more than occasionally overpaid) already-wealthy mercenaries every bit as rashly as their rivals from New York ever did. A top Sox pitcher who fancied himself an entrepreneur defaulted on a $75 million loan from the state of Rhode Island, and later got fired from a cushy sportscasting job by continuing to speak and/or tweet inappropriately. And at least two of the best hitters on Boston's championship teams were fueled by banned performance-enhancing substances.

The 2016 season saw the Sox improve by 15 wins over the previous year, and go from last place in their division to first in the process. But less than 24 hours after their elimination from the American League playoffs in three straight games, bloviating talk-show hosts, pot-stirring columnists, and much of the team's rabid fan base were demanding the ouster of the manager who had spearheaded their remarkable improvement.

The success they spent decades hungering for has turned Red Sox Nation into Evil Empire North. These days the only discernable difference between Red Sox rooters and Yankee fans are the accents.

No one outside of New England currently considers the Red Sox and their followers underdogs, or even remotely lovable. The only group of North American sports aficionados more despised than shrill Boston baseball fans are shrill New England Patriot football fans. But that's not hard to explain, at least to anyone with a memory spanning more than 12 years. Everyone, it seems, hates a too-frequent winner.

Good luck to the Chicagoans on breaking their 108-year title-less streak. But careful what you wish for, Cubs fans.

You just might get it. ●

On Reading and Aging

March 10, 2009

Years ago my parents and numerous public school English teachers earnestly tried to interest me in a variety of literature, but no amount of effort from any adult I knew could sway me from my determined distaste for reading. Then as now it was tough to impact a child willing himself to be unreachable. My preferred pastimes were athletic in nature. The only words I'd even glance at voluntarily were either published on the sports page or printed on the backs of baseball cards.

That's why it's ironic that today my favorite leisure activity is poring over printed words, despite the fact I have far less free time with which to do it than I did during my long-since-departed youth. Even odder: the person who finally sold me on reading did not to my knowledge own a teaching certificate, although his photo did on occasion appear on the front of one of those baseball cards I used to memorize.

Forty years have passed since professional baseball pitcher Jim Bouton, a former 20-game winner with the New York Yankees, put together, with the assistance of New York sportswriter Leonard Shecter, a diary of his 1969 season with three professional baseball teams that he titled *Ball Four*.

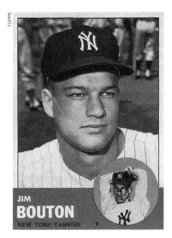

Jim Bouton circa 1963, the year he won 21 games for the New York Yankees, and six years prior to authoring the book that made me a reader.

Major League Baseball commissioner Bowie Kuhn publicly harrumphed when the book was published in 1970. He and numerous sycophants in the media indignantly implied the material contained in Bouton's book was so salacious it would ruin baseball, and by extension our great nation. It was in no small part thanks to their shrill objections that I decided I had to read *Ball Four*. However, I did not possess what a hardcover bestseller went for back then (a stratospheric $6.95!) and our town library hadn't acquired a copy.

My father wasn't a big baseball fan, but recognized his oldest child was. One weeknight the following spring he came home with a paperback edition of *Ball Four* that had set him back $1.25. Prior to his handing it to me he gave me a stern cautionary lecture regarding certain words contained in the book that neither he nor my mother endorsed.

I nodded soberly, thanked him, excused myself from the dinner table, retired to the semi-privacy of the room I shared with my brother, and commenced reading. I finished the 371-page book at about 5 o'clock the following morning, pausing only to deal with my tired sibling's protests that all the chuckles and bed-shaking belly laughs emanating from the top bunk were keeping him from getting any sleep.

Ironically, *Ball Four* might not even get into print today due to the *lack* of the sort of allegedly prurient details Commissioner Kuhn so piously objected to 39 years ago. In its pages Bouton did indeed reveal that many ballplayers spent their free time chasing and/or looking up skirts, and that more than a few regularly partook of alcohol. He further related that some even tried enhancing their on-field performance with little pills not readily available at their local pharmacies. Imagine that! In short, he wrote that major league baseball players weren't gods; rather, they were ordinary men enjoying an extended adolescence thanks to their ability to skillfully play a child's game.

What he didn't do, at least with specific incidents that could have gotten individuals in hot water, was name names. The only exception was his disclosing that longtime Yankee superstar Mickey Mantle could get surly from time to time, and that he enjoyed a drink or two. Many who had placed the handsome, muscular, drawling Caucasian superstar on a pedestal just below God were outraged.

Bouton's perceived blasphemy earned him pariah status in the baseball world, even though no credible person ever claimed anything he wrote wasn't true. Ironically, in his declining years Mantle himself openly admitted to his severe drinking problem in numerous broadcast and print interviews.

Jim Bouton turned 70 this past Sunday. Four decades ago that seemed impossibly old to me. Today it's an age I no longer fear, but rather one I can only hope to attain myself in less than two decades.

Accurately and sensitively defining "old" is a tricky business, as well as an ongoing process. As a teenager I thought 30 was past one's prime, 40 was ancient, 50 was Paleolithic, and 60 was prehistoric. I lacked the adjectives to describe anyone over 70. It wasn't until I was well into nominal adulthood that I came up with what I thought was a reasonable and flexible description of elderly. "Old" was by my definition what anyone born 20 or more years before one's grandparents was.

Thanks to Jim Bouton and countless others, I now know better. An old person is someone who, regardless of chronological age, decides that he or she is no longer interested in reading. ●

How Far Has Baseball Receded?

April 8, 2015

What was once a significant annual event for most die-hard athletic aficionados has become almost an afterthought, barely noticeable amongst the forest of events the multi-billion-dollar professional sports industry assaults Americans with 24-7 in order to keep them hooked on the exploits of grossly overcompensated athletically gifted young men.

Coming on the eve of the finals of the NCAA men's and women's basketball tournaments, the imminent Masters golf tournament, the rapidly approaching National Hockey League and National Basketball Association playoffs, and whatever was on the upcoming NASCAR schedule, it's a minor miracle the St. Louis Cardinals' 3-0 blanking of the Chicago Cubs on April 5th, Major League Baseball's official opening night, even made the next morning's sports page.

Even here in the heart of Red Sox Nation, a surprisingly large bloc of otherwise rational sports fans (which some see as a contradiction in terms) barely acknowledged the annual starting date of a sport which not all that long ago was unquestionably America's favorite.

Baseball was literally *and* figuratively the country's "National Pastime" for at least the first two-thirds of the 20th century, yet 15 years into the 21st it's become marginalized, barely noticed until the conclusion of the basketball and hockey playoffs, and even then only followed with any hint of passion until July, when the insidiously well-marketed National Football League opens its training camps in preparation for its five-month NFL season that begins in earnest each year around Labor Day.

Longtime baseball fans genuinely wonder how and why so many younger people follow other athletic endeavors with far greater ardor than they do the game that produced truly influential cultural and historical icons like Babe Ruth, Jackie Robinson, and Roberto Clemente. Perhaps they've been following other things. Paying closer attention to nuclear arms limitation talks, potentially life-altering climate change developments, or the ongoing equal rights for everyone battle(s) is understandable. But New England sports fans more concerned with a first-round Memphis Grizzlies playoff game than with how the Red Sox are faring is inexplicable.

As bewildered as veteran baseball watchers are with younger sports fans, Twittering, Snapchatting, selfie-taking, instant-gratification addicts are probably equally curious about why so many venerable types still obsess over a three-hour, often action-free game that moves at a snail's pace.

Here's a thought: fifty years ago, TV sets had three channels at most. Personal computers didn't exist. Leisure hours were, for some, likely more plentiful than they are today. But the imagination required to fill that idle time had to be self-generated, rather than artificially created by some electronic device(s). Young people made their own fun, and much of that involved actually *playing* the sports they watched live on a fuzzy black-and-white video screen once in a great while, if they were lucky.

Marketing was also a part of the equation, although the baseball industry's efforts in that regard half a century or so ago seem quaint by today's standards. One tiny but nonetheless significant portion of selling the game in the early 1960s took place on the back of cereal boxes.

Because my mother had a random yet uncanny knack for bringing home containers of Post Toasties with at least one Detroit Tiger trading card on the back, I began rooting for the Motor City's American League team. Today I sometimes forget which days of the week my children have concerts or soccer practices, but those two-and-a-half-inch by three-and-a-half-inch cardboard images of Rocky Colavito, Al Kaline, Jake Wood, Dick Brown, Bill Bruton, Don Mossi, Steve Boros, and Chico Fernandez are still burned into my memory. Thank goodness Mom didn't purchase boxes featuring numerous members of the Milwaukee Braves, Washington Senators, or Kansas City Athletics. Then I'd have been stuck rooting for a defunct team a few years later. Who knows what that would've done to my psyche?

Cereal box baseball cards disappeared after 1963, but by that time the sport had hooked me, and, as it turns out, had done so permanently despite my initially sporadic and later more determined efforts to outgrow it.

Trading cards on the back of cereal boxes ought to make a comeback, but when they do they ought to feature societal impact makers instead of grossly overpaid professional athletes. It used to cost at least two really good cards, like a Kaline and a Colavito, to swap for a superstar like Willie Mays, and if the guy you were trading with drove a hard bargain, you'd have to throw in a Norm Cash to complete the transaction.

I wonder if packaging a Rosa Parks and a Thomas Edison together would get me an Abraham Lincoln, or if I'd need to add a Jonas Salk to close the deal? ●

Happy Birthday Moe

July 20, 2006

On a hot August afternoon in 1983 I was at Olympic Stadium in Montreal for the Expos' Old-Timers game, and thanks to a press pass an enterprising friend had arranged for I was amidst a few dozen former major leaguer baseball players. I wanted to write a slew of freelance stories that night, but unfortunately I wasn't quite sure how one approached active or former professional athletes. As a result I stood near the batting cage sweating profusely, speaking to no one, and feeling like a doofus.

The press credential I had been issued proclaimed that I represented the *Winsted Evening Citizen*, which at the time was Connecticut's smallest daily newspaper. It was my good fortune that a pleasant-looking guy in a baseball uniform glanced at my badge and exclaimed, "Hey! You're from Connecticut! *I'm* from Connecticut!" The man's name was Moe Drabowsky.

I had collected baseball cards religiously as a youth, so I knew that the fellow speaking to me had been born in Ozanna, Poland, lived in Highland Park, Illinois, and had pitched for eight different major league teams in a career that spanned parts of 17 seasons.

Moe patiently answered all my questions and regaled me with stories that were often self-deprecating and contained not the slightest hint of braggadocio. He happily recalled the October day in 1966 when he established a World Series record by coming out of the Baltimore bullpen to strike out 11 Los Angeles Dodgers in the opening game of that year's Fall Classic. What made his performance even more remarkable was that he had entered that season, his first as an Oriole, with a lifetime major league record of 48 wins and 81 losses.

He talked about his reputation as being one of the game's premier practical jokers. Some of Moe's stunts included filling the opposing team's water cooler with goldfish, arranging for snakes to slither out of bread baskets at various banquets, and using the bullpen phone at Baltimore's Memorial Stadium to order take-out Chinese food…from a restaurant located in Hong Kong.

Moe related that he and his mother emigrated from Poland to Hartford when he was three years old. His father joined them a year later, and shortly thereafter the family moved to nearby Windsor. Moe grew up loving the Red Sox. He wanted to be a second baseman like Bobby Doerr, but instead Drabowsky ended up pitching when he went to Trinity College in Hartford. His hurling was impressive enough for the Cubs to sign him and insert him directly into their big league starting rotation at age 21 in 1956. When his playing career ended in 1972, he took a sales position with a paper company.

A decade later he made another career change, going to work for a Canadian telecommunications company.

I ended up writing a feature story about Moe that appeared in the Willimantic *Chronicle*, which was at the time Connecticut's *second*-smallest daily newspaper.

Fifteen years later I ran into Drabowsky again, this time at a minor league ballpark in Bowie, Maryland. In player development with the Orioles at the time, Moe was on hand to counsel some of the home team's promising pitchers. I asked if he'd do an interview for the pregame radio show I was doing, and he graciously consented. After we finished recording, I asked if he recalled our previous encounter in Montreal. Moe claimed he remembered it clearly, which meant either he possessed the world's best memory or he was the world's kindest man.

Moe Drabowsky died last month. He had been battling bone marrow cancer.

These days I occasionally encounter people who look down on sports in general and baseball in particular. When someone opines that in the grand scheme of things the national pastime doesn't really amount to much, I can't argue. However, when someone suggests that persons who play, coach, umpire, or cover the game for a living are wasting their time, I stridently disagree. Baseball may be meaningless to some, but to those who devote significant portions of their lives to it, it most definitely is not.

Moe would have turned 71 this week. His record of 11 strikeouts by a relief pitcher in a World Series game still stands today. More significantly though, he was an ordinary, extraordinary human being who did his best to make the world a more enjoyable place. ●

Moe Drabowsky with the Kansas City A's, the fourth of his eight big league teams.

Will Bill Buckner Get the Legacy He Deserves?

July 2, 2019

One of the outstanding Major League Baseball players of his era, Bill Buckner is unfairly remembered by far too many people for a single play, one that constituted perhaps one ten-thousandth of a percent of his otherwise distinguished 22-year career in Major League Baseball.

It turns out Buckner, who died at age 69 this past Memorial Day, was just as upstanding, successful, and honorable off the field as he was a standout on it.

Few human beings are capable of showing the grace under fire Buckner did after his 10th-inning misplay of Mookie Wilson's ground ball in the sixth game of the 1986 World Series finished (note: "finished," not "caused") a crushing Red Sox loss, one that took on even greater significance the following night, when the New York Mets won the decisive 7th game and extended Boston's baseball championship-less streak to 68 years.

Buckner's miscue made him a national punchline and a New England punching bag. Unfairly and shrilly vilified for the better part of two decades afterward, a lesser man would have turned bitter, or just disappeared, but Buckner did neither. Instead, he immersed himself in his roles as a prosperous Idaho businessman who was active in his community, a caring parent, and an avid outdoorsman.

Those who defined Buckner by his one notorious misplay did a disservice to him not only as a human being but as a baseball player. The National League batting champion in 1980, Buckner rapped out 2715 hits in his career, a figure topped by only 65 of the 19,564 (and counting) players in Major League Baseball history. In addition, the outfielder/first sacker who played the latter portion of his career on legs similar to (or perhaps even worse than) Mickey Mantle's helped lead teams from both the National (Dodgers) and American (Red Sox) Leagues to a World Series appearance. He was also one of baseball's most difficult batters to strike out, never whiffing more than 39 times in a season. How remarkable is that? *New York Times* baseball columnist Tyler Kepner tweeted that on the last full day of Buckner's life, 16 different players struck out three times in a major league baseball game, something Buckner *never* did in *22* big league seasons.

Sadly, Buckner's impressive numbers may not be quite enough to make him a baseball immortal; three of his left-handed hitting contemporaries, Rusty Staub, Vada Pinson, and Al Oliver, and another lefthanded hitter who came along later, Johnny Damon, all rapped out more hits than Buckner, and none of them have been enshrined in the sport's Hall of Fame in Cooperstown, New York. Neither have Steve Garvey, Mickey Vernon, or José Cruz, all outstanding players whose career numbers are similar to those complied by Buckner. But perhaps there's hope.

Consider "Sunny Jim" Bottomley, whose perpetually cheerful disposition earned him his nickname. He played in the major leagues for sixteen distinguished seasons in the 1920s and '30s, and compiled career numbers not unlike Buckner's. The National League's Most Valuable Player in 1928, when he led the circuit in home runs and RBI, Bottomley played for two World Series–winning teams with the St. Louis Cardinals. He achieved lasting fame on September 16, 1924, the day he drove in 12 runs in a single game against the Brooklyn Robins. That established the single-game record for runs batted in that still stands 95 years later, although it's been tied once (by another Cardinal, Mark Whiten, on September 7, 1993). When Bottomley retired after the 1937 season his 2313 hits ranked him 38th on the all-time list, and although 31 of those ahead of him on the list were ultimately enshrined in Cooperstown, Bottomley, who died in 1959, never received serious consideration for that honor himself.

Until fifteen years later. In 1974 Bottomley was elected to the Hall of Fame by baseball's Veterans Committee, which at the time included one of his influential ex-teammates, 1947 Cooperstown inductee Frankie Frisch.

Could history repeat itself? Consider the possibility that in 2034, one of Buckner's Hall of Fame ex-teammates, like Jim Rice, Ryne Sandberg, or maybe even Roger Clemens, occupies a spot on the group charged with selecting Hall of Famers from bygone days, and decides to do a little persuading of his fellow committee members. Perhaps then Buckner will deservedly gain inclusion to the Hall, and with it ultimate vindication from being unfairly and inaccurately characterized as merely a historical footnote, the guy who let Mookie Wilson's ground ball go through his legs. ●

SECTION 6

At/On the Field

Just Let Them Play

July 2, 2013

Many years ago a baseball team I was coaching led our opponents 9-4 as we batted in the top of the 7th (and last) inning. With one out I flashed the "steal" sign to the runner at first base, who easily pilfered second on the ensuing pitch. That moved the opposing coach to call time, walk from his dugout directly to the third base coaching box where I was standing, and berate me about what a bad example I was setting by trying to run the score up like that. Once his righteous indignation had been expressed, he turned and stomped back to his bench.

In professional baseball many believe stealing a base with a five-run lead in the last inning does indeed constitute rubbing the other team's nose in it. However, this was a Western Connecticut Conference freshman game, and that opposing coach didn't know our team had lost all four of its previous games, allowed 15 runs or more in each drubbing, and was badly in need of a morale-boosting victory. But I did. That's why I was employing strategy designed to turn a five-run lead into a six-run lead.

Some time later I was an assistant coach for a high school basketball team destined to finish its season with 20 losses in 20 games. We took some fearful trouncings that year, but none worse than a 104-39 pasting at the hands of the eventual conference champs, whose starters were still full-court pressing at the start of the fourth quarter. Our apoplectic head coach was beside himself, sensing our opponents were "rubbing it in."

But how did *he* know the other coach's rationale for such strategy? Our more talented opponents had a big game coming up later that week against significantly better opposition. Was it their fault we were that weak? Their coach apparently thought playing his starters for the last eight minutes was more beneficial than inserting the JV team just to avoid the appearance of running up the score. Was outscoring an already humiliated opponent 30-4 in the fourth quarter appropriate strategy that night? I probably wouldn't have done it, but the fact was their coaches were better qualified than I to determine what was best ***for their team*** that night.

Coaching young athletes to the satisfaction of their parents is even more challenging these days than it was a generation ago. No rational adult hires a plumber to fix a leaky faucet and subsequently second-guesses him over which wrench he uses, nor does anyone reasonable take a car to a mechanic and then tell him how to change the oil. Why then would any parent openly second-guess the coach of a youth athletic team? When an individual acts as though a game with five, six, nine, ten, or eleven players on a side revolves solely around his or her youngster, it's unsurprising when the child in question ultimately begins believing it as well.

Loudly questioning or criticizing an opposition coach at a youth sports event sets a poor example, but it's not nearly as counterproductive as people openly or furtively casting aspersions on the adults in charge of their own offspring's team. There's far more to coaching youth sports than knowing what the pros would do in a given situation. The dynamics of any team in any sport at any level are unique; achieving optimal results requires players to fully believe in the coaching staff as completely as they do in one another. It also requires said team's supporters to refrain from trying to insert themselves into an endeavor that they are not (and should not be) directly involved in. Failing to remember that undermines everyone involved.

A youth sports coach truly deserves criticism or outright censure when he or she engages in behavior that belittles, humiliates, or questions the integrity of players or officials, but such actions should be handled through proper channels. In an ideal world, "adults" who are first and foremost intent on building dynasties with teenage and/or pre-teenage athletes would be weeded out. However, since most youth leagues depend upon volunteers, this doesn't always happen. It would be nice if one of the requirements for coaching a sport at any sub-collegiate level were the successful completion of a year of officiating it first. Such a regulation would likely curb at least some inappropriate behavior on the part of those aspiring mentors who take winning a tad too seriously.

Parents, friends, and others who follow local high school and youth sports: let the officials officiate and let the coaches coach. But most importantly, let the kids ***play*** without interference. ●

Accurately Gauging How Victory Feels

July 7, 2017

My 11-year-old son was a member of the 2017 Cumberland/North Yarmouth Little League champion Red Sox, and I was one of the coaches. It was my second involvement with a Little League championship team. The first was in 1966, when I rode the bench for the Easton (CT) Little League champion Hawks. Oddly, after the CNYLL Red Sox won their championship game last month, I couldn't help but think of a certain former Major League Baseball player.

Jim Kaat was an outstanding pitcher who had an exceptionally long career. I wasn't yet potty trained when he debuted with the Washington Senators, but by the time his big-league playing days concluded I was a college graduate. Kaat is one of only eleven hurlers in Major League Baseball history to have pitched in four different decades, and his 283 career wins exceed the totals compiled by any of the other ten, except for Hall-of-Famers Nolan Ryan and Early Wynn.

But Kaat wasn't known solely for his longevity. The 6'4" native of Zeeland, Michigan, won 15 or more games in a season eight times between 1962 and 1975, including a 25-victory effort in 1966. He amassed 200 or more innings pitched in a season 14 times, which, given changes in philosophy regarding the care and handling of pitchers, is unlikely to be equaled (or even approached) in the future. He won the Gold Glove, emblematic of being his league's best-fielding pitcher, a record 16 times. He also reinvented himself in mid-career, morphing from a flame-throwing left-hander with high strikeout totals to a pitcher whose experience, guile, quick delivery, and ability to keep batters off stride more than made up for the inevitably decreasing velocity of his pitches.

Like millions of other boys who grew up dreaming of athletic glory but had no realistic chance of achieving it, I often wondered what life in the big leagues would have been like. How did Jim Kaat feel on June 17, 1957, when he signed his first professional contract with the Washington Senators at age 18, or on August 2, 1959, when he made his major league debut at Chicago's Comiskey Park against the World Series–bound White Sox?

What it was like a little over a year later when his team uprooted all its employees and moved from the nation's capital to a new home in the Upper Midwest, rechristening themselves the Minnesota Twins?

How great was it on June 19, 1962, in Chicago (again!) when, batting against Dom Zanni of the White Sox, he walloped the first of his 16 major league home runs?

Was the elation he felt after Game 2 of the 1965 World Series, a 5-1 victory over the Dodgers and Sandy Koufax, more intense than his disappointment of losing Games 5 and 7 to Koufax and his Los Angeles teammates four and seven days later?

Was Kaat nervous taking the mound for the American League in the 4th inning of the 1966 All-Star game in St. Louis, when the first six batters he faced were future Hall of Famers Willie Mays, Roberto Clemente, Hank Aaron, Willie McCovey, Ron Santo, and Joe Torre? He was probably calmer nine years later when only the first *three* hitters he faced, Lou Brock, Joe Morgan, and Johnny Bench, were Cooperstown-bound.

After more than 17 years with the notoriously stingy Senators/Twins organization, getting waived in August of 1973 had to hurt. Was being released for the final time, on July 6, 1983, worse?

Stealing a base at age 41 during a complete game victory had to be great, but was it better than the 16th and final home run of his big league career, which came two months later?

Jim Kaat, Chicago White Sox, 1973

But maybe the most rewarding thing about Kaat's career was returning to the World Series 17 years after his only other appearance in the Fall Classic, and helping his team win it.

Let's face it: I never played pro baseball, and as a consequence I have no way of *really* knowing how Jim Kaat felt when he signed to play professionally, got uprooted when his team moved, hit unexpected home runs or stole even more unexpected bases, won (and lost) World Series games against Sandy Koufax, pitched in front of millions of viewers in two All-Star games, or got unceremoniously dumped by his team in the middle of a season after 17 years with them.

But thanks to simple math I believe I know how he felt when he and his St. Louis Cardinal teammates won the World Series 17 years after his only previous appearance there.

About one-third as good as I did when the CNYLL Red Sox earned their title last month, 51 years after the Easton Hawks won theirs. ●

Delusions of Grandeur on the Pitch

August 9, 2011

Growing up in my world boys played baseball, football, and basketball.

Period.

Individual "sports" like golf, tennis, and swimming were for rich kids who belonged to country clubs. Hockey was seasonal, and even then only when the nearby ponds were sufficiently frozen over. Lacrosse existed solely on Indian reservations and at prep schools, and only small, balding men who spoke heavily accented English played soccer.

But where I attended college the nationally ranked men's soccer squad drew overflow crowds at their home matches, and as a result the student body was enthused about playing the game themselves. There were hundreds of intramural teams there, but due to a dearth of appropriate playing surfaces on campus, the games were all contested under the lights on a grassless, cratered football team practice field appropriately referred to as "The Moon."

I was recruited to play for my dorm's team partly because I was fast but mostly because I was unencumbered with trifles like attending classes, studying, or paying attention to a girlfriend. As far as my teammates were concerned, my availability and willingness to do what I was told more than compensated for my utter lack of discernable skills.

Besides, intramural soccer bore little resemblance to the sport the rest of the world was familiar with. Games were played on three narrow, parallel mini-fields on The Moon's surface. The nets weren't anywhere near regulation size, which was why goalies weren't allowed to use their hands. The teams played six per side for two 20-minute halves. As a defender my instructions were to charge directly at any ball coming my way and boot it as far and as hard as I could, either up the field or out of bounds. Under no circumstance was I to try to dribble, or even worse, attempt to pass the ball across the middle.

Our team was reasonably good. Three adroit forwards provided the scoring. Our goalie, a refugee from the university's rugby club, gleefully turned aside enemy shots by throwing his body in front of them, and my defense partner and I limited ourselves to aggressively attempting to get in the way when the opposition had the ball and even more zealously trying to stay *out* of the way when our team got possession of it.

As the season went on, I began thinking I had been wrong about soccer, and about those rotten high school gym teachers who made us play it every autumn when the vast majority of the all-male class would have preferred beating each other's brains out playing the American brand of football. We were enjoying (and winning) the majority of our matches, but unfortunately that success began deluding me into thinking I was actually good at the game. One night in the midst of a tightly contested tilt I collected possession of the ball deep in my own end and prepared, as per instructions, to forcefully send it out of bounds. But then I had an inspiration: rather than blast the ball over the sideline or up the field as I habitually did, I'd surprise our opponents by going on the attack! I pictured myself skillfully dribbling, zigging and zagging through the entire flabbergasted opposition, then punctuating my incursion by artfully launching a 25-yard blast with a banana curve on it that would elude the goalie's desperate leap and dent the twine at the net's upper corner.

As I was visualizing getting mobbed by my ecstatic teammates, I failed to notice a member of the opposition bearing down on me. Panicking, I attempted to pass the ball across the middle of the field to an invisible teammate. The other team's striker neatly stole it, raced unmolested toward our goal, and then from a distance of no more than ten feet from the net violently launched a rocket of a shot which our goalie, whose arms were locked behind his back, couldn't have dodged even if he had wanted to.

The speeding ball hit him flush in the face, nearly separating his skull from his shoulders. A ghastly welt appeared nearly instantly above one of his eyes; it got blacker and bluer by the second as he inexorably morphed into the Elephant Man while my teammates and I looked on in horror.

Hastily telling him I was genuinely sorry; his response, delivered in an indiscernible mumble, was either "Don't worry about it," "Where am I?" or "I'm going to kill you, you stupid $@%& *%@#%^er!"

My oldest boy's youth soccer season starts later this month. Most kids assume their dad was a reasonably accomplished athlete himself. I sincerely hope my son takes that on faith, rather than asking me any specific questions about my own brief and undistinguished career on the pitch. ●

Seeing an All-Time Great Before He Was Famous

October 1, 2013

Before becoming a high school English teacher and occasional essayist, I earned a modest living as a radio play-by-play announcer for a series of minor-league professional baseball teams. As part of that job, I saw plenty of ballgames: about 1700 of them, more or less.

But it's been several years since I've seen people get paid to play baseball. In fact, the last major league game I attended involved the Florida Marlins, who've since changed their name, and the Montreal Expos, who no longer exist.

My previous experience was probably what prompted a friend to offhandedly ask me recently if I had ever called a game in which Mariano Rivera, the just-retired New York Yankee relief ace, was the pitcher. In fact, I have. However, I never witnessed him earn any of his all-time record 652 major league saves, ply his trade at any major league ballpark, or perform anywhere as a relief pitcher.

In 1992 I was calling the play-by-play for the Vero Beach Dodgers of the Florida State League, and as such was behind the microphone for the team's game against the Fort Lauderdale Yankees on May 30th. The starting pitchers that Saturday night were two right-handers who could not have been more physically different. The Dodger hurler was Eric Weaver, a 6'5," 230-pound 18-year-old who looked like a National Football League tight end. The home team countered with a young man who from a distance looked a bit like Ichabod Crane on a hunger strike. At 6'4" tall and an alleged 168 pounds, Mariano Rivera looked more capable of hiding behind a broom handle than he did of confounding aspiring major league hitters. But it quickly became apparent that the Panamanian beanpole had some talent; Tim Griffin's third-inning single was the only hit Rivera allowed in seven shutout innings.

The FSL played an unbalanced schedule in those days, which is why the Dodgers found themselves at Fort Lauderdale Stadium facing Rivera again just 12 days later. This time the visitors actually scored a first-inning run on Vernon Spearman's single, a stolen base, a sacrifice bunt, and a sacrifice fly, but they were stymied the rest of the way as Rivera hurled a four-hit, no-walk complete game, winning 4-1.

So did I know back then Rivera was destined to be one of baseball's all-time greats?

Well, um…no. Lots of pitchers look good in the minor leagues, but things can change in a hurry. When Rivera next faced the Dodgers at Vero Beach's Holman Stadium in the first game of a June 19th doubleheader, the home team lit him up like a Christmas tree. Roberto Mejía and Jay Kirkpatrick slugged back-to-back home runs in the first inning, and consecutive singles by Mike Boyzuick, Anthony Collier, Billy Lott, and Freddy Gonzalez finished Rivera's evening in the bottom of the third inning. All told he gave up five runs on eight hits that night, while only managing to record eight outs.

It turned out there was an explanation. Shortly after the drubbing, the Yankees shut Rivera down. He subsequently underwent surgery on his damaged right elbow that August, which finished his season.

It turned out that what my friend *really* wanted to know was if I had ever actually spoken with Mariano Rivera, and if he was a nice guy.

Since the radio station airing Vero Beach Dodger baseball in 1992 broadcast to a virtually 100% English-speaking audience, Rivera, who spoke only Spanish, was not high on my list of potential pregame show interviews.

I did become friendly with a Spanish-speaking Fort Lauderdale player that year, a utility infielder who'd seek me out to practice his English with. But because he never made it out of the Florida State League, no one ever asks me about Andres Rodriguez.

New York Yankee fans would undoubtedly have preferred Mariano Rivera's final pitch had come later this month, and produced a World Series-ending whiff of some fearsome hitter on the National League champions, finishing Game 7 of the World Series and clinching the Bronx Bombers' 28th World Championship.

But there was no Hollywood ending. Rivera's actual final offering was popped up to second base by Tampa Bay's Yunel Escobar, the second out in the top of the 9th inning of yet another dreary Yankees' defeat.

I'm not overly concerned with how Mariano Rivera's retirement will go. He's a sure bet for first-ballot admission to the Hall of Fame in five years, and after that I'm sure his post-baseball life will be just fine.

But I ***do*** wonder about what Andres Rodriguez did in the final at-bat of ***his*** career. ●

How Others See Us

August 11, 2009

The world's most famous arena was sold out, and the building literally shook as I grabbed yet another defensive rebound. Turning, I fired an outlet pass to Walt Frazier and hustled up the floor, and thanks to my perpetual alertness was in position to opportunistically pick up the loose ball when Clyde's pass for Bill Bradley was deflected away. I head-faked left, stutter-stepped, then blew past a beleaguered Jerry West for what seemed like the tenth time. When seven-foot one-inch behemoth Wilt Chamberlain took a step in my direction I fired a one-bounce, no-look pass to our captain, Willis Reed, who banked in yet another unmolested two-pointer from underneath the basket.

Not satisfied, I hungrily darted in behind West and intercepted Chamberlain's careless inbound pass. Immediately converged upon by two angry, frustrated Lakers, I dribbled twice, stepped back, and tossed up an off-balance, high-arcing two-hander as I tumbled backward. "Yessss...and it counts!" shouted Knicks broadcaster Marv Albert, screaming to make himself heard over the din created by the capacity crowd. The roar continued

After taking a no-look pass from Andy Young, Walt Frazier of the New York Knicks eludes Seattle's Lucius Allen for a layup.

unabated, reaching a crescendo as the exasperated visitors called time out, but when play resumed my domination continued. I drove the lane at will, slashing in for multiple acrobatic, jaw-dropping lay-ups, and when the defense collapsed on me I coolly found Dick Barnett, Cazzie Russell, Dave DeBusschere, or whichever one of my white-shirted teammates was open in his favorite spot for a wide-open jumper. Defensively my quick feet and pickpocket hands were making the evening a nightmare for West, a perennial all-star. Then without warning I heard a clear and distinct voice. It was that of a young male.

"Mr. Young? I didn't know you played basketball."

Deflated, I thudded back to reality. The venue wasn't Madison Square Garden, there weren't 19,500 ecstatic fans watching, and I wasn't orchestrating a dismantling of the powerful Los Angeles Lakers. It was a winter morning in 2009, and I was trying to break a pre-school sweat in the Kennebunk High School gymnasium at 6:45 AM by firing up jump shots without opposition. The only sounds other than those created by my squeaking sneakers and the ball bouncing rhythmically off the floor were an occasional "swish," and more frequent "clangs" caused by one of my rotationless attempts caroming off the back iron.

Getting jarred back to reality was sobering enough, but then I remembered Chamberlain and DeBusschere are dead, Bradley is a decade or so removed from the U.S. Senate, and everyone else involved in my 1970-era fantasy is in his dotage. Talk about a reality check!

I had no idea anyone else had been in the gym. A boy who had been in a class I had taught a couple of years earlier had come in through a side door to use the weight room. He had made his comment because, well, he hadn't known I played basketball. Why should he have? As far as he knew I was just what he had observed in the classroom, a middle-aged man who talks a lot about books, pesters young people to care about their writing, and demands they get their assignments in on time.

It's good to step back periodically and assess how others see us.

Twenty-five years ago I was coaching three different sports at my old high school. Some of the kids I was working with were the younger siblings of people I had graduated with only a few years before. My daily attire consisted of sneakers, white socks, sweatpants, a t-shirt, and an omnipresent whistle around my neck. I was universally addressed as "Coach," and assumed anyone mentioning "Mr. Young" was referring to my father. Back then if I wasn't working or sleeping, I was involved in some sort of competitive athletic pursuit.

The reaction I got that winter morning in Kennebunk from the boy who was surprised when he saw me in the KHS gym before school was similar to the one I'd have gotten a quarter-century earlier if one of the players on the junior varsity baseball team had discovered me reviewing a copy of *The Merchant of Venice*. More than likely he'd have exclaimed, "Gee Coach, I didn't know you could read!"

Conversely, the sight of me playing basketball 25 years ago would have elicited the same response from the people who knew me then that seeing me pore over *The Autobiography of Malcolm X* does from my colleagues today, which is to say none at all.

Imagining we are who we'd like to be is a healthy thing to indulge in once in a while, provided that the fantasy involved isn't illegal, or harmful to others.

I wonder if Walt Frazier ever fantasizes about being a high school English teacher in Maine? ●

September 23, 1967

August 18, 2007

You never forget your first time.

Forty years ago this month 11,031 people, among them my father, my brother, two cousins, and my Uncle Eddie, were present at the consummation of my initial love affair.

It was a Saturday night and the Houston Astros were playing the New York Mets at Shea Stadium, a not-yet-four-year-old palace of a ballpark. Never mind that the visitors began the evening in ninth place, 32 1/2 games behind the pennant-winning St. Louis Cardinals and only five and a half games ahead of the last-place Mets. It was our first trip to a major league baseball game and we were in Heaven.

My uncle and my father were the evening's chaperones. Our party's half-dozen tickets would have cost an outrageous twenty-one dollars had we gone for box seats, but fortunately reserved seats were only two-fifty each. The six dollars we saved bought a lot of 25-cent hot dogs, 50-cent hamburgers, and 30-cent pizza slices. My father and my uncle might have had a 50-cent beer or two, but we kids were limited to 15-cent sodas. We certainly weren't going to splurge on 35-cent milkshakes!

I bought a scorecard for a quarter, then painstakingly filled in the names of each squad's nine starters. With both teams hopelessly out of contention, both lineups included several young unknowns hoping to make an impression during the season's waning days. Hal King and Lee Bales were in the Houston batting order, while Joe Moock, whose major league career ultimately consisted of just 13 games, was at the hot corner for the Mets.

Given that New York ace Tom Seaver was on the mound for the home team and four of the nine starters in the Met lineup had batting averages under .200, the pitchers' duel that developed was not wholly unexpected. After four scoreless innings each team had accumulated just two singles. Perhaps anticipating his teammates would need some assistance solving Houston starter Dave Giusti, Seaver hit his mound opponent on the hand with a pitch with two out in the top of the fifth, forcing him to leave the game for a pinch runner. However, the Mets fared no better against reliever Dave Eilers, who shut them out over the next four innings while allowing just one hit. Fortunately Seaver maintained his effectiveness as well. Entering the ninth inning each team had identical totals of no runs, three hits, and two errors.

However, at that point we had much more to worry about than whether or not Seaver would get his 16th win. Wanting to both beat postgame traffic and maintain their sanity, our chauffeurs decreed that our evening at the ballpark would be concluding at the end of nine innings, regardless of the score.

When Seaver retired the Astros in order in the top of the ninth we begged the adults to stay for the inevitable extra innings, but they were intractable. If we were to see the game's conclusion the Mets had to score in the bottom of the ninth.

Fortunately the fates smiled on us. The Mets loaded the bases with no one out on a leadoff double, an intentional walk, and a hard-hit single. At that point Larry Sherry, the MVP of the World Series for the Dodgers in 1959, was summoned from the Houston bullpen. Perhaps he'd have been equal to the task of extricating himself from a bases-loaded, none-out jam eight years earlier, but on this night Jerry Buchek, the first batter he faced, hammered a long, game-winning single beyond the reach of Houston's leftfielder.

40 years later Sherry is dead, as is Ron Davis, the outfielder over whose head Buchek's game-winning blow flew. Everyone else who participated in that game is at least 62 years old today; three are in their 70s.

I was ten years old in 1967. There were flirtations in my future with football, basketball, hockey, and, much later, women. But it's true what they say about your first love. You never forget it, even if in some cases (like this one) you have to look up some of the details. ●

Falling In and Out of Love with the Mets

May 14, 2007

Time marches on. Shea Stadium is being razed this fall. It opened in 1964, three years before I saw my first major league baseball game there.

I was born the same year the two original New York–based National League baseball teams relocated to the west coast cities of Los Angeles and San Francisco, and thus was just five years old when the Big Apple's current senior circuit team began its existence. Growing up in a family of underdog lovers made me a natural New York Mets fan.

In the wake of their handing the Eastern Division title to the Phillies last fall, I did some thoughtful and reflective soul searching, and was not totally unhappy with what I discovered. It turns out the nature of my connection with the Mets provides something of a map of my own evolution as a human being.

I was twelve in 1969 when the eminently embraceable Miracle Mets of Gil Hodges, Ed Kranepool, Cleon Jones, and Ed Charles won the World Series. I have no doubt that had they lost the fall classic to the favored Baltimore Orioles (or for that matter the initial National League Championship Series to the Atlanta Braves) that year I'd have wept, and probably for days.

I was nearly 30 in 1986 when that year's edition of the team brought home their second world title. Had it not been for the tenth inning ineffectiveness of Calvin Schiraldi, the subsequent wildness of his replacement, Bob Stanley, and an unfortunate muff of a seemingly harmless ground ball by their star-crossed teammate Bill Buckner in Game Six, the Mets would have lost the World Series to the Red Sox, but I'd have consoled myself with the knowledge that Lenny Dykstra, Wally Backman, Darryl Strawberry, and the other sociopaths playing for skipper Davey "See no evil, hear no evil" Johnson simply got what was coming to them.

Late last September when the Mets completed their late season collapse by losing to the Marlins on the season's final day I scarcely noticed. And while it's hard to pinpoint the precise reason(s) for my lack of interest, I have a few educated guesses as to why.

Maybe my need to teach my three children how to be good neighbors and good citizens takes priority over following the doings of a few young, entitled millionaires. Perhaps my desire to excel in my job as a high school teacher and also serve as a good role model for the kids I deal with as a youth sports coach takes precedence over following the fortunes of any group of professional athletes. Maybe my concern with making a significant mortgage payment each month, as well as fulfilling other financial and social obligations, ranks higher on my priority list than following the doings of 25 young men whose average annual salary is approximately 134 times what mine is.

Of course, I'm not the only one who's changed. In 1969 there was no 24-hour all-sports talk radio. There were no irritating blow-dried infotainers trying out their new catchphrases every night on ESPN. No one knew what steroids were, no player had his own theme song, and only true superstars like Willie Mays, Hank Aaron, Roberto Clemente, and Frank Robinson were earning anywhere close to $100,000 per year. Baseball parks were named for cities or human beings, not corporations, and their names didn't change every five years. Four decades ago most big league players had off-season jobs to supplement the income they earned as athletes. A pack of five baseball cards cost a nickel. The other day I noticed there was a sale on Topps baseball cards at the store where I shop for groceries. The price was $3.49 for 22 cards.

Playing Little League and Babe Ruth League baseball assisted me in developing self-esteem. Being a baseball-crazed teenager helped me get through adolescence with relatively few physical and emotional scars. As a young adult, spending quality time at the ballpark or around the television set with like-minded individuals helped enhance social skills that have proven advantageous to me in far more ways than I could have imagined at that time. And the 14 years I spent doing radio play-by-play for minor league professional teams afforded me the opportunity to work alongside more dedicated, unique, and decent people than I'd have met in a lifetime of lifetimes otherwise.

But as someone who's finally "grown up," it's hard to find reasons to care about people who play major league baseball. Even the ones who've got M-E-T-S emblazoned across the front of their shirts. ●

One Thing Baseball Taught Me

March 26, 2019

For the entirety of my forty-year childhood I was obsessed with baseball. Never mind Christmas, Thanksgiving, or my birthday; the most eagerly-anticipated event of the year was Opening Day.

Wide-eyed from start to finish, I witnessed my first live big league game more than a half-century ago at a sparkling, barely three-year-old 55,000-seat, state-of-the-art stadium in New York.

I wrote about baseball for my college's student newspaper, called the school's games on the campus radio station, and later got a job doing radio play-by-play and publicity for a semi-pro team in Fairbanks, Alaska.

That led to similar opportunities with professional teams in North Carolina, Florida, Montana, and ultimately Maine. All told I spent 14 years doing my dream job.

But my interest in the pro game waned after I became a dad; the last big league contest I attended was in Montreal, where professional baseball ceased to exist in 2004. Four years after that the now-decrepit old stadium where I had witnessed my first big league contest was demolished.

These days my connection with baseball is limited to coaching and/or umpiring youth games.

But the game and the people in it taught me some valuable life lessons, many of which had nothing to do with athletics. One remarkable fellow taught me about the foolishness of prejudice.

As the new radio "voice" of the Carolina League's Durham Bulls in the mid-1980s, I attended an informal pre-season press conference at Durham Athletic Park, the facility where the team played their home games. Between sips of beer in his pint-sized office, the team's new field manager was duly responding to generic questions from local reporters about the team's prospective infield, outfield, and starting rotation when one of the writers asked about a specific player, one I'll call "X." A former 1st-round draft selection, X was beginning his third year in Durham. (Generally more than one year at the Class A level means the player in question should be actively working on a Plan B.)

Puffing on his cigarette, the team's nominal on-field mentor matter-of-factly replied,

"That little African American won't play an inning for me."

Except the term he used to denote the player's race was, then as now, one no decent human being should ever use. I spent the rest of the session in a fog. I couldn't believe I'd be spending the following five months riding buses with (and running errands for) such an ignorant bigot.

Once the season got underway the manager was good to his word. X took batting practice with the other scrubs, then shagged flies or hit grounders until the visitors took over the field for their pregame workout. Once the actual contest began, he and I did exactly the same thing. The only difference: *he* wasn't on the radio describing what we were both watching.

But players got injured, reassigned, or released, as they always do during a 143-day, 140-game minor league baseball season. One night, short of able bodies, the manager pressed X into service. It turned out that while he might not have been a budding superstar, X did a lot of little things well. An outfielder who always hit the cutoff man, he never missed a sign at the plate. As a hitter he could spray the ball to any field on command, and he was a fearsome baserunner; if he was occupying first base when a Bulls batter hit an infield grounder, the opposition would NOT turn a double play.

Late in the season the team was going nowhere; the guys who hadn't been promoted or released were pretty much playing out the string. Then one night Atlanta's farm director called, informing the Bulls' skipper that two outfielders had gotten hurt in Greenville (the Braves' AA affiliate at the time), and reinforcements were needed pronto. He requested a specific player, a large, photogenic Caucasian who'd received a sizable bonus to turn pro not long before. "You can have that fellow if you want him," our skipper said. (Except he didn't say "fellow," instead using a slang term nearly as offensive as the one he'd spouted four months earlier in his office.) "But if you want my best player, you'll take X."

X was indeed promoted, and performed impressively enough to land a AAA spot the following spring. And all because a beer-swilling, chain-smoking, epithet-spouting manager had recommended him.

I thought back to that early April press conference, when I quickly and without any doubt labeled someone an ignorant bigot because of his coarse, inappropriate vocabulary.

Maybe he *was* prejudiced. But in retrospect, he wasn't the only one in that tiny room who had been guilty of unfairly prejudging someone he didn't know. ●

Opening Day 1984

April 7, 2009

Last Tuesday 37,057 fans showed up to watch the Red Sox beat Tampa Bay 5-3 in Boston's home opener.

However, unlike many of the 14,266,485 or so other New Englanders who didn't attend the game that day I had no desire to, and not just because I'd have had to take out a second mortgage to afford the tickets.

When my friend Bill, a lifelong Detroit Tiger fan, asked if I wanted to accompany him to the Bengals' contest against the Red Sox in Boston's home opener on April 13, 1984, I couldn't shout "Yes!" fast enough. It was to be my first trip to Fenway Park.

A quarter-century ago our Opening Day reserved seats, numbers 21 and 22 in Row 1 of Section 24, cost $6.50 each. That's only $1.75 more than what it costs for a Fenway Frank at a Sox game today! The plan was for me to meet Bill at his office in Hartford at 11:30. He'd drive the two or so hours from there to Fenway, meaning we'd arrive well before the scheduled 2:15 first pitch.

When I appeared where Bill worked at 11:20 he was on the phone, but grinned and signaled he'd only be a moment. Forty-five minutes later he was no longer smiling, but still engaged in business from which he could not extricate himself, since those were the days prior to when every breathing individual above the age of 12 had a cell phone. When we finally left sometime after noon, we were well behind schedule.

Bill lead-footed it all the way to Boston, but the combination of it being a sunny Friday afternoon **and** the day of the Red Sox home opener slowed traffic to a crawl as we approached the city, and then the venerable stadium itself. It was clear we'd never be able to both park the car and arrive on time for the game's start. As we neared the ballpark Bill broke what had been an awkward silence.

"It's my fault we're late, buddy," he said. "Why don't you get out now so you can see the first pitch?"

With transparent insincerity I responded, "You don't have to do that."

"No, really; I insist," he said.

"Okay!" I yelled, although I doubt he heard the second syllable of my response over the slamming of the car door.

Sprinting into the stadium just as the Star-Spangled Banner concluded, I bought a program for $1.25, hurried to my seat, and frantically began filling out my scorecard. However, before I could do so the Tigers had loaded the bases with no one out. Detroit cleanup hitter Lance Parrish looked at a third strike, but that was the only out the Red Sox starting pitcher would record that afternoon. The next three batters reached base, as did the first five to face reliever Mike Brown, who was summoned from the bullpen to replace the spectacularly ineffective Bruce Hurst. Parrish mercifully ended the inning on his second at-bat by grounding into a double play, leaving the Sox down by a mere eight runs!

Incredibly, the first five Boston batters reached base in the bottom of the inning before Tony Armas grounded into a double play, the first of six twin killings Detroit's defense would manufacture that afternoon. However, Rich Gedman followed with a home run that made the score 8-5 and finished Tiger starting pitcher Milt Wilcox. In the bottom of the second Dwight Evans hit a two-out solo home run and the crowd roared, but not nearly as loudly as the people around me in Section 24 did moments later when Bill, who had parked somewhere near New Hampshire, arrived at the start of the third inning and asked breathlessly, "Did I miss anything?"

The visiting team's 13-9 win that afternoon was a harbinger of things to come for both squads. The Tigers won the American League East, finishing 18 games ahead of 4th-place Boston, and while Detroit was beating the San Diego Padres in a five-game World Series that fall the Sox were shopping for a new skipper to replace the retiring Ralph Houk. They ultimately settled on John McNamara, who was destined to become infamous two Octobers later by failing to use Dave Stapleton as a defensive replacement for Bill Buckner in the bottom of the tenth inning of Game Six of the 1986 Fall Classic.

For me it'd be tough to top the 1984 Red Sox home opener, which I still believe is the best game I've ever seen at Fenway.

In fact, since I haven't been back since then, I *know* it is! ●

Want to Coach? Go Behind the Plate First!

July 17, 2019

As someone who has coached and officiated baseball, soccer, and basketball since the late 1970s, I think Ron Kramer's "Maine Voices" piece* regarding youth sports reaching a potential tipping point due to a lack of qualified officials is relevant, eloquent, and accurate. Those currently serving as referees and/or umpires will indeed "age out;" some, like me (and, I gather, Mr. Kramer) will do so sooner rather than later.

Re-stocking the officiating pool is indeed an issue, thanks largely to the all-too-often accurate perception that far too many involved "adults" cannot or will not behave appropriately, and routinely disrespect those officiating their children's athletic contests.

In his essay Mr. Kramer suggests a series of tangible, eminently sensible steps that might help to alleviate the problem, including establishing a "zero tolerance" policy regarding bad behavior from parents, coaches, and/or players; requiring all involved parties to sign an official code of conduct, establishing stiff (and enforceable) penalties for those who violate said code; and instituting more extensive training for officials regarding effectively dealing with sportsmanship issues.

I wholeheartedly endorse each of those proposals, but I'd like to respectfully add one more. I recommend the governing bodies of youth baseball, football, basketball, hockey, soccer, and lacrosse *require* a year's officiating experience of all prospective coaches (or assistant coaches) before they are allowed and/or licensed to mentor youngsters in whatever their sport of choice is.

For the past five years I have umpired Little League Baseball games in the town where I live, and the only thing I've heard from any spectator after (and often during) games has been, "Thank you." I believe a big part of the reason for that civility is the local Little League strongly urging coaches to serve as umpires at games not involving their own teams. I know it's worked for me; as a coach I can recall seeing questionable calls on numerous occasions, but knowing *I'd* be calling balls and strikes myself the next night initially kept me from lodging any protest(s), and before long gave me the ability to refrain from reacting negatively, outwardly *or* inwardly, to any and all calls made

---

* "Maine Voices" contains guest editorials that appear in the *Portland Press Herald*, Maine's largest daily newspaper. This essay was prompted by one of those columns.

by an official. Behavior exhibited by coaches and parents will, for better or for worse, inevitably trickle down to the players. It's also likely that behavior will be perpetuated, also for better or worse, by the young people observing it.

Here's something else I've learned after over four decades of involvement with four different youth sports: in the long run, what matters most is the participants (primarily the players; to a lesser extent, the spectators) *enjoying* the experience, which makes staying positive of the utmost importance. Take it from someone who has coached both an undefeated high school soccer team and a winless basketball squad, *and* was a member of the 1966 Easton (CT) Little League champion Hawks: **in the long run** it *really doesn't matter* who wins any particular youth sports tournament or league championship. ●

SECTION 7

Other Sports

The Teflon League

July 27, 2008

When the New England Patriots opened their training camp last week, the largest player present was 6'7", 330-pound Ryan O'Callaghan. The third-year offensive tackle is one of 19 players on the team's pre-season roster weighing in at over 299 pounds. This doesn't include 305-pound Stephen Neal, 315-pound Nick Kaczur, or 325-pound Oliver Ross, all of whom are currently on the Physically Unable to Perform list.

According to The Sporting News 1972 National Football Guide, the biggest player on New England's pre-season veteran roster that year was defensive end Ron Berger, a 6'8", 285-pound behemoth who had played his college football at Wayne State. Tackles Rich Moore and Dave Rowe each tipped the scales at 280 pounds, but none of the other 48 men listed weighed more than 265.

Last year's Patriots had what was arguably the most memorable season in the National Football League's history. They won 18 consecutive games before a heartbreaking loss to the New York Giants in the Super Bowl. Including the practice squad, there were 65 players listed on New England's roster for last season's final game. Sixteen of them tipped the scales at 300 pounds or more, and another five weighed in at more than 270. Can human beings have naturally gotten that much bigger over the past 35 years?

Die-hard NFL fans say only conspiracy theorists would suggest that numerous professional football players have done things over the past three and a half decades to artificially accelerate their growth. "Where's their evidence?" the League's defenders ask.

The 1971 Patriots weren't all that hot, winning six games and losing eight. Their lackluster record could have been attributable to any number of causes. One possible reason: the idea of secretly taping upcoming opponents' practice sessions hadn't occurred to head coach John Mazur and his staff. Or perhaps they lacked the foresight to obtain the hand signals opposition coaches were using, something done with apparent regularity (not to mention disregard for ethics or legality) by the team's brain trust three decades later.

Was a more plausible cause for New England's less-than-stellar record in 1971 that their team was undersized by the standards of the day? In a word, no. A comparison of New England's 1972 pre-season roster with that of the previous year's Super Bowl champions discounts that possibility. The average 1971 Dallas Cowboy was smaller and lighter than the average Patriot was that year. The heaviest man on Dallas's 45-man roster was 265-pound offensive tackle Ralph Neely, although the Cowboys did have seven others who weighed in at over 250. In contrast, the *average* listed weight of the 55 players on the 2007 Dallas roster was 252, which is 28 pounds heavier per Cowboy than it had been 35 years earlier. Fourteen 300-pounders wore Dallas uniforms last season, and an additional 14 weighed 250 or more. Has the average professional football player *really* gotten 12.5% heavier in the last 35 years solely through increased lifting of weights and drinking protein-rich milkshakes?

Many fans associate senseless violence in professional sports these days with the National Hockey League, even though more acts that border on assault and battery take place during a single play in an NFL game than do during most NHL contests. When inappropriate and/or criminal behavior of professional athletes is the subject, as often as not it is National Basketball Association players whose names are cited, even though the number of felons currently active in the NFL dwarfs the number employed by NBA teams.

When the subject of banned or illegal substances in sports comes up, many current fans immediately think of disgraced baseball stars like Mark McGwire, Barry Bonds, Roger Clemens, José Canseco, or Rafael Palmeiro. Others associate steroid use with cyclists competing in the Tour de France. However, the first athletes thoughtful sports fans *should* associate with the use of illegal, performance-enhancing substances neither play baseball nor pedal bicycles.

It's hard to believe the NFL keeps getting a pass on these issues. If John Gotti was the Teflon Don and Ronald Reagan was the Teflon President, can there be any doubt about the identity of the Teflon League of Professional Sports? ●

A Sport in Need of Repair

March 14, 2011

High school basketball has become painful to watch, at least to those of us of a certain vintage.

The recently completed Maine boys state tournament featured scores like 41-38, 41-40 (in overtime), 42-30, and 30-27, and those were all regional title contests featuring some of the state's nominally best teams.

Basketball players of a certain era (okay; *my* era) learned to play by *playing*. That meant four-on-four, three-on-three, two-on-two or one-on-one on half courts at school, on a street or, if you had connections, in someone's driveway. Weekends were for full-court games in crowded gyms. You called your own fouls; the first team to reach 15 stayed on and the losers walked, with no guarantee they'd play again that day. If you were covered by someone smaller you posted him up. Being matched up against someone bigger and/or stronger meant you ran him until he collapsed. Guarding a player with a weak left hand? Force him to go that way by overplaying him to his right. When a teammate got open, you found him. Improvisational skills were crucial; those without them usually ended up on losing teams. And the more your team lost the less often you got invited back on the court. Pickup basketball was classic survival of the fittest.

But today pickup games are by and large a thing of the past, and youth basketball has become, particularly in the suburbs, survival of the wealthiest. For those who can afford personal coaches and home gyms there's plenty of competition, not to mention cool uniforms and plenty of travel.

Another problem: too often there's too much coaching and not enough freelancing going on. Basketball games should be more about the participants and less about suit-wearing orchestrators on the bench. Too many of today's young hoopsters are over-coached by aspiring Bob Knights, some of whom run the same patterned offenses and use the same defensive sets every year, regardless of the capabilities of their personnel.

None of the multiple factors involved in the current state of affairs is easily remedied. Today's teens have a plethora of leisure time alternatives, and too many of those options (think PlayStation, X-Box and similar electronic time-wasters) involve little to no physical exertion. There's also the curse of unrealistic parents who push their kids too hard, not to mention ambitious and/or unscrupulous youth coaches who all too often self-servingly (and usually unwisely) counsel aspiring young athletes to specialize in one sport.

Today's most fundamentally skilled professional basketball players invariably come from foreign countries, where youth is less readily influenced by NBA, NCAA or network television executives far more concerned with sales and marketing than with two-hand chest passes, boxing out, or cultivating a reliable 15-foot jump shot.

In the late 1960s basketball on TV meant a single NBA game on Sunday afternoons, usually featuring the Celtics against whichever team Wilt Chamberlain was playing for at the time. Today dozens of televised college and pro games are viewable every night, as are ubiquitous highlight packages on ESPN, which understandably have American kids thinking all basketball players are tattooed, chest-bumping trash talkers in expensive name-brand sneakers, and that all games consist of slam dunks, behind-the-back passes, and occasional half-court heaves that swish right before the buzzer.

Recently Channel 6 sportscaster Bruce Glasier suggested a 20-second shot clock for boys' high school games, and that's not a bad idea. But it's a slam dunk that implementing the five innovations below would ultimately improve the quality of basketball, and more importantly enhance the enjoyment of it for all involved. Here they are:

1. Abolish <u>all</u> organized leagues for children under age 15, but open public gyms on Saturday mornings from 9 to 12 and just let kids play. For the sake of liability have one adult on hand, but don't allow him/her to do anything other than mop the floor and inflate the balls.
2. Parents: unplug your TV, or at least discontinue cable service. The less show business disguised as basketball your kids watch, the better. Not only will they be more active and creative, they might grow up thinking life is about more than beer, cars, washboard abs, and being winked at fetchingly by scantily-clad women.
3. No names on the back of jerseys. Ever. It's a team game, so a number, along with the squad's name on the *front* of the shirt, should suffice.
4. No one will be allowed to coach basketball (or any other youth sport, for that matter) until he or she has officiated it for at least a year. That should help curb sideline histrionics, bullying of referees, or similar inappropriate actions on the part of overly competitive mentors at the local level.
5. For all televised games at all levels: coaches must dress out in full playing uniform, just like in professional baseball. Youth coaches need healthy role models just as much as kids do. Think Rick Pitino or John Calipari would still preen for the TV cameras and vehemently berate the officials the way they do now if they were clad in shorts and a tank top instead of a $2500 suit? ●

Random Thoughts on Soccer

July 13, 2006

The World Cup soccer final was played this past Sunday. Contested every fourth year, it's the Super Bowl, World Series, Daytona 500, and Kentucky Derby all rolled into one in most European, South American, African, and Asian nations.

There are some things I'd change about soccer, and the first one would be the tie-breaking procedure. Deciding the winner of deadlocked matches with penalty kicks makes about as much sense as having a three-point shooting contest to settle basketball games that were even at the end of regulation time. If they did that in the NBA there's a pretty good chance 50-year-old Larry Bird would still be wearing a Celtics uniform.

What Americans call "soccer" is known as "football" (or "futbol") in the rest of the world. And while both the game the National Football League plays and soccer have 22 players at a time on the field, the similarities end there.

NFL teams have a 53-man roster. Eleven competitors play offense, 11 others play defense, and substitutes are used liberally. In World Cup soccer there are eleven players on a team, but all of them must play offense *and* defense, and teams are limited to three substitutions per game. In addition, NFL teams usually have at least five behemoths who weigh in excess of 300 pounds on the field at the same time. It is not unusual for skilled soccer players to weigh less than half that.

As a youngster all I knew about soccer was it was played by small men who, if they spoke English at all, did so with heavy accents. Boys played three sports where I grew up: baseball, football, and basketball. Soccer wasn't one of them, usually because high school athletic directors, most of whom were football and/or basketball coaches, feared a soccer program would ultimately siphon off good athletes from teams they themselves coached. And looking back, it seems those fears were justified in many parts of the country.

The United States was officially eliminated from the World Cup last month when they lost to Ghana 2-1. I was in my car early in the afternoon on the day of the game, and turned to the local all-sports radio station at 20 minutes past the hour to get an update. I was unaware that during the middle of the day there aren't sports updates every 20 minutes. Instead the Jim Rome Show was on. Jim Rome is the Sports Talk radio equivalent of Howard Stern or Rush Limbaugh, a blowhard some find entertaining. His fans want to hear outrageous opinions, and to the delight of his intended audience Mr. Rome obliges them on a daily basis. On this particular day he was ranting about how dull soccer is, how it's not a real sport, the USA should never lose to Ghana in *anything*, blah, blah, blah.

I'm not sure how much (if any) of what Mr. Rome says he actually believes, but if his remarks that day were serious, he deserves our sympathy. Much of the fun of following sports is seeing an underdog beat a prohibitive favorite. I was thrilled when the American ice hockey team upset the vaunted Soviets in the 1980 Olympics. I also enjoyed seeing George Mason University beat all those Goliaths in last March's NCAA basketball tournament, even when one of their victims was my old Alma Mater.

For those who missed it, Italy won the World Cup last Sunday. They beat France in the championship game.

On penalty kicks. ●

A Sports-related Epiphany

October 12, 2006

Recently I had an epiphany which helped me get over something that had been bothering me for quite some time.

A few years ago ESPN, the all-sports cable television network, ran a series in which the greatest 100 North American athletes of the 20th century were selected. Obviously there was a lot of subjectivity involved in compiling this list, since just about everyone has his or her own idea(s) about sports.

I figured that the top athlete of the century had to be either Babe Ruth, Muhammad Ali, Jackie Robinson, Jim Brown, or Jim Thorpe.

The network counted down their top 100, and none of my choices appeared until Robinson inexplicably was rated number 15. I consoled myself with the knowledge that had the list been of the 100 most *influential* athletes of the 20th century, the man who broke major league baseball's unwritten "color barrier" in 1947 would surely have been atop it.

The next of my choices to appear was Thorpe, who was voted best athlete of the half-century by the Associated Press back in 1950. A native American who played professional football, professional baseball, and won the decathlon at the 1912 Olympics, Thorpe's biggest shortcoming was making the mistake of dying before many of the people currently in charge of contemporary sports marketing were born. The experts at ESPN had him rated at number seven on their list.

Brown came in at number four. Serious students of professional football consider him the greatest running back of all time. Less known but equally impressive is the fact he was considered by many to be the greatest lacrosse player of his generation when he played at Syracuse University. I took some solace in the fact he was listed higher than any of the other 19 football players on the list.

Ali, who for all practical purposes *was* boxing from the early 1960s through the late 1970s, was number three. In addition to being a gifted prizefighter who could "float like a butterfly and sting like a bee," the loquacious pugilist's principled stand against the Vietnam War, which ultimately cost him three and a half years of his boxing prime, won him worldwide admiration.

Ruth, whose home runs in the 1920s put baseball (and indirectly all other professional sports) permanently onto the national stage, was listed as ESPN's second-greatest athlete of all time. I was puzzled. All of my choices had been accounted for. A moment later the network revealed their selection for greatest North American athlete of the 20th century: Michael Jordan.

Huh?

While Jordan was a five-time National Basketball Association Most Valuable Player, a ten-time scoring champ, and a member of six NBA championship teams, I had a hard time agreeing with ESPN's choice. I'm not so sure Jordan is the 20th century's best basketball player, let alone best athlete.

Long before there were TV networks showing sports highlights 24/7, the NBA had players who were every bit as good in their time as Jordan was in his. Wilt Chamberlain held every league scoring record in the books when he retired in 1973. He once averaged over 50 points per game for a complete season, and the only reason he doesn't still have the top scoring average in NBA history is because he spent his final few years altering his game for the good of the teams he played for.

These days basketball enthusiasts rave about players who register a "Triple Double" (double-digit totals of assists, points, and rebounds in the same game). Oscar Robertson *averaged* a triple double in the 1961–62 season, and that was before the advent of the three-point shot.

Impressed with Jordan's six championships in thirteen seasons? Google "Bill Russell." He led the Boston Celtics to 11 titles in a 13-year career that ran from 1956 to 1969.

Of course, there are plenty of reasons for ESPN to name Jordan the 20th century's greatest athlete. But probably the biggest is his having directly or indirectly generated more revenue for the sports industry in general, and cable TV sports networks in particular, than did all those legendary athletes from previous generations, combined.

Until recently I was still having a hard time accepting the coronation of someone who isn't even irrefutably the best player in his own sport being crowned as the greatest athletic performer of the 20th century.

But then I had my epiphany.

I realized it doesn't matter. ●

Super Bowl 41

January 25, 2007

This Sunday night most of the country will be watching Super Bowl XLI, which will be played in Miami. The National Football League championship game will feature National Conference champions, the Chicago Bears, battling the winners of the American Conference title, the Indianapolis Colts.

Heavy-hearted Patriots fans are still smarting from their team's last-minute loss to the Colts two weeks ago. They were hoping Tom Brady could lead New England's professional football team to its fourth championship in the last six years. It's ironic many people bemoaning the failure of the Pats to make it to the Super Bowl are the same folks who until 2004 were spending far too much time and energy decrying the unfairness of the Boston Red Sox not having won a single World Series since 1918. The Detroit Lions, Cleveland Browns, New Orleans Saints, and St. Louis/Arizona/Phoenix Cardinals haven't even made it to the National Football League's ultimate game once in 41 years of trying. (Okay, it's only been 40 years for the Browns. So sue me!) You'd think Red Sox/Patriot loyalists would be more sympathetic toward the long-suffering football fans in Detroit, Cleveland, New Orleans, and wherever it is both those Cardinal fans live.

The Colts have an opportunity to exorcise some large economy-sized demons on Sunday. The biggest upset in Super Bowl history took place in Miami in 1969 when the Colts, who represented Baltimore at the time and were 18-point favorites, were the victims. They fell to the lightly-regarded New York Jets 16-7, and by doing so also suffered the ignominy of being the first NFL team to lose to the champions of the upstart American Football League, which most fans of the established NFL looked down their noses at back then. The AFL was absorbed by the older league after the following year's Super Bowl, but not before getting a final bit of satisfaction. The last AFL champions, the Kansas City Chiefs, smoked the heavily favored Minnesota Vikings 23-7 in Super Bowl IV.

As is the case every year in the two weeks preceding the Super Bowl, the city where the game is being held is crawling with media types looking for human interest stories with at least an oblique connection to the game or to one of its participants. One interesting note this year involves Bears defensive tackle Tank Johnson, who an Illinois judge is allowing to play in the game despite his being arrested last month and charged with ten different gun-related offenses. Mr. Johnson had already been arrested twice in the previous year and a half. Once was for scuffling with a police officer; the other time involved multiple misdemeanor weapons charges. I can't help wondering if I'd be allowed to continue my teaching career at a local high school without interruption if I had been arrested three times on violence-related charges within an 18-month period.

The big story of this year's game began developing at around 6 PM two Sundays ago. When the Bears finished off the Saints in the NFC title game, it meant that an African-American head coach, specifically the soft-spoken but highly respected Lovie Smith, would lead a team into the Super Bowl for the first time. Hours later America was assured that for the first time a minority head coach would coach a Super Bowl champion, since Tony Dungy, the head coach of the AFC champion Colts, is also African-American. Much has been and will be made of this, and while both men deserve all the positive attention they're currently receiving, it should be due to their outstanding achievements and upstanding character, not their race.

While the NFL, aided by countless media sycophants, publicly congratulates itself on this significant bit of history, neither Smith nor Dungy was hired because of the color of his skin. Each got his job because he was judged (correctly, as it turned out) to be the person best qualified to lead his team at the time it had an opening for a head coach.

It's been 39 years since Bill Russell of the National Basketball Association's Boston Celtics became the first African-American coach to lead a team to a championship in a major professional sport. Since then five other NBA teams coached by a Black man have won the league championship. Happily, with each succeeding occurrence the coach's race became increasingly less relevant.

While it's significant that both of Sunday's Super Bowl teams will be directed by an African-American, it'll be a truly Super day when the race, religion, and ethnicities of the game's participants are considered a non-issue. Or, better yet, not considered at all. ●

Eagerly Anticipating My Yearly Football Game

January 26, 2005

This Sunday I'll be watching the Super Bowl, or at least as much of it as I can see from the buffet table at the get-together I'll be attending. Most people can't tell you the *exact total* of televised National Football League football games they've watched in the last ten years combined, but I can. Assuming I get to view some of the Eagles-Patriots game this Sunday, my number will be ten.

My interest in professional football peaked when I was in high school. Expansion and a merger with their former American Football League competitors in 1970 had swelled the NFL's membership by ten teams. Pro sports were a big deal in my social circles at the time. I could recite the names of the entire offensive backfield and defensive line of any one of those 26 squads. I also could have named any of the 26 place-kickers in the league, since back then it was the norm to employ one person to handle those duties for an entire season. These days a couple of missed kicks are grounds for immediate dismissal, and accordingly it seems as though a kicker or two is replaced almost weekly, for real or perceived shortcomings. There was one team for which I could name all 22 of the starters: the Baltimore Colts. I liked them mostly because I had read a ghost-written autobiography of their quarterback, Johnny Unitas, some years earlier; doing so convinced he was the most heroic man on the earth. I also liked the Minnesota Vikings, because what other team had cool purple uniforms?

Not everyone whose interest in pro football has lessened can point to an exact time when their devotion to the sport began to wane. But I can. In fact, I can give you the *exact date* I realized it was time for me to find a new hobby. My epiphany took place on October 19th, 1975, in the all-male dormitory at the University of Connecticut where I was residing at the time.

Our dorm had someone who distributed little sheets listing all of the NFL games each weekend, along with the point spreads. Although technically it was illegal, taking bets on NFL games provided inexpensive amusement for countless young men looking for weekend entertainment. For those unfamiliar with gambling, here's how a point spread works: if the Patriots are playing the Jets and New England is favored by seven, those betting on the Pats must have a New England victory *by more than seven points* in order to collect on their wagers. Conversely, one could bet on the Jets and collect even if

New York loses, *provided that the margin of defeat is less than seven points.* And what, you may ask, happens if New England wins the game by *exactly* seven points? Ahhhh. Now you've gotten a bit of insight into how the people who set the odds make money.

It cost just a dollar to purchase one of those sheets each week. Anyone who could pick a mere four games correctly against the spread without getting any wrong won ten dollars, a handsome return on their original bet. Sounds easy, right? Ahhhh. Now you've gotten a bit *more* insight into how oddsmakers make *lots* of money.

In 1975 on October 19th, virtually the entire dorm selected the underdog Detroit Lions to cover a seven-point spread against those purple-clad Vikings at Minnesota's Metropolitan Stadium. But by the end of the third quarter, we were in despair. The Vikings had a seemingly insurmountable 25-3 lead.

Minnesota was clearly the better team, but with the game's result no longer in doubt, the Lions "rallied" against the Minnesota second stringers, and late in the game added a meaningless score that made the final tally 25-19. It was only afterward that I realized how ridiculous it was for my friends and me to celebrate a touchdown that, while having no bearing on the outcome of the actual game, had caused Detroit to lose by *only* six points. Wasn't the idea of playing a competitive sport to win?

As it turned out all of our excitement was for naught, since as usual each of us picked one or more of our other games incorrectly. In the long run though, those dollars I lost at the rate of one per Sunday each week in 1975 were a great investment. They helped me discover earlier than most that there are a lot of things more worth doing on Sunday afternoons than sitting inertly in front of a TV set watching football. ●

How Soon Will Society Evolve?

October 15, 2013

I grew up playing, watching, and loving football.

Currently a lot of great kids play the game at the youth or high school levels, and many, thanks in part to the influence of some fine mentors, will grow into solid, productive "team players" as citizens. I've observed positive leadership and role modeling by several youth football coaches that have unquestionably impacted numerous boys and young men in a positive (and long-term) manner. But the dark side of America's most popular spectator sport is becoming increasingly evident to anyone willing to open his or her eyes.

Ongoing research has demonstrated to all but the most willfully obtuse that competing on the gridiron is inherently dangerous. Bigger, faster, and stronger players are concussing and crippling one another at alarming rates not only at the professional and college levels, but in high school and youth games and practices as well. Research published late last month by the Virginia Tech-Wake Forest University School of Biomedical Engineering found that football players as young as seven years old absorb blows to the head comparable in magnitude to those sustained by high school and adult players.

Perhaps playing football should be viewed the same way as tobacco use. As recently as 1966, 51.9% of American men were cigarette smokers, thanks largely to clever, ubiquitous, and insidiously effective mass-marketing featuring endorsements from celebrities (including athletes) slyly implying that puffing on a Winston, Camel, or Lucky Strike made males more manly and desirable.

But then science intervened, proving to all but the most inflexibly dense that smoking is dangerously unhealthy. Consequently tobacco usage is far lower today than it was five decades ago, and the prevailing image of smokers, male or female, is anything but attractive.

Ample evidence now exists indicating playing football has potentially nasty health consequences, both immediately and down the road. A recently completed Centers for Disease Control study showed professional football players are three-times more likely to die from neurodegenerative diseases like Alzheimer's and Parkinson's than the rest of the general population. The suicides of former National Football League standouts Junior Seau, Dave Duerson, Andre Waters, and Ray Easterling are all sobering (if anecdotal) evidence of the perils of football-related traumatic brain injuries. Even more chilling are the self-destructions of ex-NFL players Jim Tyrer, Mike Current, Jeff Alm and Jovan

Belcher. All violently took the lives of others before snuffing out their own.

Longtime Oakland Raiders center Jim Otto straps on an artificial leg he wears 12 hours each day, one he was fitted with after enduring nearly 70 surgeries. The late Baltimore Colts quarterback Johnny Unitas didn't sign autographs in his declining years; his arthritic hands, crippled by years of pounding, couldn't grip a pen. His longtime teammate John Mackey died in 2011 after years of requiring round-the-clock care; the cloud of dementia began enshrouding him less than a decade after he stopped playing. Disquieting cases such as those of these three Hall-of-Famers have become distressingly common. The number of former NFL players whose post-athletic lives were shortened or compromised by their choice of profession is probably in the thousands. Include those who played the game at the high school or college level and it's likely in the tens of thousands, or even higher.

Forget "game plans"; football games are, at every level, nearly always won by the team which best intimidates, overpowers, and physically dominates and/or disables their opponents. The sheer number of life-altering injuries suffered in an athletic competition contested at the professional level by young, huge, fast, physically aggressive, and often chemically aided modern-day gladiators is staggering, likely dwarfing the amount of permanently crippling injuries suffered by athletes in every other major American team sport combined. And the cumulative effects of participating in a concussive activity once known as a "contact" sport that today is more accurately categorized as a "collision" sport, while not yet fully quantifiable, are clearly horrific.

Like tobacco apologists and climate-change deniers, logic-challenged football lovers loyally cling to what they believe, and for similar reasons: tradition, resistance to change, and of course, money. No NFL team owner or major college athletic director has any desire to see his or her portion of a multi-billion-dollar revenue stream dry up, and toward that end they'll spare no expense to ubiquitously market their product.

They'll cite legitimate statistics pointing out football players aren't the only people who commit suicide; welders, librarians, and nurses do so as well. And young people get hurt playing soccer, baseball, basketball and other sports, they'll add, which is true. But those are, like other false equivalencies, utterly irrelevant.

Would anyone aside from tobacco company hired guns seriously recommend smoking cigarettes just because a few *non*-smokers have gotten lung cancer too? ●

Which Contemporary Athletes Merit Admiration?

February 5, 2013

Five decades ago impressionable American boys were encouraged both openly and covertly to emulate the nation's greatest athletes. But looking back, it seems that, with a few exceptions, they were duped into idolizing caricatures rather than actual human beings.

Arthur Ashe was one of those anomalies. Born in 1943, he grew up in a single-parent household. His mother died when he was six years old and his brother Johnnie was an infant. While Ashe initially gained renown as an athlete who overcame poverty and prejudice, the impact he made on America and the world was far greater than that of a mere world-class athlete, albeit one who won three Grand Slam tennis titles. The prowess he first exhibited on the segregated courts of Richmond, Virginia, his hometown, earned him a college scholarship. He also served in the U.S. Army during the Vietnam era.

Though hardly radical or extroverted, Ashe actively advocated for civil rights, both in his home country and overseas. He visited South Africa during the period when that nation was making the difficult transition from apartheid to racial integration. He was voluntarily arrested for taking part in a protest outside the South African embassy in Washington in 1985, and again was taken into custody in 1992 near the White House for participating in a peaceful demonstration on behalf of Haitian immigrants. A loyal husband and doting father, Ashe also became a tireless advocate for AIDS education, and somehow found time to write a three-volume book chronicling the history of African-American athletes, a project that took him nearly six years to complete.

Ashe was a freshman at UCLA in 1963 when athletes like Mickey Mantle, Jim Brown, Wilt Chamberlain, and Bobby Hull were being lionized for their sports-related achievements by a reverential press corps doing its utmost to create and then maintain squeaky-clean images for America's athletic elite. Who knew some of those gods gambled, tippled, philandered, or physically abused multiple spouses? The men (there were no women) reporting on sports in those quaint times were as interested in sanitizing the auras surrounding America's popular athletes as today's media seems concerned with sullying them.

There were no electronic devices capable of spewing out sports-related information 24 hours per day, seven days a week during the JFK administration, nor were there ubiquitous TV and radio talking heads sharing shrill, often ill-considered opinions with a nationwide audience consisting primarily of credulous, gullible individuals permanently addicted to athletics by a multi-billion dollar per year professional sports industry for which no amount of profit is ever enough.

Arthur Ashe's autobiography, *Days of Grace,* reads like he spoke: thoughtfully, logically, and eloquently. What makes his memoir even more remarkable: it was being written by someone who knew his earthly time was running out. A blood transfusion he had gotten during heart surgery performed nearly a decade earlier was tainted with HIV. Ashe had developed full-blown AIDS by the time he began putting his autobiography together in June of 1992. He died 20 years ago this week.

Today only the most willfully naïve amongst us idolize professional athletes unconditionally. Recently an internationally-renowned cyclist who had previously denied all allegations of impropriety with a strident combination of anger, self-righteousness, and litigiousness confessed to having cheated to win seven Tours de France.

No one was elected to the Baseball Hall of Fame this year because of the sport's ongoing drug issues. A top college football star was humiliated because the "girlfriend" he maintained an intense, long-distance relationship with turned out to be imaginary.

A disgruntled professional golfer publicly and indignantly expressed unhappiness over the unfairness of having to pay a higher rate of taxes on his estimated annual earnings of $48 million. Another pro golfer, the sport's top money maker and a serial adulterer who generated an estimated $80 million last year through endorsements and licensing fees, just won another tournament that earned him another $1,098,000.

A parade of egotistical, semi-literate behemoths spent the week leading up to the Super Bowl reminding us of their greatness while simultaneously denying use of any banned substances, including the one Major League Baseball's highest-paid player, a pathological prevaricator and confessed drug cheat, stands accused of utilizing.

A 25-year-old snowmobiler suffered fatal injuries while competing in a made-for-TV "athletic competition" that was invented for the sole purpose of generating programming and even more profits for a 24-hour sports cable network. And all of that occurred during just the first month of the current calendar year! Phew!

Arthur Ashe's contributions to the planet that had nothing to do with sports far exceeded his impressive athletic achievements.

It's worth considering which of today's wealthy, entitled athletic elite will ultimately impact society in his or her lifetime like Ashe, Jackie Robinson, Roberto Clemente, Pat Tillman, Billie Jean King, Muhammad Ali and Jesse Owens did in theirs. More tellingly, which (if any) of them are truly interested in doing so? ●

Finally Kicking the Habit

March 8, 2011

Although I've never used tobacco and have lived without alcohol for decades, I can sympathize with those who desperately want to escape some sort of odious addiction, but are, for whatever reason(s), unable to do so. For what seems like forever I've been trying to stop doing something that is needless, counterproductive, and at times can cast me in a less-than-flattering light. I'm unquestionably not the only middle-aged male who has wasted thousands of hours of valuable time over the years being preoccupied with professional sports, but the fact numerous others have the same problem doesn't make it any more attractive.

My infatuation with games played by mercenaries has bordered on obsession for a long time. Before my tenth birthday I knew the names and batting averages of the three Alou brothers on the San Francisco Giants; that the Houston Oilers were in the Eastern Division of the American Football League, but the Baltimore Bullets were in the Western Conference of the National Basketball Association; and that anyone wanting to play in the National Hockey League had to be born in Canada. And that was without all-sports talk radio and ESPN, two obscenely profitable phenomena which thankfully weren't around during my childhood.

Sports were what boys did in the area where I grew up. Period. Back then you were on the baseball field, football field, or basketball court every afternoon after school unless you had a prosthetic limb, vision that was worse than 20-200, or a splintered bone sticking through your skin. And it was understood any neighborhood male whose excuse for non-participation didn't include one of those acceptable three reasons would supplant the kid who wore shorts, dark socks, and black tie-up shoes to his piano lessons as the prime subject of ridicule on the school bus for at least the next week.

Since then there have been plenty of good reasons for me to de-emphasize pro sports, if not put them in my life's rear-view mirror. Learning to read books without color pictures in them, discovering the existence of girls, getting acceptable grades, and finding suitable employment were just a few of them. But I resisted them all until my adolescence ended a mere three decades or so after it had begun.

Like addicted smokers or drinkers, I could not get away from my unattractive habit. I tried to appear respectable, but whenever I was alone or out of sight, I'd go back to it. When carpooling to work with other adults, my car radio was on NPR, but when traveling alone the push of a button tuned me in to a Boston Sportstalk station, where Joe from Natick could publicly air his dissatisfaction with whichever Red Sox, Bruins, or Celtics player hadn't gotten the job done in the previous evening's game. I could feel my brain melt as I listened to the program's knuckle-dragging "hosts" loudly compete to see who could best disparage their dim-witted callers. The high-decibel arrogance grated on me, so much so that one afternoon I shut them off and swore off sports-driven talk radio forever. But then I learned Portland had *its* own Sportstalk station, and it too had a call-in show during afternoon drive-time hours. Like an alcoholic who's been on the wagon for six months and thinks he can handle just one little drink, I turned my car's radio to 96.3 FM one afternoon and got hooked again.

At first I enjoyed getting my afternoon fix. The genial co-hosts of the Portland afternoon show sounded like two young guys who genuinely loved what they were doing; listening to them was far easier on the ears than it was to endure the shrill pontificating of the swaggering Neanderthals in Boston. They also went out of their way to not denigrate their callers, which in many cases probably wasn't easy. But their show's subject matter was still the same, and I began to realize again I just wasn't interested in hearing about the exploits of million-dollar mercenaries in billion-dollar businesses anymore.

Knowing I was wasting my time was the fuse. The spark that lit it came on February 14th. On my afternoon commute home, I absentmindedly turned on the radio. The two voices coming out of it were earnestly discussing who they felt was "hotter," Cameron Diaz or Jennifer Aniston. Apparently a previous "sports-minded" caller had opined that neither actress interested him; between snorts and snickers the show's two hosts were wondering aloud about his mental health.

Questioning my own sanity, I double-checked the radio dial. It was indeed the all-sports station. I shut it off.

I have not turned it back on since that Valentine's Day epiphany, which I truly believe has allowed me to kick my unattractive and needless habit cold turkey. ●

SECTION 8

The Way It Is

Gracias Edgar. Ahora, adiós!

November 9, 2010

Major League Baseball fans able to overlook the rampant greed of the sport's owners, players, and sponsors, steroid scandals, night games in November, obscene ticket prices, and even more obscene player salaries have much to celebrate about the recently completed World Series.

For one thing, it marked the first championship for the Giants in 56 years. They won their last one while playing their home games at Harlem's legendary Polo Grounds, a ballpark that was demolished 46 years ago. With the possible exception of Clevelanders (62 years since their last World Series title) and Chicago Cubs fans (102 years and counting), all true baseball aficionados outside the Lone Star State should be celebrating San Francisco's triumph. And the Giants won representing the National League, which to its credit still eschews the execrable designated hitter rule, an innovation adopted by the American League in 1973 that's still far better suited for slow-pitch softball than it is for competitions that involve actual athletes.

But my personal reason for celebrating involves the Most Valuable Player of the 2010 World Series. Fifteen years ago Edgar Rentería and I were both rookie employees of the Portland Sea Dogs. He was a 19-year-old shortstop prospect; I was the radio play-by-play announcer.

At the welcoming dinner the evening before the season opener, ticket-buying fans were treated to hot dogs, ice cream, and other ballpark delicacies, but the main attraction was a chance to sit and chat with a real live Sea Dog player. Eight people were assigned to each table: seven ticket buyers and one actual team member.

However, there was one potential logistical problem: two players spoke only Spanish. One was Dominican pitcher Antonio Alfonseca; the other was Rentería, a Colombian. Since I had spent a brief period in Central America nearly a decade earlier, I was nominated by those in charge to sit with one of the two young Latinos that night.

Since it was my first year with the team and the players had arrived from Florida only hours earlier, I had no idea what any of them looked like. But when I got to my assigned table there wasn't too much doubt about who Edgar Rentería was. Six people chatted amiably amongst themselves; a dark-skinned, athletic-looking young fellow sat with them, mutely and expressionlessly.

I approached the quiet young man. "Edgar?" I said. He responded wordlessly, acknowledged my presence with a nod. Seizing upon his silence as a window of opportunity, I began reciting the fractured-Spanish soliloquy I had been practicing all afternoon.

Edgar: yo soy Andres. Mi trabajo es con los Sea Dogs. Ocho anos en el pasado yo vivi en Guatemala con Cuerpo de Paz, y a este vez yo hable un poquito de espanol, pero ahora yo no recuerdo mucho. Pero su necesitas ayuda, yo voy a tratar. (**Very** rough translation: "Edgar, I'm Andy. I work for the Sea Dogs. Eight years ago I was in the Peace Corps in Guatemala and spoke a little Spanish at that time. I've forgotten most of it, but if you need help I'll try to assist you.")

Edgar listened impassively. When I finished he looked me in the eye and said, "Don't worry, man. I speak English."

Once a slender 18-year-old Portland Sea Dog, here's a wealthier, fleshier Edgar Rentería, pursuing a ground ball for the San Francisco Giants in 2009.

Edgar didn't need to say much that summer; his play spoke for him.

Near the end of the season, he did a ten-minute pregame show interview with me in Binghamton, New York. And despite the likelihood that no one besides the two of us understood a word of his earnest but heavily-accented English, we both enjoyed it immensely.

By the following May, Rentería was the Florida Marlins' shortstop. The year after that he rapped out the game-winning single in the bottom of the 11th inning of the seventh game of the World Series. He was 21 years old at the time.

And thirteen years later he belted a series-clinching three-run home run off of one of the game's elite pitchers, making him a World Series hero again, albeit one with slightly more flesh and a lot less hair than he had sported as a summering Mainer 15 years ago.

Three days after being named World Series MVP, Edgar was released by the Giants, although they did give him the $500,000 buyout his contract called for. ●

Business as Usual in the Sports Business

January 16, 2010

It's been an all-too-typical month in the world of play-for-pay athletics. The only person benefiting from the most recent spate of narcissism, greed, arrogance, and bad decisions on the part of high-visibility sports figures is the individual who's most likely earned more money through professional sports than anyone else in the industry. Thanks to a pistol-packing National Basketball Association star, a carpetbagging college football coach, and a crocodile tear-shedding former home run hitter, Tiger Woods finally saw his name disappear from the tabloid headlines for the first time since a Thanksgiving night car accident that ultimately exposed the planet's best golfer as a libidinous, world-class hypocrite.

Gilbert Arenas is employed by the Washington Wizards of the National Basketball Association. Last year he signed a contract with the team worth $111 million over six years. However, both his exorbitant salary and his freedom are currently at risk after he pleaded guilty to felony gun possession last week in D.C. Superior Court. The charges stemmed from a locker room disagreement between Arenas and a teammate which culminated with a display of firearms. Arenas's original reaction to the affair was to joke about it via Twitter, but it's no laughing matter to the authorities in the nation's capital, to say nothing of the NBA flacks who've been working for years trying to sanitize the image of a league too many view as unsavory.

Arenas may be guilty of bad judgment, but if greed, hypocrisy, and treachery were crimes numerous Division I college football coaches would be doing life without parole. The latest example is Lane Kiffin, who thirteen months ago was signed to a six-year contract worth over $13 million by the University of Tennessee to turn their underperforming team around. It was quite a coup for a brash young (34) mentor whose only previous head coaching experience had been an underwhelming (five wins in 20 games) stint with the NFL's Oakland Raiders. Last week Kiffin rewarded Tennessee's faith in him by bolting for the head coaching position at the University of Southern California. Two of his assistant coaches left for USC with him, but not before calling several of the athletically gifted recruits they'd lured to Tennessee to let them know they'd be welcome to follow the new USC coaching staff out to Los Angeles.

Kiffin's lack of loyalty was bitterly decried by Tennessee's athletic department, not to mention the assistant coaches (including Kiffin's brother-in-law) who aren't going with him, and whom he didn't contact before hurriedly leaving town. However, the Tennessee athletic department's justifiable outrage about another school's stealing their head football coach didn't stop them from hiring a new one three days later, one they lured away from Louisiana Tech in the same clandestine, whirlwind manner with which USC had enticed Kiffin.

And then there was Mark McGwire, whose 70 home runs broke Major League Baseball's single-season record in 1998 (though it was re-broken three years later by another player with a cartoonish, likely synthetic physique). After years of denials McGwire finally admitted last week that he had indeed used performance-enhancing substances during most of his career. His admission was about as surprising as a retired professional wrestler confessing that most of what he did was staged.

Is McGwire truly sorry? Probably, if the tears he shed while being interviewed on The Baseball Network are to be believed. But he's also deceiving himself if he really thinks, as he professes, that using banned substances which transformed him into a 6'5" Charles Atlas had nothing to do with his shattering of Roger Maris's 37-year-old single-season record of 61 home runs. That's the equivalent of Donald Trump claiming he'd have starred in a hit TV show even if he didn't have a famous name and a gazillion dollars first, or Rush Limbaugh maintaining he'd still be the king of talk radio even if he limited himself to quietly saying things that were true.

So how much of the approximately $74 million the allegedly contrite Mr. McGwire earned in salary from 1990 to 2001 is he planning on turning over to the relief effort in Haiti, or to soup kitchens in St. Louis, or to cancer research? Probably about the same amount as baseball's team owners and executives, all of whom profited immensely from the torrent of chemically-aided home runs swatted by previously pedestrian big leaguers during the same time period in which McGwire acquired his synthetic muscles.

Yet despite all this many who witnessed McGwire's long-overdue acknowledgment of his deception were sympathetic, which proves that the people who orchestrated the delusional, self-worshipping former slugger's lachrymose, choreographed mea culpa did a brilliant job.

Tiger Woods ought to give them a call. ●

Why Baseball Won't Punish Steroid Users

August 3, 2009

A generation ago the only people needing to willingly suspend disbelief before watching their favorite athletes compete were followers of professional wrestling. Maintaining that the antics of paid grapplers were genuine rather than staged involved taking a voluntary vacation from reality, something most wrestling aficionados were (and still are) more than willing to do.

Baseball, football, basketball, and hockey fans looked down their noses at the bloated behemoths who took part in weekly televised wrestling shows and sold-out extravaganzas at venues like Boston Garden, Chicago Stadium, and New York's Madison Square Garden. It wasn't just that bizarrely clad, unnaturally gargantuan specimens like Terry Bollea, Sylvester Ritter, James Janos, Gino Marella, and William Myers were engaging in staged performances; they did so while using bogus names. Only the most devoted wrestling enthusiasts would recognize the quintet listed above as the alter egos of, in order, Hulk Hogan, the Junkyard Dog, Jesse "The Body" Ventura, Gorilla Monsoon, and George "The Animal" Steele.

Wrestling devotees no longer need to take abuse from fans of any of America's supposedly "legitimate" sports regarding the use of substances which artificially and radically change the shape and capabilities of the human body. Performance-enhancing products (as well as chemicals which mask them from showing up on drug tests) have been a fact of life in all the major sports for years. Who really believes professional football linemen weighing in excess of 350 pounds got that big simply through improved eating habits and extra work in the weight room?

Lately the use of banned substances by highly-paid professional athletes has become a sensitive issue in these parts, given the report in last week's *New York Times* that Manny Ramirez and David Ortiz, who comprised the middle of the Boston Red Sox batting order when the team won two World Series earlier this decade, had both tested positive for performance-enhancing substances in 2003.

Neither Ramirez, now a Los Angeles Dodger, nor Ortiz, who is still with Boston but whose production has fallen off precipitously in the past two years, have bothered denying the allegations. Most New England baseball fans love the Sox even more than they hate the New York Yankees, their despised rivals who amassed 26 championships in between Boston's titles in 1918 and 2004. The Sox will be at Yankee Stadium this

Thursday through Sunday, and given that smug members of Red Sox Nation have been mercilessly razzing Yankee fans about the steroid connections of current or former Bronx Bombers Alex Rodriguez, Roger Clemens, Jason Giambi, Andy Pettitte, and Gary Sheffield, the weekend is unlikely to be very pleasant for New England's beloved "Big Papi."

No one should be stunned that Boston's top two home run hitters used pharmaceutical performance-enhancers in the past decade; in fact, it would be more surprising if they hadn't. It's likely the vast majority of baseball's power hitters availed themselves of such products in the late 1990s and the early part of the 21st century. Why wouldn't they? It was reasonable to assume most of their competition was using anabolic steroids and similar substances that were easily obtainable. It was also readily apparent that the lords of Major League Baseball, the leaders of the all-powerful Major League Baseball Players Association, and the mainstream media serving as MLB's de facto publicity arm were determined to look the other way where drug usage was concerned, particularly as long as the turnstiles continued clicking and the television money kept on coming.

Angry fans feeling cheated by ongoing steroid revelations, outrageous player salaries or both have no one but themselves to blame. Those disliking what the National Pastime has become need to stop supporting the owners and performers who comprise MLB, which would mean no more buying tickets, tuning in to game broadcasts, or doing business with those who sponsor them.

Despite the public fretting of players, owners, and media members whose jobs depend on Major League Baseball's continued financial health, it's unlikely any of them are terribly worried about an imminent massive fan exodus. Professional wrestling and the National Football League have each had numerous steroid-related scandals and tragedies over the past two decades, many of which have been highly publicized. If MLB commissioner Bud Selig is truly concerned about impending fiscal disaster due to fan outrage over steroids, he can always call World Wrestling Entertainment Chairman of the Board Vince McMahon or NFL commissioner Roger Goodell to ask what effect widespread use of performance-enhancing substances have had on their organizations.

It's doubtful Selig will contact either man, though. He already knows what rampant steroid usage has done for professional wrestling and football.

It's made them both significantly more profitable. ●

On Setting (and Breaking) Records

August 11, 2007

Not long ago someone asked me what I thought about the recent milestones reached by three veteran major league baseball players, Barry Bonds, Alex Rodriguez and Tom Glavine. My guess is he was interested in my opinion not because he thinks I'm all that smart (he doesn't, and I'm not), but because he's aware that in a previous life I worked in a variety of off-the-field capacities for a half-dozen different professional baseball teams.

All three of the above-mentioned players are handsomely compensated for being amongst the best ever at what they do. Mr. Rodriguez, who plays third base for the New York Yankees, struck his 500th career round tripper on August 4th. He'll gross $22,708,525 this season. He could pay off the cumbersome mortgage my wife and I will be working the next 29 years to do with less than one of his weekly paychecks. Mr. Bonds broke the career home run record when he hit his 756th three days later. The once-lithe, now burly outfielder will be paid $15,533,970 this season, although that's a major cut from the $22,000,000 he earned just two summers ago. Mr. Glavine, who is just the sixth-highest paid player on his team, will have to get by on a mere $7,500,000 in 2007. That means about $250,000 per game, assuming he gets into 30 contests this season. He'd probably have to make three starts to pay off my mortgage, although he could buy our house for cash and still have a good chunk of change left over after just two appearances.

Although I earned just over $20,000 (with no benefits such as health insurance) in my 14th and final season working in organized baseball, please don't think I feel these three gentlemen are overpaid. I don't. Like all of us, Bonds, Glavine, and Rodriguez are entitled to collect whatever they can get for their services, and like all of us they are free to find another employer or field of endeavor if and when the time comes that they are unhappy with their job conditions. I *may* feel that health care providers, firefighters, police officers, and others who serve the public are by comparison grossly *under*paid, but that's another topic for another day. I also understand that were it not for all the health care providers, firefighters, police officers, and others who choose to spend their discretionary income on attending ballgames and buying a multitude of baseball-related products, the gap between their annual income and that of professional athletes would be much less wide.

Diehard baseball enthusiasts have always had a fascination with numbers. National pastime fans of my generation knew the significance of 56, 511, .406, 714, 4191, and 2130, all of which represented unbreakable baseball records. Forty or so years later 56 (Joe DiMaggio's hitting streak), 511 (Cy Young's career wins) and .406 (Ted Williams's batting average in 1941, the last year anyone hit over .400) are still significant, but the other three numbers that were once considered unreachable have been topped. Ty Cobb's 4191 hits and Lou Gehrig's 2130 consecutive games played have both been bettered, and Babe Ruth's 714 career homeruns has been surpassed twice, though only once by a player who was unenhanced chemically.

My family is into numbers as well, and I set a record this summer I feel is comparable to Cal Ripken's 2632 consecutive games played. Due to a variety of coincidences, I was nominated to give my airplane-phobic mother-in-law a ride back home to Maine from Michigan, where she had been tending to a family emergency. I drove 789 miles to Sarnia, Ontario, on a Sunday night, then shattered that mark by driving 1012 miles the next day to pick her up and get her back home at a few minutes before midnight. The number 1012 should be in the Young family record book for quite some time, although I fervently hope that if and when it is surpassed, its eclipser is someone other than me.

And as for the recent milestones achieved by Tom, A-Rod, and Barry, the amount of time I'll spend celebrating the records they've set is in all likelihood exactly equal to the amount of time each of them will put into celebrating mine. ●

An Autumn Gift from the Red Sox: Time!

October 5, 2014

Last year New England sports fans were consumed by baseball's post-season, but when the World Series finally ends late this (or early next) month it's likely few locals will even notice. One-third of Major League Baseball's 30 teams will participate in the 2014 playoffs, but the Boston Red Sox, who finished dead last in the American League's Eastern Division, won't be one of them.

The defending World Series Champions laid an egg this year. Some key performers were injured, a number of highly-touted youngsters failed to live up to their advance notices, and several prematurely wealthy veteran players performed below expectations as well. But thoughtful citizens of Red Sox Nation have reason to celebrate.

Thanks to the dreadful just-completed season, thousands of loyal Boston baseball fans now possess a significant chunk of leisure time they didn't have a year ago. Last fall it took the Red Sox 16 games to win their third World Series title in the last ten seasons. Those choosing to watch every televised minute of those contests deprived themselves of 56 hours and 42 minutes, all of which could undoubtedly have been utilized more productively, or at the very least squandered more imaginatively. Nearly all of last fall's Red Sox post-season baseball "action" took place at a time of night when most people on the east coast would ordinarily be preparing to turn in, or would have already retired for the evening. And those fans unable to do without the pre- and post-game chat-a-thons gave up even more of their leisure and/or nominal resting hours.

Things are different this fall, though. Not only did the Sox gift New England's baseball faithful with significantly more leaf-peeping time, they gave plenty of advance notice they'd do so by figuratively waving the white flag in late July, selling or trading off as many handsomely-compensated underachievers as they could find takers for. Boston management clearly signaled their intention to stay out of post-season play by dealing off three-fifths of their starting rotation, a quality relief pitcher, an outfielder, and a shortstop, all of whom were being paid princely salaries which team management judged to be too high. The team's mathematical elimination from post-season play on September 10th was such a foregone conclusion that it passed virtually unnoticed.

There are a variety of reasons local folks and a great many other Americans living south and/or west of here will be doing something other than watching baseball this month. One of the biggest is the length of time a contemporary nine-inning contest takes to play.

It took the 1967 "Impossible Dream" Red Sox and the St. Louis Cardinals 16 hours and 39 minutes to play the seven games of that year's World Series, an average of 2:22 per game. That included the Game 6, which lasted an impossibly long two hours and 48 minutes.

Last year's World Series between the Red Sox and Cardinals took 19 hours and 57 minutes to play…and it only lasted *six* games! Game 5, which took two hours and 52 minutes to complete, was the *shortest* game of Boston's post-season, and was the *only* one of the team's 16 playoff and World Series contests last year that lasted less than three hours. The average time of those 16 games: a snooze-inducing three hours and 33 minutes.

Televised National Football League regular-season matchups generally attract larger audiences than baseball's nominally most meaningful games, and that's despite the recent flood of news coverage spotlighting a spate of incredibly ugly incidents involving some of the NFL's highest-profile players and executives.

And there's more bad news for those charged with running America's nominal National Pastime: when it comes to disinterest in the World Series, New Englanders are not alone.

"The games are so slow," an old friend and lifelong Boston fan complained to me recently, adding, "how can anyone with a job stay up past midnight to watch this stuff?"

And he's got other issues with America's grand old game: the overabundance of preening, pharmaceutically-aided players, night playoff games in cities where after-dark temperatures often drop below 40 degrees, and the difficulty he has tossing his hard-earned dollars to a multi-billion-dollar industry where the minimum player salary is now ten or more times the annual earnings of police officers, firefighters, teachers, nurses, members of the military and others who do far more for society than professional athletes or entertainers.

Too many overpaid performers (some of whom cheat), interminable games that go on long past bedtime, and nighttime weather that's often more appropriate for skating than baseball are all valid reasons for passing on baseball's Fall Classic.

And here's one more thing for die-hard Red Sox fans to consider: would Boston's Major League Baseball team being *in* this year's Fall Classic change any of those things? ●

What Makes People Angry?

December 23, 2005

Last week an article in the *New York Times* revealed that the president of the United States had given authorization for certain government agencies to spy on American citizens. Wiretapping phone conversations without first obtaining a warrant granting permission to do so is illegal.

The president didn't bother to deny the allegations, instead choosing to excoriate the people at the *Times* responsible for bringing the clandestine activities to light.

Given these and other recent events, it's not surprising nearly everyone I talked with during the week before Christmas was filled with outrage. Was all the righteous anger I heard from neighbors and co-workers directed at the president for his administration's violation of the rights of everyday Americans? Was their wrath directed at the *New York Times* and other publications for giving aid and comfort to our enemies? Was nearly every informed student in the classes I teach at a local high school appalled by the most recent example of the Bush administration running roughshod over the constitution? Or were these young people upset by the continuing interference of the media in our nation's affairs?

The answers to the above questions are no, no, no, and no.

What so many New Englanders were consumed with last week was a 32-year-old man named Johnny Damon choosing to terminate his employment with the Boston Red Sox in order to accept a similar position with the New York Yankees. Mr. Damon expressed some regret at leaving Boston, but also pointed out his new employer was happy to pay him three million dollars *more* per season (for each of the next four years) than the Red Sox were willing to.

The Red Sox and Yankees are not sovereign nations. They are rival baseball teams, each consisting of 25 individuals whose average annual compensation for publicly playing a game 162 times each year has seven digits to the left of the decimal point.

Mr. Damon may be a self-proclaimed "Idiot" (that's the title of the autobiography which was ghost-written for him last year), but he's no fool. Professional athletes have a very limited window during which they can command princely wages. Who among those cursing the erstwhile Red Sox centerfielder would say no to a job offer from a competitor who was offering a pay raise of 30 percent? Or $3 million per year, for that matter?

When I hear someone decrying the lack of loyalty on the part of today's professional athletes, I simply assume the individual speaking is either from another planet, or has, by choice or involuntarily, lost contact with reality.

When Johnny Damon was 18, he was drafted by the Kansas City Royals, meaning the recent high school graduate had the choice of either joining the Royals organization or finding a job outside of professional baseball. Not surprisingly, Damon elected to sign a Kansas City contract.

After serving a minor league apprenticeship of more than three years playing for teams in Davenport, Florida; Rockford, Illinois; Wilmington, Delaware; and Wichita, Kansas, Damon arrived in the big leagues in mid-1995. He hit .292 while playing in the outfield for the Royals over the next five-plus seasons.

As a reward for his fine performance, the Royals traded him to Oakland after the conclusion of the 2000 season. That meant he had to pick up the life he had made for himself in Kansas City and move it to a city with which he was unfamiliar. Of course, he didn't have to go to Oakland. His other option was to find employment that didn't involve playing baseball professionally.

In professional sports, loyalty is a two-way street that leads to a dead end from both directions.

The hysterical reaction to the Johnny Damon situation made me want to contact an old friend in Ohio with whom I worked some years ago in the professional sports field. I'd have liked to get the perspective of someone from outside Red Sox Nation on Damon's defection. However, after some consideration I decided against calling him.

I wasn't sure who might be listening. ●

Baseball's Changing Status

April 17, 2009

Eight-year-old Cardinal Thomas Young (2009)

My oldest son is a Cardinal.

Not a senior ecclesiastical official or a seed-eating red bird, but a baseball player. He's now a rookie in the farm league, after spending last year with the Pony League Phillies and the previous season with the White Sox of the T-ball League. He is all of eight years old.

Baseball and the role it plays in the lives of American youth has changed significantly since my childhood, when we used wooden bats and only rich kids wore cleats. The lone opportunity my sneaker-clad friends and I had to play any organized sport prior to starting high school was Little League Baseball.

At age nine I made one of the four Little League teams in my town, and even though I rarely played I felt lucky to warm the Hawks' bench, occasionally coaching first base and chasing foul balls during games against the Rams, the Lions, and our arch-rivals, the Bears. And although I wasn't an instant superstar (I didn't register my initial legitimate hit or catch my first fly ball until I was 11) I ate, slept, and lived baseball. Even before I was old enough to try out I knew the names of all three Alou brothers. I was familiar with Babe Ruth's called shot, Bobby Thomson's home run, and Don Larson's perfect game. I knew Yankee fans had big mouths, but that no matter how loudly they shouted there was no way Mickey Mantle was better than Willie Mays, never mind Hank Aaron, Roberto Clemente, or Frank Robinson. I could not only recite what positions John Roseboro, Dick McAuliffe, Ruben Amaro and Harry Bright played, I knew which team(s) they played them for as well. Knowing baseball was essential for boys growing up in the late 1960s, at least where I lived.

However, that was then and this is now.

Eight months after my Little League career began, the first Super Bowl was played. While professional football's executives of that era were looking into the future, baseball's staid and unimaginative lords were mired in the past. Television, a medium for which football was seemingly designed, was becoming a major player in professional sports. In an effort to cash in, Major League Baseball transformed its All-Star Game and the World Series from daytime affairs into "prime time" events, a strategy that brought them money in the short term but was disastrous in the long run, since baseball's two signature events now concluded far too late at night for most young people to stay up and watch them to their conclusion.

For more than forty years since then American youth has been wooed far more successfully by ambitious and energetic people marketing football, basketball, hockey, soccer, auto racing, golf, and professional wrestling than by agents of the self-proclaimed National Pastime. Professional baseball's belated efforts to peddle itself have been aimed more at securing corporate dollars than at winning over new generations of fans.

I recently realized how long it's been since baseball lost its hold on me when I saw a headline trumpeting "Sox Hoping for Comeback from Papi." I initially read the last word as rhyming with "happy" rather than "hoppy." That the first image I had gotten was one of Stan Papi, the utility infielder acquired in a 1978 trade for Bill Lee whose brief and uneventful Red Sox career consisted of 125 plate appearances, rather than current Red Sox DH David "Big Papi" Ortiz confirms that my interest in the game I grew up loving probably peaked three decades ago.

Boston's Big Papi

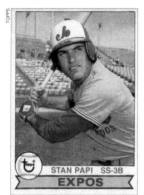

Boston's original Papi

In my youth the term "play date" didn't exist any more than the word "airport" had fifty years earlier. Kids wanting to play baseball, football, or basketball routinely walked, ran, or rode their bikes to the nearest backyard, schoolyard, or vacant lot and chose up sides.

To my knowledge none of my three children has ever played a sport in a situation that wasn't formally structured. Maybe that's because we don't have a big backyard, we don't live close to a schoolyard, and vacant lots are tough to come by these days. But more likely is because here in the 21st century, youth sports are painfully over-organized.

When I was eight, I knew the infield fly rule. My son, who is far smarter than I was at a similar age, doesn't know how many balls there are in a walk. In fact, on the way home from practice the other night I found myself having to explain to him exactly what a base on balls is.

America in general and New England in particular are no better or worse than they were half a century ago when baseball was the undisputed king of sports; they're just different.

Sigh. ●

NBA Work Stoppage is an Opportunity to Learn

November 7, 2011

Judging by the wailing and hand-wringing of media members who cover the professional sports business, you'd think the current National Basketball Association labor impasse is an epic economic disaster with potentially catastrophic consequences, both in the United States and internationally.

Fortunately that's not true. The current dearth of major league professional basketball isn't Armageddon. In fact, it may be quite the opposite.

The NBA season was supposed to start last Tuesday. But because the billionaires who own and operate the 30 NBA teams have decided to lock out the players, many of whom are, at least on paper, millionaires themselves, it didn't.

The owners hope to crush the NBA Players Association and ultimately resolve the current labor dispute in management's favor. Currently the major sticking point seems to be how best to divide the obscene amount of basketball-related income generated by the league each year. Under the recently-expired collective bargaining agreement (CBA) the players were receiving 57% of it, while the owners had to make do with a mere 43%.

But when the CBA both sides agreed to in 2005 ended last spring, the indignant plutocrats decided to take a hard line in dealing with their elongated hired hands. They want no less than a 50-50 split of the monies generated by the league's gate receipts from all exhibition, regular season, and playoff games; novelty, program, and concession sales; mascot and dance team appearances, arena-naming rights, broadcast rights, and a myriad of other sources of revenue which make the league's annual income measurable in the billions of dollars.

Management's unsurprising public stance regarding the current impasse is that the players are greedy, entitled ingrates. Equally predictably, the players' union correctly maintains no one ever paid triple-digit ticket prices to see avaricious, middle-aged men in thousand-dollar suits (other than former NBA superstar Michael Jordan, currently one of the owners of the Charlotte Bobcats) play basketball.

Some nominally bad things will continue taking place as long as NBA labor and management persist in locking horns. Arenas around North America and their adjacent parking garages will stay dark. Bigwigs accustomed to entertaining clients in corporate luxury boxes during games won't be able to close deals over chateaubriand and caviar. NBA staffers who sell tickets and/or advertising will stay laid off, or perhaps be permanently terminated. And game-night employees who earn modest hourly wages pouring $9 beers, grilling $7 hot dogs, or hawking $10 programs will stay on indefinite furlough, which is truly unfortunate.

However, another consequence of a lengthy labor standoff would be that fans who for whatever reason(s) feel the need to pay exorbitant ticket prices to get a professional basketball fix every so often would find themselves looking for other ways to spend not only their time, but money that was previously earmarked for the already too-deep pockets of an NBA team owner or one of his far-too-rich young employees. And that's potentially a very *good* thing.

Without the distraction of the NBA, basketball fans will be getting a windfall of spare time which, if managed correctly, should end up being *quality* time. Some might discover or rediscover the joy of socializing with friends and neighbors, or visiting with relatives they haven't seen enough of recently. They might opt to play pickup basketball themselves, join a bowling league, or volunteer at a local hospital, church, synagogue, or library. They could help coach or chaperone their children's activities, dedicate themselves to some worthy cause they believe in, or plan some special family activities. Idle NBA fans could go to the movies, read a book, or phone, write, or Skype with old friends. They could learn to play a musical instrument, start their own blog, or update their existing one. The list of things to do with all the time (to say nothing of all that found money) the NBA owners and players are handing over is literally endless.

It's true there are less productive ways to spend one's idle hours than watching large men try to throw an orange ball through a metal hoop. But at least sitting on the couch watching "Dancing with the Stars" doesn't require viewers to pony up a couple of car payments worth of cash for the privilege.

And while the rest of us are busily finding activities other than watching rich young men in shorts and tank-tops running up and down a 94-foot-long, 50-foot-wide flat surface, the owners of all 30 currently inactive NBA teams and their erstwhile players might be learning something too, which is that when there's nothing to divvy up, there's no difference whatsoever between 57% and 43%. ●

The Legacies of Two Red Sox Outfielders

May 11, 2009

In ten full seasons with the Boston Red Sox, Dominic DiMaggio batted .298, slugged 98 home runs, added 618 runs batted in, stole an even 100 bases and played superior defense. But despite DiMaggio's stellar contributions the Red Sox appeared in only one World Series during his tenure. The St. Louis Cardinals bested Boston in 1946 in heartbreaking fashion; the winning run came home in the bottom of the 8th inning of the seventh game on a botched relay that began with center fielder Leon Culberson, who had been pressed into service after DiMaggio had been hurt running the bases in the top of the frame.

The day before DiMaggio's death last Friday at the age of 92, another former Boston outfielder was in the news. Manny Ramirez, who these days draws an annual salary of almost $24 million for plying his trade with the Los Angeles Dodgers, was suspended 50 games for violating Major League Baseball's drug policy. During his nearly eight-year stint in Boston, Ramirez batted .315, crushed 294 homers, drove in 921 runs, pilfered seven bases, and played memorable defense. The Red Sox won a pair of World Series Championships during Manny's tenure, thanks in no small part to his extraordinary contributions. The dreadlocked left fielder clubbed six homers, amassed 27 RBI, and hit .349 in the 28 post-season games the Red Sox played in 2004 and 2007.

There's no point comparing the career statistics of these two former Red Sox, even if they did both play their home games at Fenway Park. DiMaggio, who was listed as 5'9" tall and 168 pounds in his heyday, probably wouldn't even get a tryout today due to his diminutive size, not to mention the scholarly-looking spectacles he wore that earned him the nickname of "The Little Professor." Conversely, there weren't any dark-skinned players in the big leagues when DiMaggio debuted in 1940, and there were no native Dominicans in the majors when he left the game in 1953, nearly 19 years before Ramirez was born.

Some maintain Ramirez's admitting to having taken a banned substance (one he says was prescribed to him by a doctor) and his subsequent acceptance of a mandatory 50-game suspension without appeal show admirable character. Earlier this year New York Yankee superstar Alex Rodriguez owned up to having used banned substances some years ago (after incontrovertible evidence of it was revealed by a national magazine), and humbly apologized for his poor judgment.

But is the regret for their actions being shown by baseball's two highest-paid players sincere? Or have those in charge of shaping the public's perception of Rodriguez and Ramirez determined—from watching Roger Clemens, Mark McGwire, Barry Bonds, Sammy Sosa, Rafael Palmeiro and others make fools of themselves denying the obvious—that public contrition is a better form of damage control?

Thanks to the business acumen he showed after his playing days were over, Dom DiMaggio died a wealthy man. However, the total he earned for playing in 1399 major league baseball games was a tiny fraction (perhaps one fortieth) of the $7,650,273 salary that Manny Ramirez will forfeit as the result of the 50 contests he'll miss due to his mandated vacation.

Only those who still believe in the tooth fairy can think Ramirez wasn't getting pharmaceutical augmentation during his seasons with the Red Sox, or that he was the only Boston player availing himself of such assistance during that time. It would be far more surprising to learn any particular home run hitter or muscular pitcher of the late 1990s or early 21st century *wasn't* using some form of chemical enhancement. Why wouldn't he? Such help was readily available, virtually all the competition was availing themselves of it, and neither Major League Baseball nor the "journalists" covering it seemed terribly interested in learning anything about the use of performance-enhancing substances, how it may have been affecting the game, or how widespread it was. Given MLB's announced attendance figures over the so-called Steroid Era, the sport's drug controversy didn't turn off many fans, either.

It's doubtful many of the handful of people still alive who saw Dom DiMaggio patrol center field for the Red Sox in the 1940s have any desire to attend a game today, even if they could afford the stratospheric price of a ticket.

For younger fans unaware of or unopposed to steroid use, there's no problem. But for those who piously and shrilly profess to abhor what they see as the rampant cheating and greed in professional sports, here's a question: why do you still care? And even more significantly, why are you still buying tickets to Fenway Park, watching major league baseball on TV, or purchasing Red Sox apparel bearing the name of your favorite 30-year old multi-millionaire on the back? ●

PART 3

Pungent Social Commentary

There weren't any politically themed essays included in *Young Ideas,* mostly because I learned from reading years of old essays that non-political columns have a far longer shelf life than those commenting on various politicians and/or their enablers. That said, I've included a few here (in the "Unvarnished opinion" section) because, well, I guess I want whatever descendants I have to know that back in the early part of the 21st century, great-great Grandpa Young was on the right side of history.

SECTION 9

Outside the Box

Born in November? Don't Seek the Presidency!

November 3, 2015

Renowned humorist Samuel Clemens (DOB: 11-30-1835), better known by his pen name "Mark Twain," didn't just write classic novels like *The Adventures of Tom Sawyer* and *The Adventures of Huckleberry Finn*. His observations on life in general and human beings in particular are still widely cited. Two of Twain's acerbic gems, "All you need in this life is ignorance and confidence, and then success is sure," and "Get your facts first, then you can distort them as you please," are clearly still relevant.

Apparently Twain's gift for irony isn't as fully appreciated today as it was when he was penning his thoughts during the late 19th and early 20th centuries, though. Most (if not all) of the 18 individuals currently vying for the Democratic or Republican party presidential nomination would be doing America a favor if they'd stop taking the above sentiments so literally.

But Twain also dispensed wisdom displaying a more thoughtful, sensitive side, like "Kindness is the language which the deaf can hear and the blind can see" and "The best way to cheer yourself up is to try to cheer somebody else up."

Given that publicly-stated capacity for empathy, if Twain were alive to mark his 180th birthday later this month it's likely he'd try to cheer himself up by directing some kindness toward Scott Walker, who formally ended his bid for the Republican presidential nomination on September 21, citing low polling numbers and a lack of money. However, careful research reveals what *actually* brought about the union-busting Wisconsin governor's meekly bowing out of the race for the White House, and it had nothing to do with funding or polls.

Walker was born November 2, 1967, in Colorado Springs, Colorado. But it wasn't the *place* of his birth that brought him down; it was the *date*.

The last American president born in November was elected in 1920. Most reputable scholars consider Warren Harding (DOB 11-2-1865) America's least effective 20th-century chief executive. Known best for a corruption-wracked administration and some torrid extramarital affairs that were uncovered long after his death, Harding served less than two and a half years of his term before succumbing to a cerebral hemorrhage while on a speaking tour in 1923.

Prior to Harding four other United States presidents were born in November. James Garfield (11-19-1831) was struck by an assassin's bullet less than four months after taking office in 1881; he died two months later.

Franklin Pierce (11-23-1804), whose policies as president (1853–1857) helped bring about the Civil War, was a profoundly unhappy man whose wife battled illness and depression most of her life. None of their three children lived past age 11. Not surprisingly Pierce was a heavy drinker who died of cirrhosis of the liver in 1869.

Zachary Taylor (11-24-1784) took the oath of office in March of 1849; he died suddenly of a stomach ailment less than 18 months later. His immediate predecessor, James K. Polk (11-2-1795), served one term (1845–1849) as commander-in-chief and acquitted himself well, but the job took such a toll on him that he died at age 54. The 103 days he lived after leaving office constitutes the shortest post-presidency in American history.

At this writing, not one of the 18 remaining 2016 presidential aspirants (3 Democrats and 15 Republicans) has a November birthday. Hilary Clinton (10-26-1947), Martin O'Malley (1-18-1963), Bernie Sanders (9-8-1941), Carly Fiorina (9-6-1954), Donald Trump (6-14-1946), Bobby Jindal (6-10-1971), Mike Huckabee (8-24-1955), Jeb! Bush (2-11-1953!), Marco Rubio (5-28-1971), Ben Carson (9-18-1951), Rand Paul (7-7-1963), Rick Santorum (5-10-1958), Jon Kasich (5-13-1952), Jim Gilmore (10-6-1949), Chris Christie (9-6-1962), Ted Cruz (12-22-1970), George Pataki (6-24-1945) and Lindsey Graham (7-9-1955) were all born in one of the other eleven months.

It's not just presidential timber November is short on. There have been 88 best-actor Oscars bestowed since the award began in 1929, but of those honorees only Burt Lancaster (11-2-1913), Art Carney (11-4-1918), and Matthew McConaughey (11-4-1969) were born during the eleventh month on the calendar.

This eerie scarcity doesn't just exist in the drama field. Of the 68 living members of baseball's Hall of Fame, only Whitey Herzog (11-9-1931), Bob Gibson (11-9-1935), and Tom Seaver (11-17-1944) began their lives in November.

But that's not cause for Novemberites to hang their heads. Any month that produced

Marie Curie, Billy Graham, Charles Schulz, Winston Churchill, and the three Turners (Ike, Tina, and Ted) can't be all bad. As Twain presciently observed, "All generalizations are false, including this one."

He also wrote, "It is better to keep your mouth closed and let people think you are a fool than to open it and remove all doubt," a thought to which a significant number of the remaining presidential wannabes ought to pay more heed. ●

Why Not, Indeed?

August 6, 2014

Want to feel good about life? Go to a wedding. Virtually everyone there is happy, upbeat, and optimistic, and on top of that is looking his or her best. Wedding attendees exude enough positivity, generosity, and wholesomeness to light up a large city for a year. Aside from the occasional shotgun-toting prospective father-in-law and the groom his weapon is trained on, the only sour people at a wedding are those who arrived bound and determined to be that way, and such individuals are as easily avoided as they are recognizable.

The only problem with relying on such joyous occasions for their outlook-enhancing value: attendance at such events is by invitation only. And for those of us of a certain age, securing one can be a bit of a challenge.

When it comes to weddings, I'm at an awkward age. I'm too old to have chronological peers taking the plunge. Nearly all of my friends and co-workers are either happily married or happily single. Everyone I grew up with who was interested in publicly pledging lifetime fidelity to another took care of it long ago; in fact, several have done so multiple times. Many of *their* children have already been married as well, but it'll be a long time before any of their children's children are ready to take the plunge. As for my own three progeny, the oldest is still trying to decide whether or not it's worth five dollars to attend middle school dances. As a result of these circumstances, I find wedding invitations in my mailbox about as often as I get telegrams from Publishers Clearing House telling me I've won their grand prize.

The few weddings our family has attended over the past decade have all been memorable. One of my cousin's daughters got married over Labor Day weekend in Pennsylvania a few years ago; the highlight was someone snapping a photo of my then-four-year-old daughter smilingly holding an empty Heineken bottle, an image that will probably prevent her from ever seeking elective office. A year or two later another cousin's daughter got married on a stormy, sultry evening where the lively, festive reception had even more positive electricity than the lightning-filled sky. We spent last year's Labor Day weekend in New Jersey at the wedding of our nephew, where the groom's 85-year-old grandmother was movin' and groovin' on the dance floor long after the limousines that had transported her to the reception had turned into pumpkins.

The most recent wedding I had the good fortune to attend took place earlier this month. Outwardly it featured a lot of what other such ceremonies did: an outrageously attractive happy couple, a handsome and friendly best man, a luminous maid of honor, an impossibly cute flower girl, an equally adorable pint-sized ring-bearer, and a large group of family and friends, each of whom was indescribably happy for the soon-to-be-wedded duo standing at the altar.

Several factors made the sunny, humid day memorable, not the least of which was the air conditioning inside the church. The singers and musicians were *exceptionally* good, although given that the couple getting married are both music teachers that wasn't all that surprising. Another unusual (and less easily explained) phenomenon: there were at least half a dozen children under the age of three in attendance, yet not one misbehaved or cried out during the entire ceremony. There was a reading from scripture that was as moving as it was inspirational, and a dramatization of a children's story that was both entertaining and relevant. Celebrating a special day of joy, hope, love and peace with friends, colleagues, and lots of really nice people who'd previously been strangers was both a privilege and an honor.

At the conclusion of the ceremony the pastor pronounced the happy couple husband and husband. My oldest child, who enjoyed the festivities immensely, quietly commented, "Daddy, I didn't know the church performed same-sex weddings." I briefly explained to him that not every church does. When he asked if the one he attends performs such ceremonies I had to truthfully respond that it did not.

He paused, furrowing his 13-year-old brow. Then he asked, "Why not?"

Sometimes kids say the darnedest things. As a parent and teacher, I spend a lot of time trying to get young people to heed my words. But every so often something occurs which reminds me that the importance of *my* listening to youthful individuals is *at least* as significant as them listening to me.

Why not, indeed? ●

Getting Down to 24

January 1, 2017

Few double-digit integers are more interesting than 26. Salaried employees who get paid biweekly get 26 paychecks per year. There are 26 red cards in a standard deck, and oddly enough 26 black ones, too. There are 26 cantons in Switzerland. There are precisely 26 bones in the normal human foot and ankle. Baseball Hall of Fame members Billy Williams and Wade Boggs had their #26 jerseys retired by the Chicago Baby Bears and Boston Crimson Hose, respectively. And of course everyone knows 26 is the only number that's one greater than a perfect square AND one *less* than a perfect cube.

But while there's much that's attractive about the product of thirteen and two, it's clear 26 is wholly inappropriate for the number of letters in an alphabet. It could be worse; the Hawaiian alphabet contains a mere 13 letters, which are clearly too few. Conversely those accustomed to the modern English alphabet see one consisting of 29 (Turkish or Vietnamese), 33 (Russian or Dinka) or 44 (Hungarian) letters as far too confusing to even think about.

But for the sake of organization, our system of printed writing would be much better off with precisely 24 characters. Twenty-four letters can be neatly grouped evenly and easily. Four identically-sized sets of six letters would work, as would a half-dozen foursomes, three octets, eight trios, two dozens or twelve pairs. Good luck subdividing the current alphabet into small, evenly divided groups. Your choices are thirteen couples or two ungainly baker's dozens.

But getting down to a more ideal twenty-four symbols involves eliminating two of the current ones, and some would say that's not possible. "You can't alter anything that's been around that long," the change-resistant naysayers will indignantly claim. Really? Ask any disappointed devotee of the former planet Pluto about that!

So which symbols get voted off the island? The 10th letter would be a candidate, but it might chust be too hard to chunk. American history books would have to be re-edited in order to include Chessee Chames and Chanis Choplin. Contemporary Americans like Choan Chett, Hoolio Iglesias, Cherry Seinfeld, Michael Chordan and Vice-president Choe Biden would all obchect to that, as would Chacksons like Chessee, Chanet, and Chermaine, not to mention the descendants of Andrew, Stonewall, and Michael.

The letter immediately after the one referenced above is another candidate for removal, although it would involve some disadvantages, particularly for Chris Christopherson and the Cardashians. On the other hand, it's possible eliminating the current alphabet's 11th letter might do society some good. The white supremacists who burn crosses and wear pillowcases over their heads might permanently disband if the letter between J and L were eliminated, as it's entirely possible no one involved with the organization has the imagination or creativity necessary to rename the group were its one initial permanently eradicated.

The last letter of the current alphabet rarely seems necessary, but it likely would be agonising to eulojighs a letter that's vital at Kwansuh, not to mention Bar Mittsvahs. Without the current alphabet's last letter dussins of laysee boosers would have to find a new way to snews if too many drinks had them feeling dissy.

The bottom line: there are two letters that could be dropped from the alphabet tomorrow without creating even the slightest problem. Without them young people could still answer kwestions on kwizzes. Their parents could still kwell and/or kwench their thirst by kwaffing a beverage or two. Muslims could still kwietly worship at a mosk of their choice. Kwartets of Kwakers could go anteeking. Brusk people prone to kwarreling could try conckering croakay, or kwilting. The 17th letter isn't needed for ducks to continue kwacking, snakes to go on skweezing, or for the San Andreas Fault to, on occasion, start kwayking.

The other letter to go wouldn't be missed by members of either secks, including musicians who play the sacksophone or the zylophone. You don't have to be smart as a focks (or strong as an ocks) to know that the neckst letter bound for ecksamination (and ultimately eckstinction) lies between W and Y. There are plenty of ecksamples of words that currently contain this letter; you could fill a bocks with them. But in reality there's no eckscuse for ecksizbbiting this letter any longer. It should be ecksized. And once that's done it shouldn't ever be eckzumed.

Don't consider a 24-letter alphabet viable? Think again. You just read a 748-word essay that used it! ●

A	B	C	D	E	F
G	H	I	J	K	L
M	N	O	P	R	S
T	U	V	W	Y	Z

Continuing Litterology Research

June 9, 2009

On weekend mornings when it's not pouring rain, I start my day with a brisk walk. Each Saturday I take a left out the driveway, go to the end of the street, up Tuttle Road to the Twin Brooks Recreation Area, through the park, and back down Greely Road. Then I take a right onto Middle Road and return home. On Sundays I hike the same four-mile loop in the opposite direction. At the hour I exercise (usually between 5 and 6 AM) it's both peaceful and beautiful.

Last Saturday morning was typical, and not only did I get some needed physical exertion, I made nearly three dollars doing it. As Yakov Smirnoff used to say, "What a country!" Unfortunately, the manner in which I generated the revenue is more than a bit depressing.

I started my walking habit a year ago, but after one stroll realized I could simultaneously use the time to do a bit of community improvement as well. I began taking a couple of shopping bags along and filling them with litter I picked up along the way. The first time I did this I quickly found two bags weren't nearly enough to effectively do the job, given the amount of trash along the sides of these rural byways. I subsequently decided to limit myself to picking up recyclable materials such as discarded cans and bottles. The good news: since making that decision I've been generating a bit of money for the local food pantry while simultaneously doing my part to clean up the environment. The bad news: I can't keep up with the litterers.

Last weekend I returned to our house with two cloth shopping bags, both of which were overflowing with cans and bottles. When one of my children asked why I was carrying two bags of returnables, I replied it was because I lacked enough hands to carry four of them.

No accredited American university currently offers a major in Litterology, but when I find one that does I'll be the first to apply for a professorship. My informal but extensive research shows there's no such thing as an average litterbug. Bottle-and-can-flingers discard vessels containing water, diet soda, fruit juice, "energy drinks," and alcohol-based beverages. Their primary missiles seem to be 12-ounce or one-pint containers, although they don't mind tossing 20-ouncers either. Thinking about investing in the stock market? Put your money into plastics rather than aluminum, since the ratio I've found on my walks is generally about three to four discarded bottles for every one pitched can.

Every so often I see signs threatening litterers with hefty fines, but how many people heave empty cans of Foster's Lager out the window within sight of law enforcement personnel? Cumberland County police officers probably issue littering citations about as often as their colleagues in rural Aroostook County hand out jaywalking tickets.

Making people care about the environment isn't easy, and curing the laziness and selfishness of those who willfully don't concern themselves with it is even harder. However, there are ways that haven't been tried yet.

Suggestion number one: how about making part of the community service requirement for those convicted of OUI picking up trash along the sides of state highways?

Another thought: since the current five-cent deposit required for buying a bottled or canned beverage in Maine apparently isn't enough to move people to return empty containers, how about raising it? Wine bottles, which I rarely see on the roadside, require a 15-cent deposit. How about a deposit of 25 cents on all plastic bottled water containers, 40 cents on all individual canned or bottled soft drinks, and 50 cents on cans or bottles containing "energy drinks" or any liquid refreshment containing alcohol?

Those who make their living peddling such beverages would undoubtedly object to these adjustments and decry what they'd surely refer to as "new taxes," but such changes would only levy charges on those who opt to purchase canned or bottled libations *and* who subsequently decide, for whatever reason(s), not to return their drink's container.

America was built on **everyone** making sacrifices. It's time for both consumers and purveyors of beer and soft drinks to start doing their part. If the proposals suggested here are enacted I'll be doing mine, since the weekend income I've been obtaining on my nature walks would in all likelihood disappear.

But that's a price I'd be more than willing to pay. ●

Time to Kiss Wednesdays Goodbye

December 1, 2009

America's workweek keeps getting longer and more stressful, but no one seems to be doing much about it.

Complaining about one's employment when many are jobless is unseemly. However, suggesting ways to make our nation's workforce more productive while not simultaneously crippling the economy is admirable.

Everyone loves three-day weekends, but permanently reducing our country's workweek to four days (even four *ten-hour* days) would make too many already-entitled Americans even lazier. Currently United States workers have 104 Saturdays and Sundays off, plus approximately ten additional holidays. Permanently adding Mondays to the weekend would reduce the number of regular work days by 40 annually, which would slow productivity to a crawl. That won't do.

But how about eliminating one work day entirely?

The Gregorian calendar has been the internationally accepted method of marking time since 1582. It was created by some remarkably astute individuals who somehow calculated exactly how long it takes the earth to revolve around the sun, how to synchronize the months with our planet's seasons, and why it was necessary to add an extra day every fourth year so that when the 21st century arrived we weren't having snowball fights in August, or trying to find space at the beach on Valentine's Day.

But as brilliant as Giambattista Benedetti, Giuseppe Moletti, Aloysius Lilius, Christopher Clavius, Pope Gregory XII, and the other 16th-century mathematicians who came up with our present-day calendar were, they clearly weren't able to think outside the confines of their late-1500s box.

Simply put, the time has come for the six-day week.

The adoption of a calendar consisting of 60 weeks and five days wouldn't cause the planet to spin off its axis. A day would still consist of 24 one-hour segments. Three out of every four years would still contain 365 days, with every fourth one getting 366. All twelve months would retain their current complement of days. The only difference would be an increase in the number of weeks, each of which would, under the new system, consist of a sextet rather than a septet of days. April, June, September, and November would contain exactly five six-day weeks.

Seven other months would last five weeks and a day, and funky February would be comprised of a mere four weeks and four days. The end result would be shorter work weeks, but a more productive and less-stressed population. A calendar consisting of six-day weeks would contain 120 Saturdays and Sundays (up from the current 104), but we'd lose less than a dozen work days annually, since there'd be no Monday holidays on the new and improved calendar. Christmas, New Year's Day, and July 4th would be celebrated annually on whatever day of the week they actually fell, but Memorial Day, Martin Luther King Day, Labor Day, and all other national holidays would be observed on Saturdays, which would already be a day of rest for most of the population.

The rejuvenated working class and their delighted employers wouldn't be the only ones who'd benefit from this radically revamped system. Priests, reverends, pastors, rabbis, and imams would all get an additional eight formal days of worship per year to inspire and/or add to their flocks.

So which day should get the ax if our calendar were permanently altered to eliminate the current system of grueling seven-day weeks?

Saturdays and Sunday are obvious keepers. Eliminating Fridays would force the closing of numerous TGI Fridays restaurants, and another wave of unemployment is the last thing the country needs. Many people whine habitually about Monday mornings, but eliminating the current whipping boy of days would merely pass the title of least-liked-day to Tuesday by default.

Returning to work Monday is always tough and always will be. By Tuesday you've accepted that the weekend is over. On Thursday afternoon there's light at the end of the tunnel. Fridays always have been and always will be the gateway to the weekend.

The most logical candidate for downsizing is Wednesday, which is to days what March is to months: endless. Americans head into work Wednesday mornings knowing that by lunch the week should be half over, yet by the time five o'clock arrives it mysteriously seems as though the next day should be Friday. But it never is! At Thursday's conclusion we're spent; the week seems like it should have concluded, but it hasn't. We trudge home, only to find that we're due back at the salt mine the next day. And it's all Wednesday's fault!

Let's stop complaining about the length of the current work week and do something about it. The time has arrived to adopt the 60-week (plus five days) calendar, and to dump Hump Day! ●

An Eminently Adjustable Number

February 4, 2018

I'm trying to remember the name of the guy who wrote *Romeo and Juliet, Macbeth, Julius Caesar*, and a bunch of other famous plays.

Was it Oscar Wilde? Edgar Allan Poe? Molière? Or some obscure English guy?

Well, to paraphrase whoever it was, I come to praise February, not to bury it.

Shame on those who decry the second month of the Gregorian calendar for its trifling imperfections, rather than celebrate it for its many assets.

True, February's nights are too lengthy and its hours of daylight too few. The air temperature is ceaselessly frigid and the driving perennially hazardous. Mere walking is treacherous, thanks to perpetually slick surfaces pedestrians must surmount. Even the most sure-footed are at risk, since the burden of snow and ice removal, which by mid-February is as much a part of daily life as brushing one's teeth, can precipitate frostbite, heart attack, or impalement by snow shovel. And the most grievous of the month's warts: a diabolical "holiday" invented and perpetuated by a nefarious cabal of florists, greeting card producers, and the all-powerful chocolate lobby. Valentine's Day is far more despised by discerning, rational, pragmatic types than it is breathlessly anticipated by the romance-addled, courtship-obsessed segment of the population.

But there is far more justification for celebrating February than there are reasons to condemn it. It is, after all, the shortest of the winter months. And as those who pine for spring, summer, and/or autumn are keenly aware, February's first week marks the midway point of what is, for non-skiers, non-snowboarders, non-snowmobilers, and non-ice fishermen, the least desirable season.

February is the month when countless important inventions, including the steamboat, the self-starting automobile engine, and the removable steel plow blade were originally patented.

Adolf Hitler wasn't born in February. Neither was Osama bin Laden, Benito Mussolini, or any Kardashian sister.

Who **was** born in February, you ask? Abraham Lincoln. Rosa Parks. George Washington. And me.

I've never understood people who complain about getting older. The alternative (being too dead to have a birthday to celebrate) isn't attractive, and besides, who doesn't love an excuse to party? My birthday is always memorable, even when lighting the candles on the cake set off not only *my* smoke alarm, but all the neighbors' alarms as well.

I used to get flustered on my birthday when some insensitive individual had the temerity to ask me my age, but those days are long gone, thanks to a revolutionary new calculation system recommended to me a decade or so ago by a thoughtful friend several years my senior. It seemed a little overly complicated at the time, but as I was taught to always respect my elders (an increasingly dwindling group) I decided to try it. It wasn't until after I had undergone hip replacement surgery several years later that I fully appreciated the depth of his wisdom.

For years when I was asked how old I was I had to mentally subtract the year of my birth from the current one, then blurt out the answer. But then I began, as advised, calculating my age differently: by adding the ages of a pair of matching body parts (i.e. legs, eyes, thumbs, ears, etc.), then dividing their sum by two. For example, a person with a 40-year-old right arm and a 40-year-old left arm has a BPS (Body Part Sum) of 80, which, when divided by two, reveals a chronological age of 40.

But now when someone tactlessly expresses curiosity regarding my chronological age I give a completely logical and nearly truthful response. This year when, inevitably, someone impertinently asks how old I am I'll reply with a smile (and in an upbeat voice), "33!" (Left hip: 61; right hip: 5; sum: 66. Which, divided by two, equals....)

The reactions one gets from those unable to absorb this cutting-edge age computation method vary. Last year when I told an intrusive young co-worker I was turning 32 she responded with wordless incredulity. Because of her rapidly-changing facial expressions and equally numerous shifts in body language, I couldn't tell if she was thinking, "No, seriously" or "You're such a liar!" or "Did you actually *hear* my question, old man?" or "Did he think I asked him his IQ?"

And besides, age is just a number. I'm thrilled to be celebrating another birthday in reasonably good health and in control of all my faculties, including my steel-trap memory, which just recalled the name of the English guy who wrote *Julius Caesar*.

Now if only I could recall some of George Bernard Shaw's *other* famous plays! ●

How I Almost Joined the Punditocracy

August 11, 2009

Not long ago my wife, perhaps envious of my summer vacation from teaching, suggested I get a second job. I told her I already had one: writing essays for this newspaper. She asked me what I was getting paid, and when I informed her she replied that I needed a third job.

I told a friend of my situation. He said I was already working too hard. "Writing weekly opinion columns is tough," he said, telling me what I already knew. "You need to get into television."

Infotaining while disguised as a journalist looked easy; just repeatedly shout what your audience wants to hear, then collect a fat paycheck. I decided to apply for a job as a pundit with an organization actively trying to appeal to people like me. I studied each major news corporation's editorial tendencies, then revamped my resumé and headed for a place I felt certain could use at least one more person from my demographic group.

When I arrived at Fox News headquarters for my interview I was greeted warmly by a slender, well-endowed blonde receptionist. Winking, she smiled, hiked up her mini-skirt, and invited me to have a seat. I began perusing the latest copy of *National Review*, but didn't have to wait long. A couple of minutes later her phone buzzed. Beaming coyly at me she cooed, "Mr. Farr will see you now."

A tall, well-dressed man who looked as though he had just emerged from a tanning booth welcomed me and introduced me to his equally nattily attired assistant, a slightly shorter fellow he addressed as Mr. Wright. I felt instantly at ease, since both were middle-aged male Caucasians just like me. "I've reviewed your credentials and they are MOST impressive," Farr said. "What we'd like to do now is conduct a social attitude assessment. We find this the most effective way of measuring a potential commentator's appeal to our viewers. We're going to play a game of word association."

"Bring it on!" I said enthusiastically. I could tell I had made a strong first impression. Farr began speaking as Wright picked up a clipboard and prepared to record my answers.

"Republican," said Farr.
"Good," I replied.

Then he said "Democrat."
"Bad" I scoffed, shaking my head disapprovingly.

"Conservative," intoned Farr.
  Warming to the task, I said "Wise."

"Liberal?"
"Misguided!"

"Conservative think tanks?"
"Problem solvers!"

"Left-wing intellectuals?"
"Eggheads."

"Right?"
"Right."

"Left?"
"Wrong."

Farr and Wright looked at one another, nodding in approval. "You've scored very well so far," said Farr. "Let's see how you do on specific issues. Marijuana legalization?"
"Bad!"

"Gun control?"
"Worse!"

"Abortion?"
"Murder."

"Death penalty?"
"Damn straight!"

"Healthcare reform?"
"Socialism."

"Tax breaks for the wealthy?"
"Birthright."

"Islamic theocracies?"
"Frightening."

"Christian theocracy?"
"Righteous. Worth considering."

"God?"
"Crusaders."

"Allah?"
"Terrorists."

"Tax and spend?"
"Democrats."

"Borrow and spend?"
"Pragmatic."

"Military spending?"
"Essential."

"Education spending?"
"Okay, but only for private school vouchers."

"Same-sex marriage?"
"Sin."

"Global Warming?"
"Myth."

"Environmentalists?"
"Drill, baby, drill!"

"Proof that presidential candidates were born in this country?"
"Imperative!"

"Proof that vice-presidential candidates have a triple-digit IQ?"
"Unimportant."

Smiling, Farr looked at Wright and nodded. "Wow!" said the shorter man. "You've got a perfect score so far. Now let's see how you react to important individuals in the news."

"Barack Obama?" said Wright.
"Inexperienced. Weak." I responded earnestly.

"Clinton?"
"Which one?"

"Hillary."
"Ruthless zealot. Power-crazed. Ethically challenged."

"Bill?"
"Monica." Farr and Wright grinned at one another. Things were going *very* well.

"Sarah Palin?"
"Joan of Arc."

"George W. Bush."
"Who?"

"Al Gore?"
"Kook. Sore loser."

"Dick Cheney?"
"Patriot. Bad shot."

The two men exchanged frowns. I vowed to myself not to make any more little jokes.

"Let's see what you know about some current opinion makers," Farr said pointedly.

"Sean Hannity?"
"Courageous."

"Keith Olbermann?"
"Outrageous."

"Rush Limbaugh?"
"Works hard."

"Al Franken?"
"Blowhard."

"Glenn Beck?"
"Idealist."

"Bill Maher?"
"Cynic."

"George Will?"
"Articulate."

"Paul Krugman?"
"Elitist."

"Ann Coulter?"
"Hot!"

"Oprah?"
"Not!"

"Media?"
"Liberal."

"Fox News?"
"Fair and balanced!"

"MSNBC?"
"Lunatic fringe."

Farr and Wright looked at one another, impressed. Brimming with confidence, I thought I was all but assured of becoming Bill O'Reilly's sidekick. "Just one more question," said Farr. "What's the most important quality a Supreme Court justice should possess?" Without hesitation I replied "Empathy."

There was an awkward silence.

Finally Farr broke it. "Nice try, Lefty. Now get…"

"…out!" finished Wright.

Dejected, I headed for the door. "How did they know?" I asked the miffed-looking receptionist as I stepped into the street.

Coldly she replied, "Next time try taking off that 'Yes, we can' button before your interview." Then she slammed the door behind me. ●

Learning about the Few and the Proud

May 2, 2017

Because I wanted to learn more about helping young people more effectively determine their future direction, I was one of sixty New England high school and college teachers, coaches, administrators, and counselors who traveled to Parris Island, SC, last month for a Marine Corps Educators workshop.

My father was a World War II veteran whose wartime experience left him wary and distrustful of many things military, so naturally I came in with some preconceived notions, both pro and con, about the Marines. The positive assumptions I had turned out to be 100% accurate, and while not all the misgivings I had harbored were allayed, the honesty and respect with which my concerns were addressed helped me see things from a different perspective.

Marine recruits expect to be challenged on Parris Island, and the same is true for those opting to participate in the educator workshop. There was much to be absorbed in three days. One important factor hiding in plain sight: there is no such thing as a "typical Marine" any more than there are "typical teenagers," "typical nurses," "typical welders," or, well, "typical educators."

Marine recruits aspiring to serve America hail from rural, urban, and suburban areas, and from various socioeconomic backgrounds. A few come from foreign countries, and can expedite the process of obtaining United States citizenship by signing up. Some enlist hoping to escape poverty and/or find direction through military service, but others with more material advantages eagerly volunteer as well. Recruits can enter the Corps after graduating from high school, spending time in the work force, or obtaining a college degree. Some will make the military a career; others do their time, earn an honorable discharge, and go on to further their education and/or obtain public or private sector employment. One high-ranking officer referred to the Corps as "The Ultimate Meritocracy," implying there are no limits to what motivated individuals can achieve once they become Marines.

No organization tops the Marine Corps when it comes to logistics and attention to detail. The three-day, information-filled workshop was fraught with physical and mental challenges for all those willing to participate. Virtually every Marine and civilian employee we encountered on Parris Island was articulate, personable, engaging, and eager to provide assistance.

According to their stated core values of Honor, Courage, and Commitment, Marines are expected to "exemplify the ultimate in ethical and moral behavior: to never lie, cheat, or steal; to abide by an uncompromising code of integrity; to respect human dignity; and to have respect and concern for each other." Corps members who live resolutely by this credo are to be commended; that many in the general population cannot or will not do so is a shame.

The basic methods the Marines use to attract new recruits are in essence no different from those used by civic organizations or religious groups. Each team's members are motivated by the certain knowledge that their institution and its members are helping make the world a better place. One troubling difference about the Marines, at least for some: the willingness to kill people one doesn't know (and to be trained to do so effectively and efficiently) isn't a requirement to join up with the Rotary Club or the Jehovah's Witnesses.

As so often is the case, educational seminars such as the one I attended can teach participants a great deal about not only the subject(s) at hand, but about themselves as well. Some individuals should have misgivings about becoming a Marine. As impressed as I was with everything and everyone I encountered, it was soberingly clear to me that for a variety of reasons, I was no more fit for the Corps four decades ago than I would be today.

In retrospect I find myself impressed even more than I had expected to be by the men and women who comprise the Corps. Many of the misgivings I harbored before taking part in the Educator Workshop on Parris Island have been allayed. And even if some individual elements of the training Marine Corps recruits go through give me pause, I cannot argue with the ultimate results of that training. The impressive men and women who become Marines personify just how much potential each of us is capable of realizing.

I have no idea how much it cost the United States government to fly sixty New England educators to and from to South Carolina, put them up for three nights, feed them, and pay the personnel required to keep them safe while enlightening them and shepherding them around Parris Island. But whatever the amount, I can confidently assure any skeptical taxpayer it was money (and time) exceptionally well spent. ●

Why Everyone Should Love Loving Day

June 3, 2017

This month marks the 50th anniversary of a significant but often overlooked moment in American history. On June 12th, 1967, the United States Supreme Court unanimously overturned a lower court decision upholding a Virginia state law that made interracial marriage a crime. The plaintiffs in the case were Richard Loving, who was white, and his wife Mildred, an African American / Native American. The couple had gotten married in 1958 in Washington, DC, where such unions were legal. They subsequently returned to their native state of Virginia, where they took up residence at the home of Mildred's parents.

Five weeks after their wedding the couple was in bed at home when, at two o'clock in the morning, the sheriff of Caroline County and two of his deputies burst into their bedroom, leveled flashlights at the couple, and demanded of Richard, "Who is this woman you're sleeping with?"

The sheriff responded to Mildred's reply ("He's my husband") by telling the couple their District of Columbia marriage certificate wasn't recognized by the state of Virginia. They were subsequently arrested, jailed and charged with unlawful cohabitation. At the time one-third of the 48 United States, including Virginia, had laws on the books prohibiting interracial marriage.

Ultimately the Lovings pleaded guilty to violating the state's Racial Integrity Act and were given a year in prison, a sentence that would be suspended if they agreed to leave their home state and not return together for the next 25 years. Presiding judge Leon Bazile stated in his decision: "Almighty God created the races white, black, yellow, Malay, and red, and He placed them on separate continents. And but for the interference with His arrangement there would be no cause for such marriages. The fact that He separated the races shows that He did not intend for the races to mix."

Initially the Lovings moved to Washington, DC, to avoid jail time, but were unhappy living away from their families, and in a setting far different from the rural one in which both had grown up. They would travel separately to visit friends and family in their hometown of Central Point, VA, but were justifiably unhappy with their situation. Finally in 1964 Mildred wrote to United States attorney general Robert Kennedy asking if the just-passed Civil Rights Act would help them. Kennedy responded that it would not, but the justice department referred the couple to the American Civil Liberties Union, which agreed to represent them free of charge.

The case of Loving v. Virginia bounced among several federal and state courts for three years before the Virginia Supreme Court ultimately agreed with the original judge's decision, reaffirming the legality of the state's miscegenation laws. The Lovings and their attorneys then turned to the United States Supreme Court, which agreed to hear their final appeal. On June 12, 1967, the court unanimously decided in their favor, and by doing so effectively struck down the nation's last legally sanctioned segregation statutes requiring separation of races in marriage. The couple neither sought nor claimed to be reformers; Richard and Mildred both simply wanted to be able to legally marry the person they loved.

It would be nice to say the Lovings lived happily ever after, but their story is bittersweet. In 1975 their car was broadsided by a drunk driver who had run a stop sign. Richard was killed in the accident; his wife's injuries included the loss of her right eye. Mildred Loving lived quietly in her hometown until she died at age 68, precisely one month before what would have been the 50th anniversary of her marriage to the man about whom she said, "He was my support, he was my rock."

Mrs. Loving shunned attention, and rarely gave interviews. However, in a statement she issued on the 40th anniversary of the Supreme Court's landmark ruling, she urged the powers that be to legalize same-sex marriage.

Neither Richard nor Mildred Loving ever believed they were remarkable, but that doesn't mean the rest of us can't think so.

There is not yet a commonly recognized commemoration of the decision 50 years ago that effectively ended state-endorsed prohibition of interracial marriage.

But "Loving Day" sure **sounds** like a holiday everyone would look forward to celebrating.

Which is appropriate, because we all should. ●

Want Me to Return Your Call? Here's How!

July 31, 2019

A few years ago I was enjoying some quality family time with my children when the telephone began ringing. The response that followed confused me, mostly because there wasn't one. Not one of my trio of offspring made even the slightest attempt to answer it.

I briefly considered several possibilities. Perhaps they were all hard of hearing, and I hadn't noticed it before. Maybe *I* was hearing things, as a result of all the undiagnosed concussions I suffered in those backyard football games many decades before. Or it could have been that while lying next to my wife Cleopatra I had been bitten by an asp, which brought about a strange dream that was taking place two millennia in the future.

But two of those three scenarios were entirely implausible, and the Egyptian one was pretty unlikely, too, so I said, not unreasonably, "Will one of you answer that?"

Their reactions ranged from puzzlement (from the seven-year-old), to minor irritation (from the ten-year-old), to incredulousness (from the twelve-year-old, whose facial expression suggested that I had just asked him to throw himself onto a live grenade).

I didn't understand their reticence then. But I do now.

According to data from several call protection companies, nearly half of all phone calls in the United States today are made by telemarketers, robots, scammers, or some diabolical combination of the three. ***Now*** I get why today's kids think cell phones are for taking photos, texting, playing video games, creating needless drama via social media, or any number of other activities not involving actually conversing with other human beings.

So what can one do about all this verbal electronic spam? Exercising restraint and kindness is a good start. Cursing out the person on the other end of the line is pointless; after all, why kill the messenger? Besides, there's an excellent chance the person making the call isn't enjoying his or her current job to begin with. How many human beings grow up aspiring to make a career of phone solicitation? The thought of spending even a small portion of one's adult life making cold calls from within a windowless building—chained to a desk inside a cubicle surrounded by hundreds of other similarly desperate drones—doesn't sound like an existence that's fraught with romance, glamor, intrigue, or significant financial reward.

Maybe my kids were onto something back when they were feigning deafness.

Fortunately, thanks to caller ID there's no reason to let a daily onslaught of junk calls upset one's customary routine. Every incoming call I get is duly noted on my cell phone's call log, and once in a great while someone *actually leaves a message* on my answering machine, invariably ending it with, "Have a nice day!" When that happens I dutifully listen to and evaluate the information that's been communicated, then thoughtfully and without prejudice decide whether or not to contact the party who left it.

On the off-chance this essay is being read by an entity who's been trying without success to get me to return his, her, or its calls, here's a helpful list of "Dos and Don'ts" for those wishing to reach me by phone. Just because I like to be different, I'll start with the "Don'ts."

1. **Don't** call and then not leave a message. The chance of my returning a message-less, unsolicited call is ZERO.
2. **Don't** tell me you've got the life insurance quotes I've asked for, since I didn't request any.
3. **Don't** offer me home improvements, particularly if caller ID indicates you're located in Arizona, California, British Columbia, Paris (France *or* Kentucky), or, for that matter, anywhere that's more than 20 miles from where I reside.
4. **Don't** read off a script. Sounding like a robot is a real turn-off, even if you're *not* a robot.
5. **Don't** tell me you want to relieve my tax burden; I don't have one.
6. **Don't** darkly suggest this is my last chance to remedy my crushing credit card debt; I don't have that, either.
7. **Don't** call me if you're from North Dakota, Hawaii, Mississippi, Wisconsin, Saskatchewan, or West Virginia. I don't know anyone who lives in those places.
8. **Don't** tell me my niece has been abducted while traveling overseas, and you need my credit card information and bank account numbers to rescue her. My niece always tells me when she's going abroad, and she assiduously avoids kidnappers.
9. **Don't** call me before 8 AM, or after 8 PM.
10. **Don't** forget to consult the list of "Dos," which I've helpfully provided below.

Oops. Sorry. There are no "Dos."

But have a nice day! ●

SECTION 10

Unvarnished Opinion

Applying a Mother's Wisdom

January 15, 2017

Even though my mother passed away nearly a decade ago, I still carry significant bits of her aura with me every day. Whatever admirable traits I possess are in large part due to her incredible patience and quiet, consistent role-modeling.

One lesson she taught my siblings and me: always say "Thank you" in a timely and genuine manner. That's why, with the inauguration of America's 45th president just days away, it seems far more appropriate to express sincere gratitude to the nation's outgoing chief executive than it does to comment on his successor.

Barack Obama's accomplishments in eight years at the nation's helm would be noteworthy even if he *hadn't* been America's first African-American president, or been obstructed nearly every step of the way by an opposition party that not only made it plain from the day of his inauguration they wanted him to fail, but did everything in its power to bring about that failure, even if it was bad for the nation they piously profess to love above all else.

President Obama's leadership rescued the country from the financial crisis of 2008 he inherited when he was elected. He ended an expensive, ill-planned, and ultimately pointless war in Iraq, another problem left to him by his predecessor. He brought about re-regulation of Wall Street, making it somewhat more difficult for predatory, greed-driven individuals and the financial institutions they control to tilt an already-rigged playing field even more precipitously in their favor. He turned around a U.S. auto industry that had been on life support when he took office. He made it possible for tens of millions of previously uninsured Americans to obtain affordable health care. He presided over the elimination of the individual who masterminded the terrorist attacks of September 11, 2001. He made it possible for gays and lesbians to serve openly in the military. He ended America's use of the "enhanced interrogation methods" considered inhumane under the Geneva Conventions. He improved America's image abroad. He boosted fuel efficiency standards, increased support for veterans, and helped pass credit card reform. He improved food safety, expanded stem cell research, and provided additional protections against hate crimes. Under his leadership four million more children got health care, a portion of which was paid for by increased taxes on poisonous tobacco products. President Obama increased investment in renewable technologies, expanded wilderness and watershed protection, and helped overthrow a corrupt and brutal Libyan dictator.

But perhaps most significant was his conduct. During eight years of living under a microscope, the nation's outgoing leader and his wife exhibited the kind of personal behavior a simpler, less polarized, less media-driven America actually expected of its first families not all that long ago. No other chief executive in the past six decades exemplified dignity and common decency like Barack Obama. His immediate predecessor was swaggering, inarticulate and ineffective, and the chief executive previous to *him* was a self-indulgent hedonist who lied to the nation about an extramarital affair with a youthful subordinate. President Reagan was publicly charming, but his family was, to be kind, dysfunctional. Richard Nixon was a liar and a criminal; Lyndon Johnson's crassness was legendary. Gerald Ford, Jimmy Carter, and George H. W. Bush were all decent men, but how effective were they as the nation's leader? Each tried to win a second term. None succeeded.

Professional discord creators openly, covertly and ceaselessly questioned Barack Obama's citizenship, his religious affiliation, and the legitimacy of his election. Interestingly, most of the high-decibel haters that unrelentingly attacked his integrity possess not a shred of it themselves. Even more ironically, these individuals seem perfectly willing to overlook countless glaring character flaws in the President's soon-to-be-successor.

And in return, what did Mr. Obama give his nation—including the dishonest, vindictive disparagers bent on destroying him personally and politically with ruthlessly scurrilous invective? Thoughtfulness. Dignity. Authenticity. Decency. Humility. Respect. Fairness. Humanity. Tolerance. Honor. Grace. Charisma. Compassion. Eloquence. Calmness. Honesty. Gratitude. Strength. Kindness. Dedication. Loyalty.

America owes a massive debt to Barack Obama. He consistently exhibited courage, integrity, intelligence and patience, traits few if any of his shrill, hypocritical attackers seem to value.

Today's USA is without doubt better because of President Obama. It would be better still if each of us conducted ourselves the way he has for the past eight years.

One other thing my mother tried to instill in her children: if you can't say anything nice about someone, don't say anything at all.

Uh-oh.

Suggesting Mr. Obama's thin-skinned, narcissistic successor is a snake oil salesman devoid of morals, ethics, impulse control, or a sense of shame would violate that particular tenet, wouldn't it?

But Mom was also a stickler for telling the truth, which is why I am one-hundred-percent certain she would not only have pardoned me for any and all of the aspersions listed in the previous paragraph, she'd have wholeheartedly agreed with them. ●

Justice or Vengeance?

May 16, 2011

Dictionary.com defines "justice" as "the quality of being just; righteousness, equitableness, or moral rightness," or "the moral principle determining just conduct." The same source explains "vengeance" as "infliction of injury, harm, or humiliation on a person by another who has been harmed by that person; violent revenge."

The two words have distinctly different meanings, yet recent events give the impression many Americans think the terms are synonymous. President Barack Obama's speech after Osama Bin Laden's carefully-planned demise proclaiming that "Justice had been done" for the victims of the attacks arranged by Bin Laden on September 11, 2001, merely furthered this apparent confusion.

The spontaneous revelry and chest-thumping which many American practitioners of Christianity, Judaism, and/or Islam took part in after United States Navy SEALS dispatched the world's most notorious terrorist earlier this month was at best troubling and at worst chilling.

Few would argue that the world was diminished by the termination of the world's most unrepentant hate-monger. But seeing sizable numbers of Americans fervently waving the Stars and Stripes while chanting "U-S-A! U-S-A!" in the impromptu celebrations which erupted after word broke Bin Laden had been slain can't have played well in certain countries, or more significantly with neutral nations which, while not being reliable American allies, are at least not dedicated to the violent overthrow of Western Civilization. Some argue anti-U.S. sentiment in many nations (particularly Islamic ones) is already a given. But open-minded people around the world were no less appalled by footage of flag-waving, chanting Americans celebrating Bin Laden's death than most U.S. residents would be if they viewed spontaneous demonstrations following the slaying(s) of American military personnel in a far-off nation where the signs in the background were printed in Arabic, and many of the swarthy chanters bearing them were sporting hijabs or turbans.

Make no mistake: the media in other nations is every bit as biased and manipulative as America's is, and often government-controlled. Producing video evidence confirming America is peopled by wild-eyed fanatics bent on world domination is child's play for propagandists in charge of producing television "news" in certain countries, particularly when the audience is already predisposed to see the United States in an unflattering light.

Unrestrained and unexamined national enthusiasm—particularly when connected with patriotism, religion, or politics—is rarely productive; it blinds people of all faiths, nationalities, and ethnicities equally.

Public displays of joy over barbarism weren't the only sad byproduct of Bin Laden's death. Spokespeople for both of America's major political parties stepped up their political rhetoric in the hours and days after the death of Al Qaeda's spiritual leader, each trying to engage surreptitiously in political opportunism while simultaneously accusing the other of openly doing so. Republican revisionist historians took a shot at crediting the rub-out to the policies of the previous administration, while Democrats tried to score political points as well, though no more so than the GOP attempted to do following the capture of Saddam Hussein in December 2003. But while critics on the right dismissed the current commander-in-chief's trip to the former site of the World Trade Center in lower Manhattan just days after Bin Laden's death as a mere photo op, the president's team took a deliberately understated approach, one in sharp contrast to his predecessor's. The decision to not have Obama speak during his brief appearance at Ground Zero was a sign his handlers learned from the mistakes of George W. Bush's advisors, who on May 1, 2003, decided it would be a good idea to send their preening, flight-jacketed boss strutting onto the aircraft carrier *USS Abraham Lincoln* with a "Mission Accomplished" banner as the backdrop to announce major combat operations in Iraq were over. History shows the statements the 43rd president made that day were nearly as spectacularly inaccurate as their presentation was transparently choreographed.

Some giddy over the government-sponsored execution of Bin Laden quickly dismissed the assertions of Middle Eastern leaders condemning the mission as an "assassination." But, per Dictionary.com, to "assassinate" is to secretively and/or suddenly kill a prominent individual premeditatedly or treacherously. And regardless of whether the depraved exterminator of thousands of innocents had it coming, that was precisely what United States Navy SEALS did to Bin Laden. Rationalizing his killing "because he deserved it" is no less a perversion of decent and moral behavior than Al Qaeda adherents claiming that all of their leader's actions were justifiable because he was a holy warrior battling the Great Satan.

Finding definitions for words like "justice," "vengeance," and "assassinate" in the dictionary is easy.

But after publicly celebrating our national blood lust and in doing so tacitly conceding two wrongs apparently do make a right, honestly defining how and why America is entitled to continue claiming the moral high ground is significantly more difficult. ●

Two Memorable American Impact Makers

June 2, 2009

For a country that's not even a quarter of a millennium old, the United States of America has produced a wide variety of real and made-up impact makers. For better or for worse George Washington, Benedict Arnold, Huckleberry Finn, Simon Legree, Rosa Parks, Scarlett O'Hara, Helen Keller and Darth Vader have all left lasting impressions on our nation.

Another example: a remarkable man whose courage and unquestioned integrity earned him nearly universal admiration. During and after America's Great Depression of the early 20th century, this single father of two young children (his wife had died young, leaving him a widower) did legal work for poor people in his hometown, a rural Alabama village where many of his impoverished clients paid for his services with acorns or firewood rather than actual cash, something none of them possessed. One particular case he took on pro bono made him a temporary pariah in much of his community, and although he didn't realize it at the time, doing so put himself and his family at great risk. He accepted a judge's request to defend a black man falsely accused of rape by a frightened young woman and her bigoted monster of a father, knowing in advance that prevailing attitudes gave him no chance of winning the case. However, his valiant actions before, during, and after the trial earned him virtually universal respect for the remainder of his days. Of all the remarkable words he ever spoke, this country lawyer's best advice, which he gave to his two children, was "You never really understand a person until you consider things from his point of view…until you climb into his skin and walk around in it."

Of more recent vintage is an individual who served as White House Chief of Staff at the tender age of 34, barely a decade after a nine-month period during which he had been arrested twice for drunk driving, and then for good measure flunked out of Yale University. Even more remarkably he later became the nation's secretary of defense despite having obtained five separate deferrals to avoid military service during the Vietnam Era. Then after five terms as his home state's lone congressman, he served as CEO of a major corporation that serviced oil fields before he become our nation's vice-president. During the eight years he was a heartbeat from nominal leadership of the free world, he rarely appeared in public, but when he did it was before carefully selected audiences of blindly loyal adherents. Mostly he chose to remain out of sight while he was in power, although at one point he did have to emerge (albeit more than 24 hours after the fact) to provide a puzzling, vague explanation of an unfortunate incident that involved his shooting a friend in the face while they were out hunting together.

These days the former policy maker is far more outgoing, enthusiastically doing the talk show circuit to deride all who disagree with him while simultaneously mocking the current president's national security policies to anyone with a TV camera or a microphone. Some see this as hypocritical, given the time he spent as vice-president loftily and indignantly labeling critics of *his* administration's national security policies as traitors and/or enablers of terrorism. He was also one of those responsible for a bellicose United States foreign policy that, while it failed utterly both diplomatically and strategically, served to enrich a select few corporations (including the one he once headed) thanks to numerous lucrative war-related contracts they were awarded, often without competitive bidding, by the designers of America's disastrous misadventures in oil-rich Iraq.

Neither the Alabama lawyer nor the former vice-president was afraid to take strong stands on controversial issues, so unsurprisingly both were lionized by their admirers and vilified by their detractors. Perhaps the biggest difference between the two men was their respective temperaments. While the attorney from Alabama is best known for a noteworthy quote which involved not judging a person until one had walked in his or her shoes, the contemporary difference-maker's most famous utterance came on the floor of the United States senate, when he memorably and angrily invited a senator from Vermont to perform an unnatural (not to mention physically impossible) act on himself.

It's a pity that Atticus Finch, the courageous protagonist of Harper Lee's classic novel *To Kill a Mockingbird* was just a fictional character, but a far greater shame that an arrogant, craven hypocrite like Dick Cheney is a real one. ●

Best of the Also-rans

March 5, 2017

That each of America's last ten unsuccessful major party presidential nominees is still alive is a tribute to modern medicine. Three of them are in their 90s; two of that trio, Jimmy Carter and George H.W. Bush, were defeated while trying to win a second term. But what sort of president might Hillary Clinton, Mitt Romney, John McCain, John Kerry, Al Gore, Bob Dole, Michael Dukakis, and/or Walter Mondale have made? Certainly all of them possessed sufficient qualifications for the White House, or at least as many as the candidate who defeated them did.

Clinton, who has devoted her entire adult life to public service, served a term as a U.S. senator from New York and later was Secretary of State, and that was after eight years as First Lady. Romney, who ran unsuccessfully for the presidency in 2012, was by capitalist standards an unqualified success, and also served a memorable term as the Republican governor of an overwhelmingly Democratic state.

McCain, defeated by Barack Obama for the presidency in 2008, had a distinguished military career prior to returning home from Vietnam and representing Arizona in the United States Senate for thirty years (and counting). Kerry, who lost the presidential election of 2004, has served the public in a variety of positions, including as U.S. Senator from Massachusetts and Secretary of State.

Gore, who won the popular vote but controversially lost the Electoral College in 2000, served his home state (Tennessee) in both Congress and the Senate prior to serving eight years as vice-president. Dole, who failed to prevent Bill Clinton's re-election in 1996, spent a combined 35 years in the United States Senate and the House of Representatives representing his home state of Kansas after being wounded during World War II. Dukakis, who lost the election of 1988, was a three-term governor of Massachusetts; Mondale, swamped in Ronald Reagan's 1984 re-election landslide, was only 32 when he was appointed Minnesota's attorney general; he later represented his home state in the senate for two terms.

Save for Romney and Mrs. Clinton, all of the above-mentioned presidential nominees served with honor in the military; in fact, McCain, Dole, and Kerry were decorated for their bravery. It's plausible any or all of these public servants would have served with honor and distinction as president. But what of another aspirant, one who sought the presidency unsuccessfully three times?

The Connecticut-born son of immigrants from Lebanon, Ralph Nader turned down a Princeton scholarship because his father felt such grants should go to students who couldn't afford college tuition, and the Naders could. Virtually unknown when he first attracted national attention in 1965 by writing "Unsafe at any Speed," Nader's indictment of the American auto industry prompted General Motors to attempt unsuccessfully to discredit him by, among other things, tapping his phone and hiring prostitutes to try and lure him into compromising situations.

Funded by the money he won for suing GM for invasion of privacy, and aided by seven volunteer law students dubbed "Nader's Raiders," his courageous, brutally honest characterization of the Federal Trade Commission as ineffective and passive led to reforms that converted the agency into a proactive advocate for consumers. Later an environmental activist and vocal opponent of nuclear power, his (and his associates') efforts convinced lawmakers to enact, among other important legislation, the Freedom of Information Act, the Clean Water Act, and the Consumer Product Safety Act.

Ralph Nader turned 83 years old last month. Still an active public-interest advocate, he lives exceptionally modestly. He never married, opting to forego family in favor of a career fighting tough battles to make life better for his fellow human beings. His three presidential campaigns, considered quixotic by critics, were based on principle. He didn't chat up potential donors, win tax breaks for big corporations, or kowtow to special interests. Paradoxically many of the people he fought for didn't fully appreciate (or even notice) his efforts on their behalf. Even worse, most didn't (and in many cases still don't) realize how badly they've needed the sort of advocacy and protection he's provided them with for decades.

The question of which still-living unsuccessful candidate might have made the best president is open for debate. The question of who has done the most for America is not. In his remarkable life Ralph Nader has improved the lot of his nation's everyday citizens more than all the other distinguished also-rans combined. ●

Fired Up about Our Fearless Leader

March 3, 2018

In June 2015 a seemingly washed-up celebrity, desperately looking to pump life into his fading brand, announced he was running for president. I yawned. Clearly addicted to fame, the orange-haired, bloated reality TV star came across as just another abrasive, narcissistic con man.

But others saw things differently. Clearly I was missing something, so I swore off liberal media and decided to get the truth from reliable sources of information like Fox News, the *National Enquirer,* and Alex Jones's Infowars. Just getting facts and ignoring all the fake news really helped clear things up for me.

I learned that for eight years an African-born Muslim who came here illegally was occupying the White House. A pro-abortion, Christian-hating zealot nearly as enthusiastic about the Gay Agenda as he was determined to repeal the 2nd Amendment, he personally invited thousands of swarthy deplorables from other countries to pour across our borders so they could rape, kill, and deal drugs to real Americans. He also promised them free health care and education, and that they'd never have to pay taxes.

Clearly change was needed, but I was still troubled by the self-absorbed non-traditional candidate's seemingly arrogant refusal to share his tax returns, his disparaging of war heroes, and his recorded boasting about forcing himself on whatever women he happened to fancy. But the other choice on the ballot, hand-picked by the treacherous Kenyan jihadist who fraudulently occupied the White House for eight disastrous years, routinely had her political opponents killed, snuck terrorists into Benghazi to murder our ambassador, looked the other way while her husband fathered dozens of children out of wedlock, and gave our nuclear codes to Russia via her non-secure personal email. Armed with that information, there was only one intelligent way to vote.

Sure, there've been a few bumps in the road, but who better to navigate a challenging learning curve than a really stable genius with a brain so tremendous he doesn't even need to read to know everything? Spending money our government doesn't have to build a pointless wall or arranging for an ego-massaging military parade may seem unorthodox, but so did the idea of clean coal, and look at the jobs **that's** creating. Plus he said he'd "drain the swamp," and there hasn't been **any** corruption since he's taken office. Well, hardly any. But people should stop complaining about nepotism. I mean, would they rather he hire incompetent and dishonest staff members from **other** people's families?

And it's not his fault that porn star seduced him. Have you seen how she dresses?

Now the Dear Leader is offering teachers like me another terrific opportunity, one I intend to take full advantage of. I'm heading for the rifle range so I can become firearm-adept enough to get a little extra pay each week for packing heat in school. There's no question I'll qualify as highly skilled; during the archery unit in gym class 45 years ago I hit that target a whole bunch of times, and just ask my kids how deadly I am with a water pistol. Plus, I once got a bull's eye in a dart game at a local saloon, and that was **after** I had a few beers. Potential shooters aren't coming anywhere near my school once I start carrying a piece. And no smart-mouthed kid is going to interrupt class while I recite Shakespearean sonnets anytime soon, either. In fact, I think a lot of my colleagues, even the uppity ones with master's degrees, are going to start listening a *little* more closely to what I have to say at faculty meetings.

Yeah, yeah, I know what some people are saying. "Mr. Young loses stuff all the time; what's gonna happen when he forgets where he left his gun?" Okay, I admit I can be absent-minded. But over the years I haven't misplaced my keys more than four or five times a month, and on each of those occasions someone's found and returned them, except for twice. And as far as my gun is concerned, I'd only take it off when I'm eating lunch, going to the bathroom, using the copier, or checking out Sean Hannity's website during my planning block. Plus, I've been on my school's faculty for nearly two decades now, and I personally know nearly every custodian in the building, not to mention more than half my fellow teachers, *and* several students. And I bet many of those people would do the right thing and return my loaded AR-15 to me as soon as they found where I had left it.

That's yuge. Believe me. I'm gonna make my school great again.

I was totally wrong about our Covfefe president. He's winning bigly.

You losers who still doubt him?

Sad. ●

Why He Must Fail

May 15, 2018

"If the president succeeds, the nation succeeds" has long been a philosophy fervently embraced by supporters of America's sitting commander-in-chief, particularly when he (or perhaps someday she) encounters rough political waters.

Such conventional wisdom makes both logical and political sense, at least on the surface. Implicit in this philosophy is the implication that anyone hoping the president fails is unpatriotic, un-American, ungodly, or some horrific combination of the three.

Each of America's last three presidents entered the White House after far fewer than 50% of the nation's eligible electorate voted for him. That's led to exponential growth in the hate- and suspicion-creating business, one that's generating obscene profits for internet, cable TV, and talk radio bomb throwers. The alarming influence high decibel, truth-challenged extremists wield over a still-increasing bloc of Americans unable or unwilling to think for themselves creates a need for the president to play defense, and in the past chanting the "If he succeeds, we succeed" mantra has been, for the most part, a reliable diminisher of dissent.

Christian evangelist Franklin Graham is urging Americans to pray for the nation's current commander-in-chief to succeed. But some don't care to take counsel from a nominal pastor who has called Islam "a religion of hatred," and who said of Hinduism, "No elephant with 100 arms can do anything for me." Others find Graham's 2011 comments regarding Barack Obama ("The president's problem is that he was born a Muslim") troubling. Many Americans would, with good reason, choose to disregard the utterer of such pronouncements.

But perhaps those disdainful of Pastor Graham would more readily heed the words of America's most recent ex-president, the very man they assail Graham and others of his ilk for defaming. On the day after the 2016 election Barack Obama met with president-elect Donald Trump and told him, "If you succeed, then the country succeeds." Defeated candidate Hillary Clinton added, "Donald Trump is going to be our president. We owe him an open mind and a chance to lead."

So if high profile spokespersons on both the right and the left believe the success or failure of the country and its chief executive are intertwined, Americans should fervently root for Donald Trump's presidency to be a triumphant one, right?

Well, no.

Having Mr. Trump's vain, inarticulate, and fact-challenged "leadership" bear fruit would in the long term be an unmitigated disaster for America. His success would be a total repudiation of the basic values our nation and the vast majority of its citizens profess to espouse. Worse yet, it would tacitly encourage those who crave elective office for all the wrong reasons to employ the sorts of tactics that are antithetical to what America was built on. Imagine a whole new generation of power-seekers, Democrat *and* Republican, eagerly embracing preening, pandering, and prevarication over courage, character, and commitment.

The current president has surrounded himself with a motley collection of obsequious bootlickers, filling cabinet posts with a blend of under-qualified incompetents (Betsy DeVos, Rick Perry, Ben Carson) and outright kleptocrats (Scott Pruitt, Ryan Zinke, Tom Price). This gives further credence to the idea that blind loyalty to one man, no matter how morally and/or mentally flawed, is far more important in the current White House than knowledge, thoughtfulness, and experience.

The current president's utter disdain for ethics, his factually inaccurate boasting, casual adultery, and unapologetic bullying are all repugnant, but no more so than his breaking our nation's word by backing the United States out of at least two painstakingly-negotiated, multilateral international agreements.

A national consensus that America's nominal leader is a success would confirm that grandstanding, insincerity, and spurious personal attacks on opponents in an effort to appeal to the lowest common denominator are far more politically effective than discussing and debating substantive issues. It would certify shamelessness as a valuable asset, not a character flaw.

Any favorable outcomes the current commander-in-chief takes credit for would further the already too-prevalent notions that the rule of law doesn't apply to the rich and powerful, that keeping one's word is for losers, and, given Trump's likely original motivation for seeking the presidency, that pursuing political power and/or national office is a sure-fire way to gain (or increase one's pre-existing) personal wealth.

Seeing an economy continue to thrive—one that was already on the rebound when he inherited it from his predecessor—is an attractive prospect in the short term, but in the long run any and all perceived successes for this president would be catastrophic. Such a scenario would verify that trust and honor are merely quaint anachronisms, and no longer prerequisites for future leaders or policymakers.

Consigning character, ethics, and truthfulness to the scrapheap of American political history seems a steep price to pay for some temporary tax breaks and the possibility of a briefly nuke-free North Korea. ●

Issuing a Much-needed Apology

July 10, 2018

America owes Canadian Prime Minister Justin Trudeau an apology, and since the person who made it necessary is unlikely to offer one himself, I thought I'd give it a try.

Mr. Trudeau: first of all, thank you for your continuing attempts to engage diplomatically with a vain, arrogant narcissist who publicly chortled over lying to you about a nonexistent trade deficit back in March.

Thank you for standing up to the swaggering, thin-skinned egomaniac who called you "very dishonest and weak" after last month's G-7 meetings. The truth: those two adjectives are as ill-fitting for you as they are apt for him. Please don't take his remarks personally; his routinely disgraceful behavior is emboldened by both his sycophantic cadre of enablers and his peculiar inability to feel shame. Thank you for firmly explaining to him that Canada will reply in kind to the ill-considered, unfair tariffs he has, for bogus reasons, decided to levy on not only your country, but on other allies which, until now, have been reliable trade partners for both our nations.

Hopefully your restrained, measured reaction will help cure the mysterious paralysis that's rendered nearly every sitting or aspiring Republican office holder unable to speak out against their party's Dear Leader. These pious individuals who in the past cast themselves as high-minded moralists have, for whatever reason(s), become too meek to speak out about the myriad transgressions of their party's ethically challenged, adulterous prevaricator-in-chief.

Most importantly though, please accept my sincere thanks to you, your nation, and all of its citizens for being ideal neighbors to Americans in general, and those of us living in border states in particular. I first visited Canada three years before you were born, and since then have been to all ten of the dominion's provinces, enjoying overnight stays in eight of them. (Don't feel bad, Manitoba and Prince Edward Island; I promise I'll be back!)

Sensible Americans know there's no better nation than yours with which to share a 8,891-kilometer border. A few obstinate, misinformed individuals, egged on by a perpetually petulant, proudly ignorant bully, would undoubtedly parrot shrill disagreement with this sentiment. But who would these people prefer to live next door to? Iran? Afghanistan? Syria? Iraq? Or maybe North Korea, a nation whose ruthless dictator our commander-in-chief has been cozying up to lately, in between issuing impulsive, insulting tweets at Democrats, entertainers he dislikes, and leaders of America's most steadfast allies.

On behalf of myself and millions of other rational residents of the United States who, unlike our president, value substance over style, I feel compelled to apologize to you, your fellow G-7 leaders, and, by extension, those who dwell in your nations. Our preening, crass president has never retracted any of his intemperate, logic-free rantings, regardless of how outrageous they are, and it seems unlikely he ever will. But please know that not all Americans are smug, boorish hypocrites. In fact, more than six decades of living here has convinced me the vast majority of us are as kind, generous, thoughtful, and hardworking as your nation's inhabitants are. But unfortunately, in contemporary America unapologetic selfishness and ceaseless, strident deception command far more attention from both mainstream and social media than diplomacy, integrity, and common decency do.

On a related topic, my 17-year-old high school senior-to-be was mightily impressed with his tours of Dalhousie, McGill, and Mount Allison Universities, all of which we visited last summer. He seems determined to attend school in Canada for a variety of reasons, not the least of which is he's embarrassed by the inarticulate, self-centered liar whose repugnant countenance is, unfortunately, seen by many on the international scene as the current face of America.

Your shining example of civility under duress has inspired me to do my own small part to strengthen U.S.-Canadian relations. I'll be coming north of the border later this summer, and while my son is exploring several universities in Ontario I'll be nearby, spending every penny of our family's modest discretionary fund. I'm totally convinced that the maple syrup, Blue Jay shirts, and good karma I'll return with will more than make up for my somewhat thinner wallet.

Finally, I'd like to apologize personally for using you as a sounding board for letting off steam, and for including several ad hominem attacks of the very same sort I've decried our president for unleashing on others. I hope you appreciate the incongruity there, because I know he won't. America's current commander-in-chief doesn't get (or do) irony.

Thanks again for your calm, level-headed stand against the screeching, pathologically dishonest oppressor to your south. If Americans and Canadians follow your dignified and courageous lead, maybe someday we can make North America great again. ●

Troubling Dreams, Both Bizarre *and* Plausible

December 7, 2018

I had hurled two scoreless innings in relief, and the lead was 7-2 when Mets' skipper Gil Hodges pulled me after the eighth inning. He reasoned the Chicago Cubs might figure out a nervous rookie's sidearm delivery and limited variety of off-speed pitches the second time through the lineup. But then he uttered five words I'll never forget: "Kid, you've made the team." My elation lasted for just a second, until it occurred to me that I'd have to call the principal at Kennebunk High School to arrange for substitute teachers during my absence.

That's when I woke up.

The human mind is capable of blending random bits of fantasy with reality so seamlessly that a sleeping person's alternative universe can seem utterly real until, after a few seconds of semi-consciousness, those nocturnal scenario(s) dissipate like morning fog.

On occasion my imagination conjures up dreams less pleasant than sports fantasies. One recurring example involves being late for something important, like work, or a job interview, or classes at the high school I graduated from over 40 years ago. And there's always a bizarre reason for my tardiness, like inappropriate attire, lost car keys, or being suspended high above my destination in a hot-air balloon that won't come down no matter how much ballast I'm carrying. Then I'll suddenly notice it's 1:50 PM, my appointment's at 2:00, there's no way I can get there in time, and panic sets in. Such dreams probably don't qualify as true nightmares, but they can be a troubling way to experience one's first groggy moments of post-sleep morning semi-consciousness.

Here's another bizarre scenario my dream-constructing imagination created recently. It was 2016, and an abrasive narcissist with an insatiable ego and his own reality TV show decided he wanted to be president. The twist: he concluded the surest way to attain the White House was to run as a *Democrat*. Widely ridiculed initially, he painted himself as a lifelong civil rights advocate and abortion rights defender who favored strong government regulation, affordable health care, and opening the nation's borders to all who wanted to come to our once-great country. While he inflamed an astonishingly gullible electorate with a fact-free litany of real and imagined national problems, he quickly reassured the increasingly rabid hordes by claiming only **he** could remedy America's currently horrific shortcomings.

Brushing aside the Old Guard with derisive nicknames like "Crooked Hillary" Clinton and "Bumbling Joe" Biden, he swept through the Democratic primaries despite mounting concerns over his never having held elective office, not to mention criticism over his refusal to share his tax returns, his publicly ridiculing a handicapped reporter, and an "October Surprise" videotape of him bragging about grabbing women by various body parts without their permission. But to the surprise of virtually every print and broadcast pundit, he swept to victory over the Republican ticket, one he had dubbed "Thieving Mitt" Romney and "Low-energy Jeb" Bush.

After the election additional unattractive information about the president-elect came to light, including his bogus eponymous university, shady business dealings with Russian oligarchs, and dalliances with adult film stars. But the incoming commander-in-chief and his army of ambitious, ethically-challenged sycophants haughtily dismissed media critics like "Windy Bill" O'Reilly, "Smarmy Sean" Hannity, and "Jabba the Hutt" Limbaugh as nothing more than shrill purveyors of "fake news." Similarly disrespectful treatment of political opponents like "Wimpy Paul" Ryan, "Un-dead Mitch" McConnell, "Surrendering John" McCain, and "Lyin' Ted" Cruz made his critics on the right apoplectic, but his reliable defenders on the left, most notably Speaker of the House Nancy Pelosi and Senate Majority Leader Chuck Schumer, explained away his frequent missteps as part of an inevitable "learning curve."

The president's daily pre-dawn, incendiary tweets energized his core supporters, the vast majority of whom resided in major cities or wealthy liberal enclaves just outside them, nearly as much as they infuriated a rural America appalled by his demonstrated lack of scruples and general amorality.

Mainstream critics on the right were beyond frustrated: the more the president lied, the more fiercely his increasingly strident base—many of whom were being negatively impacted by his policies—defended him. But Republicans ceaselessly pointing out the obvious hypocrisy of the president's spineless Democratic defenders did little to dampen the ardor of his nominal base; if anything, it further galvanized their enthusiasm for him.

Most of my dreams could never become reality. I know for certain I'll never pitch for the Mets. But I'm not so sure some of America's progressives wouldn't abandon their core principles to support unquestioningly an arrogant, ignorant, lying bully were he (or she) their party's standard-bearer, just as Republicans have been doing for the past two years.

And that's a lot more troubling than the possibility of being late because of a non-descending balloon. ●

SECTION 11
Thankfulness

An Overdue Admission
October 1, 2017

I know how my children feel when I do or say something that makes one, two, or all three of them roll their eyes in exasperation. When I was their age, I thought my father was just as out of touch as they think I am now.

Full disclosure: from the moment I was old enough to care about anything, my obsession was professional sports. I wasn't one-dimensional, though; my wide variety of interests ran the gamut from baseball to football to basketball to hockey.

I often slept in my Little League uniform. I spent every cent of my quarter-per-week allowance on sports-related collectibles, primarily baseball cards. From the time I was old enough to venture out on my own until my late teens, my friends and I spent a significant part of most days throwing or catching some sort of ball.

My dad, a casual sports fan at best, recognized and validated his oldest son's ardent interest, but he nevertheless persistently tried interesting me in other pursuits, like cars, building model airplanes, and reading. He valiantly attempted to involve me in photography, history, carpentry, or great literature, but I disdained them all. The harder he tried to make me appreciate Churchill, Shakespeare, and Dickens, the more I focused on Mays, Mantle, and Aaron.

Then one day he offhandedly uttered words that rattled me to my core. "You know, you could lose interest in sports someday. You might even stop caring about baseball," he said.

His merely suggesting such an outlandish possibility was as baffling as it was infuriating. Implying something so implausible was proof my clueless father just didn't get it. Me losing interest in baseball would have been the equivalent of Einstein disavowing physics, Sinatra discarding singing, or anyone named Rockefeller living as a pauper.

But despite Dad's tepid interest in for-profit athletics, he recognized my ardor for them, and for the most part he didn't overtly discourage me. In fact, he brought me to my first professional baseball game fifty years ago.

In 1967 six reserved-seat tickets to New York's Shea Stadium cost a **total** of $15. Dad and my Uncle Eddie couldn't go for box seats, though. Those were $3.50 *per seat* (imagine a stratospheric $21 for six tickets!), and our adult chaperones needed sufficient money to fill my brother, my two cousins and me with 25-cent hot dogs, 35-cent pizza slices and 50-cent hamburgers.

I treasured every minute of that meaningless late-September tilt between the National League's two worst teams, the Houston Astros and the New York Mets. I even forgave Dad for suggesting we leave after the 8th inning, when the game was still tied. (He was hoping to beat postgame traffic; happily for all concerned, the Mets won in the bottom of the 9th.)

But how things have changed.

Today's obsessed sports fans howl shrilly about stratospheric player salaries, outrageous ticket prices, and obscenely expensive officially licensed team apparel, among other things.

But how they themselves choose to spend their money is what's responsible not just for the aforementioned issues, but also for the even-more-indefensible profits being generated for entitled team owners who are, if possible, even less deserving of drawing eight-digit annual salaries than their highly compensated but temporary employees are. And make no mistake, even the biggest stars have limited shelf lives. Babe Ruth, Johnny Unitas, Wilt Chamberlain, and Bobby Orr, each at one time a premier player in his sport, were all ingloriously dumped once their skills began deteriorating. The same holds true today, as Barry Bonds, Randy Moss, Paul Pierce, and/or Martin Brodeur can verify.

Contemporary major league professional sports are played primarily by wealthy behemoths who have little if anything in common with those who, for whatever reason(s), pay to watch them perform. Games are high decibel, three-hour commercials scripted to maximize profits for the major professional sports cartels and their corporate partners.

And only the willfully ignorant can ignore overwhelming evidence that the disposable combatants (particularly in the NFL) are likely to live shortened, impaired lives because of their participation in these "games." Collegiate versions of football and basketball are, if possible, even less attractive products than the NBA and the NFL. That's because unlike their professional brethren, the people running these glorified gladiator shows do so without the inconvenience of having to pay the performers, an advantage allowing athletic departments and big-name coaches a virtual license to print money. There is virtually nothing attractive about big-time professional sports in 2017.

My father died more than four decades ago, but were he around today I imagine we'd have more than a few lively conversations. And the one we'd have about sports for profit would begin with me admitting to Dad that he was right and I was wrong. ●

A Hull of a Trip

August 7, 2016

The trip to Hull, Massachusetts, sounded perfect. I had been invited down for a visit by a good friend, and on two days when the rest of my family was going to be otherwise occupied. The weather looked good, and the only person needing to prepare for this trip was me. What could go wrong?

But given my history of absent-mindedly leaving important items behind, I took nothing for granted. I began packing the night before my scheduled departure so I'd be less likely to forget something significant. I made sure to put the laundry bag I had neglected to take on my last trip in my red duffel bag. Then I packed a small zippered blue pouch with my toothbrush, toothpaste, shampoo, dental floss, aspirin, razor, and comb. Next I printed, in large, legible block letters, Mapquest's 15-step driving directions to Hull and put them on the driver's seat of my car. I also tossed in my helmet, as we were planning to rent bikes and do some riding while I was there, along with some Prairie Home Companion CDs I'd been meaning to listen to. I also brought the cooler up from the basement, lined it with a towel, and left it next to my bed so I'd remember to fill it with snacks in the morning. In addition I packed a small paper bag with little jars of Maine-made honey as hospitality gifts and placed *it* in the car before going to bed, as it seemed like just the sort of thing I might forget the following morning.

Finally I filled my red duffle bag with three days worth of clean clothes. Yes, it was only a two-day trip, but it's always best to be prepared for the unexpected. I also packed an extra pair of sneakers, a book I was reading, and the little blue bathroom bag. I also took out a baseball hat, into which I put my keys, wallet, glasses and comb. I left it on the kitchen table right where I knew I'd be eating breakfast a few hours later.

The next morning I got up promptly at 6:30. I put snacks, water, and ice in the cooler, ate a hearty breakfast, then took an invigorating twelve-mile bike ride, stopping en route at an ATM to pick up a bit of emergency cash. When I came back I showered, loaded the car, and got ready to go, cautiously optimistic that for once in my life I had not overlooked a single thing prior to going on a trip.

Backing the car out of the driveway, I got 50 yards up the street, and…realized I had forgotten my cell phone! Shaking my head in exasperation I turned around, grabbed the diabolically elusive device off the table where I had left it, took one final look around and, satisfied I finally had everything I needed, took off for real.

Thanks to Garrison Keillor's skillful spinning of yarns and a plethora of snacks a mere arm's length away, the potentially harrowing 149-mile trek was a breeze. I arrived at my destination right on time, and miraculously without having made even one wrong turn!

My hosts asked if I needed any help with my luggage, but I told them not to worry. All I needed to bring upstairs was the red duffel bag. That's when I opened the trunk and saw…nothing.

I had carefully packed everything EXCEPT the red duffle bag, which contained the clean clothes, bathroom kit, book I was reading, extra shoes, and everything else I needed.

At that point all I could do was laugh, or at least try to do so half as hard as my hosts already were.

The next morning I went out, determined to either obtain new apparel OR purchase the chisel I'd need when I got back home to remove the outfit I'd have been wearing for the better part of three days. Ultimately I bought a long-sleeved t-shirt and two pairs of underwear. I also learned finding a pair of socks for a pair of size 14 feet isn't so easy in a small-town department store.

In retrospect this mini-disaster, like many others I've experienced, ultimately affected me not one whit. I saw some great sights, did a ton of biking, ate like a king, and had a quality visit with two very special friends. My ride home was totally stress-free, and sure enough, when I got back the red duffel bag was sitting right on the kitchen floor where I had left it.

The bottom line: I had a fantastic time.

And on top of that, I'm already all packed up for my next two-day road trip! ●

Hooray! Another Storm!

March 19, 2017

Last Tuesday's blizzard left more than a foot of snow on the ground, meaning there was no school that day. Now my fellow public school teachers and I won't start our summer vacations until June 27th or so, a state of affairs nearly as horrifying to us as it undoubtedly is to the young people faced with the prospect of sitting in our classrooms until then.

I never have liked winter. It's *always* been my least favorite time of year. I've never skied, nor have I snowboarded. My at-best modest hockey skills have long since disappeared. I see snowmobiles as producers of nearly as much air pollution as noise pollution. And as for ice fishing…really?

For me cold weather and accumulating frozen precipitation mean backbreaking hours of shoveling, ice-chopping and roof-raking; hazardous driving conditions; and potentially expensive problems brought on by power outages and/or frozen pipes.

Given all that, it seemed a foregone conclusion last week's Nor'easter would have me feeling angry, frustrated, sad, disgusted, and indignant, not to mention doomed to hours more labor in Arctic conditions, and envious of anyone and everyone currently residing somewhere warmer.

But just when I thought I knew myself, my emotions threw me a curveball. While my mood during the hours prior to the storm's start wasn't great, the way I felt during and after the lengthy event was a combination of fortunate and grateful.

At dawn last Tuesday, where I live nothing was falling from the sky, so on the theory I'd likely be shut in later on, I opted to hike a mile or so to the post office to mail a letter. But walking felt good, so I opted to extend my sojourn. Snow had just begun falling when I strolled another mile or so down to the start of one of the town's nature paths. Time stood still as I meandered through the woods, encountering no one and hearing nothing save for my own intermittent footsteps. Even better than experiencing the indescribable natural silence of falling snow in the midst of sylvan loveliness: knowing for certain that, on this 15-degree day at least, no minuscule, disease-carrying bloodsucker would attach itself to me, even if by some off-chance a tick-sized portion of my skin were inadvertently left exposed.

Two hours later I got home and realized I had a huge block of quality time to spend with my sons—the sort of opportunity that, given our respective ages and schedules, happens all too infrequently these days. We chatted, played cards, and had a nice lunch. Later on I called an old friend, and even managed to catch up on a bit of correspondence.

The ongoing storm was still going fast and furious when the three of us finally went out to begin shoveling late in the afternoon. Close to a foot of snow had accumulated by then, and the wind was biting. But thoughtful inward reflections, I've found, come naturally when one is simultaneously engaging in some sort of physical exertion.

Among last Tuesday's shoveling-related epiphanies:

- My two able-bodied sons were available to help me with a daunting job, worked diligently, and did so with far less complaint than I'd have made a generation ago.
- We got to interact with, help, and get help from some great neighbors who were outside cheerfully dealing with the same issues we were.
- Even the harshest Maine winter is less unpleasant than an average summer day in most of America. Thick socks, appropriate headgear, and multiple layers of clothing make staying warm possible (if awkward) on the coldest day of the year here, but there is absolutely no escaping the oppressive heat and humidity that's a daily reality south of the Mason-Dixon Line during the summer months. Which, as I recall from several summers spent in North Carolina and/or Florida, last *at least* as long as an average Maine winter does.
- Some people cannot leave their homes without aid; others spend every waking moment in the seat of a wheelchair. What right does a person with a fully functional body have to complain about shoveling snow?
- Every stormy and/or sub-zero Maine day is just more insurance against venomous snakes, scorpions, fire ants, cockroaches, and similar scourges commonly found in many other American locales ever migrating to our neck of the woods.
- Thanks to the widely-held misconception that Maine is merely a smaller, equally frigid, slightly less remote version of Alaska, our state doesn't need to build a wall to keep undesirables out! (Note: for the purposes of this article an "undesirable" is anyone who thinks Maine is a frigid, slightly less remote mini-Alaska!)

The bottom line: last Tuesday's weather event wasn't a hardship; it was a reason to rejoice.

And I plan on celebrating the next big snowstorm, too.

That is, assuming it commences shortly after sundown this coming Christmas Eve. ●

Appreciating (Not Dreading) a Milestone

February 7, 2017

Someone I'm very close to will be observing his birthday this week, but this ordinarily upbeat individual isn't in the mood to celebrate the start of his seventh decade. His body language all but shouts, "*Sixty* seems so **old**!"

This fellow and I go back a long way. We were born in the same now-demolished hospital, played on the same Little League Baseball team, graduated from the same high school, and attended the same university. He's a hard-working, enthusiastic team player who's great to my kids. And I can count on him to tell me the truth even when he knows I might not enjoy hearing it.

When we grew up *no one* was 60. Everyone's parents, it seemed, were in their 30s or 40s; grandparents were all over 70. My friend swears he never knew anyone in his or her 60s until his own mother reached that age.

My lifelong pal excels at a job he loves. He's still reasonably active; compared to others of our vintage he looks and feels pretty good. He has the love of a great family, plus the respect and affection of scores of friends, neighbors, and professional colleagues. But it's been tough shaking him out of his current malaise.

To hear him tell it he's not as physically fit as he once was. His hearing and once-excellent eyesight have both deteriorated. In crowded rooms he finds himself asking people to repeat themselves once and sometimes twice, but after that he just nods and pretends to understand whatever was said. He needs specs first thing in the morning just to recognize who's saying hello. His back creaks, as do various other joints from time to time.

I pointed out to him that in China one's 60th birthday holds special meaning and is often celebrated with lavish gifts and festivities. His doleful, Eeyore-like response was, "We don't live in China."

Appealing to his sense of humor, I cracked, "You used to remember the early 60s, and now you're in 'em." He showed about half the amusement and appreciation I would have gotten had I addressed the same good-natured remark to the Sphinx.

I've tried at least a dozen creative ways to reassure him that turning 60 isn't traumatic (at the very least it beats the alternative), yet he still hasn't bought into it.

But after an epiphany I had last night I *know* he's going to. What I need to do in order to liberate him from the doldrums is personalize the message I'm trying to convey, which is that this birthday, not to mention any and all future ones, should make him grateful, not rueful.

I'll tell him our boyhood pals David, Andy, Raymond, Kurt, and Russ would all love to have his problems, but like our college friend Stan they all died long ago.

I'll remind him that Anne Frank, Emmett Till, Samantha Smith and King Tut never got out of their teens. I'll point out Nathan Hale, Jimi Hendrix, Pocahontas and Pat Tillman never had a 30th birthday, and that Princess Diana, Lou Gehrig, Karen Carpenter, and Martin Luther King, Jr. never saw 40. I'll further mention Alexander Hamilton, Walter Payton, Jane Austen and John F. Kennedy didn't even last a half-century, and that Abraham Lincoln, Steve Jobs, Will Rogers and William Shakespeare all expired prior to reaching 60.

And if that doesn't convince him that starting a seventh decade of life is far more privilege than burden, I'll appeal to his lifelong love of the history of America's nominal National Pastime, informing him Baseball Hall of Fame members Jackie Robinson, Roberto Clemente, Don Drysdale, Mel Ott, Christy Mathewson, Gary Carter, Nellie Fox, Catfish Hunter, Kirby Puckett and Tony Gwynn never saw 60.

Then, I'll add for good measure, neither did Curt Flood, Roger Maris, Tommie Agee, Turk Farrell, Bobby Bonds, Cal Koonce, Deron Johnson, Joe Foy, Don McMahon, Harvey Kuenn, Carl Morton, Ken Boyer, Zoilo Versalles, Mark Belanger, César Tovar, Elston Howard, Chris Short, Dan Quisenberry, Vada Pinson, Tony Conigliaro, Dick Selma, Ken Brett, Dick Howser, Tug McGraw or scores of other guys whose baseball cards we used to collect not so long ago.

I'm convinced this approach will help my friend find an attitude of gratitude, so much so that I'm going to share it with him first thing tomorrow morning when I see him in the bathroom mirror.

I just hope the old guy can hear me. And that I've got glasses on, so I can be sure I'm talking to the right person. ●

Time to Take Out the Trash

March 18, 2019

The town garbage men are going to be surprised next Tuesday when they make their weekly drive down our street and see a tightly-packed green trash bag at the end of my driveway...for the first time since late December.

I'm off to a promising start in 2019 regarding household waste disposal. It took four officially marked town trash bags to contain all the rubbish my children and I produced last year, which was downright embarrassing. That was a 33% increase over the trio of bags we sent to the local landfill—or to wherever it is Cumberland's household trash goes—in 2017.

I consider myself an environmentalist, even though I haven't participated in a protest march, boycotted the oil companies, or spray-painted anyone's fur coat lately. My ongoing but still evolving contributions to the tenuous health of the only planet currently suitable for human habitation include lessening personal consumption of non-renewable resources and also voting for aspiring public servants who acknowledge not only that climate change is real, but that human behavior plays a significant role in it.

Limiting trash bag use isn't that tough. We don't eat a lot of meat in my house, and when we do it's always boneless. My compost heap is chock full of banana peels, onion skins, apple cores, orange peels, eggshells, potato skins, pepper hulls, and carrot shavings, but nothing that attracts any unwelcome vermin. (I'm not sure if sprinkling the pile's border with cayenne pepper has anything to do with the absence of raccoons, skunks, and similar wildlife, but I'm going to keep applying it anyway, just in case.)

Every month or so I send out a bin of carefully-separated paper, cardboard, plastic, and glass items, all of which I trust the town will reuse or dispose of as responsibly as possible. Between that and composting, there really isn't much left to deep-six. Frozen food bags, cereal box liners, tissues, spent toothpaste tubes, and floor sweepings (which go to the compost once it thaws) are just about it. Every week or so I'll change the kitchen trash, tossing it into the big plastic sack that'll eventually get hauled away. I can get quite a lot of refuse into those bags using my special compacter, which hyper-observant types would recognize as a size 14 sneaker with my foot in it.

Some people (okay; people who know me really well) suggest my trash bag consumption rate is less related to environmental concerns than it is to fiscal ones, and I'll admit: economics does play a role. But at last look those 33-gallon green plastic sacks with the

Town of Cumberland seal emblazoned on them were retailing at $25.00 for a package of ten, and after 2018's bag-squandering fiasco, it didn't take long to figure out that frittering away trash bags at the rate of four per 12 months would require purchasing two ten-packs every five years. To me $50.00 per half-decade seems exorbitant, so as I see it, using those bags efficiently is good for both the environment and my often too-slender wallet. It's a win-win!

Of course, there's more that responsible citizens can do to help boost the earth's health, and I could be considered something of a hypocrite on that score, since my daily round-trip commute to my place of employment is 75 miles. Working closer to home or moving nearer to work isn't feasible; my children and their many friends attend terrific schools where we live, and I teach in a different community, one full of wonderful people who make me feel both valued and appreciated. That said, I do car pool regularly, generally drive at speeds recommended for peak fuel efficiency, and do so in a vehicle that gets over 45 miles per gallon of gas. To lessen my carbon footprint even more I grocery shop with cloth bags, and during the summer do so on a bicycle rather than in a car.

I've good-naturedly chided some young folks who profess to be environmental activists, yet drive to school (and sometimes from absurdly short distances) rather than ride taxpayer-funded school buses that go right through their neighborhoods each morning. One particularly strident young fellow, perhaps fed up with being reminded of the incongruousness of his stated love of the Green New Deal and the daily half-mile drive he makes to and from school, finally told me, "All that stuff you do doesn't make any difference! No one person can make the earth healthy again all by himself!"

Of course, he's right. My efforts probably *aren't* doing the planet a huge amount of good.

But they're definitely not doing it any harm. ●

What a Famous Celebrity and I Know for Sure

August 27, 2018

Given America's cultish fascination with celebrity and the prominence of many contemporary big name "newsmakers" (think Bill Cosby, Harvey Weinstein, Roseanne Barr, and the numerous sycophantic, aspiring tell-all authors in and around the White House, to name just a few), it would be easy to conclude that fame, when handled without proper caution, is every bit as dangerous as more tangible addictive substances like heroin, cocaine, or alcohol.

Those who decide what's "news" and how it's marketed have long realized that uncovering scandal is money in the bank, and nothing sells like lurid, salacious sensationalism involving a famous name or names. Given the inherent risks of maintaining a high profile (not to mention the tremendous odds against achieving genuine renown), it would seem no rational individual would pursue stardom and all its trappings. Yet look how many ambitious people, motivated by some combination of greed and the desperate need to be noticed, try to attain and/or maintain notoriety.

But to paraphrase Mark Twain, that seeming proclivity, like all other generalizations regarding humanity, isn't always true. There are plenty of celebrities whose lives are free of scandal, and who give far more than they take from society.

Exhibit A is Oprah Winfrey.

Best known for her success as, among other things, a talk show host, an actor, a producer, a philanthropist, and a media executive, Ms. Winfrey has also authored or co-authored nine books. One, an aptly-titled, five-inch by seven-inch 228-pager originally published in 2014 called *What I Know For Sure* is filled entirely with essays about things she's certain she knows for a fact.

But what, a cynic might ask, does a multi-gazillionaire who lives in a villa on Maui know about everyday life? Well, as it turns out, plenty.

Ms. Winfrey wasn't born to wealth, privilege, or fame. On the contrary: as a child she bounced between living situations, alternately abused and/or ignored by those around her. Teased by peers for her poverty, she was a runaway at 13, and a year later gave birth to an infant who died shortly thereafter. Oprah doesn't possess "typical celebrity" roots, assuming such things actually exist.

What I Know For Sure eloquently but clearly espouses the value of joy, resilience, connection, gratitude, possibility, awe, clarity, and power in everyday life. Its short, thought-provoking essays are personal in nature, but never preachy or egocentric.

While the primary target audience of *What I Know For Sure* is most likely women, the wisdom Oprah dispenses is relevant for everyone—even veteran, lifelong males (full disclosure: like this writer).

Oprah knows for sure that whatever one puts into life is what she (or he) gets back from it. She's learned there is no strength without challenge, adversity, resistance, and (often) pain.

She knows love is all around, and that if one can survive 11 days in cramped quarters with a friend and come out laughing, that friendship is real. She's certain the results of making time for a little gratitude every day are amazing, and that it truly is better to give than to receive.

Oprah knows for sure that removing fear brings life's answers into focus. Whatever it is one fears has no power—but the fear itself does. She correctly points out that the thing itself cannot touch you, but each time you give in to fear, you lose strength, while your fear gains it.

Oprah knows for sure that if you can get paid for doing what you love, every paycheck is a bonus. She's certain it's an awesome gift to be alive, and that until one has achieved true clarity on an issue, doing nothing is often the best policy.

She knows humans sometimes travel far more difficult paths than necessary, and that once one accepts that she (or he) is a kind, decent, and giving person, there is no longer anything to prove. An individual no longer afflicted with the "disease to please" can say "No" without fearing people saying, "Who does she think she is?" because she has the courage to stand and say, "This *is* who I am."

Oprah also knows for sure life is better once one loses the "desire to acquire." Having the best *things* is no substitute for having the best *life*. (Or, "He who dies with the most toys is still dead.")

Oprah's sure doing one's best is the most fulfilling path to personal freedom. And she knows for a fact living by the Golden Rule (Do unto others as you would have them do unto you) is the right thing for all concerned. She's also realized there is never any "them"; there's only "us."

Oprah's articulate musings are simple, brilliant, and simply brilliant. One thing *I* know for sure…everyone should take the time to read *What I Know For Sure*. ●

'Tis the Season to Get Good Mail

December 16, 2018

Advances in electronic communication, the ability of private sector competitors to ship things quickly and cheaply, and a distinct falloff in America's writing skills have made the United States Postal Service an endangered species. I'm rooting for the post office to enjoy continued success, though, and not just because I own what is likely a lifetime supply of "Forever" stamps.

During my childhood getting the mail was exciting, but especially around my birthday. Early every February Grandma and Grandpa reliably sent a card containing both a nice message and a one-dollar bill, which represented a small fortune to a boy whose allowance was a quarter a week. That annual gift was appreciated *at least* 20% as much as the card containing a *five* dollar note that arrived dependably every year at birthday time from Uncle Jack and Aunt Hazel. In retrospect I'm ashamed to admit Abraham Lincoln was my favorite president not because he freed the slaves, but because his picture was worth five times what George Washington's was.

These days the post office rarely sends much that's exciting. For eleven months a year my mail is generally limited to bills, ads from insurance or credit card companies, and special offers from stores I've never set foot in.

I personally do my best to support the USPS by periodically sending out postcards that not only brighten the day of their recipients, but keep a significant chunk of Americans gainfully employed. In an ideal world everyone would enjoy his or her job, but given some unfortunate incidents in the latter part of the 20th century that gave birth to the expression "going postal," it's incumbent upon everyone to do his or her part to keep America's mail carriers as busy (and gruntled) as possible.

I used to mail out birthday cards to friends when I found a particularly apt one, and when I had an extra five dollars burning a hole in my pocket. But I haven't done so recently. Maybe they aren't making cards like they used to. Or perhaps it's these asbestos pocket liners I started wearing a couple of years back.

But for those who like getting meaningful (non-junk) mail, now really *is* the most wonderful time of the year. Since the start of December, I've been receiving daily holiday greetings from friends near and far, and it's making me feel warm all over. Sort of.

Every evening after work I collect the contents of my mailbox. Reading the return address in the upper left-hand corner of each envelope often has me quivering with anticipation as I return to the house, preparing to savor the contents of each individual card. But as years go by I'm finding there's less to appreciate.

An example: last week I heard from my friends Ben and Emily. Eagerly opening the envelope, I was treated to a generic card with a snowman on it. Inside, stamped in red ink, was "Happy Holidays." Above that, in what was unmistakably Emily's handwriting, was "Dear Andy." She also wrote something deeply personal below the printed text: "Love, Ben and Emily." Okay.

The next envelope I opened came from out of state. The Williams family and I go way back. Their card was a bit more personal, I guess. Printed on thick stock, it featured terrific color photos of their large and impossibly photogenic family, which consists of six wholesome-looking bipeds and several adorable quadrupeds. But while the card contained a brief printed message confirming everyone was still alive (and by the looks of things reasonably happy), it had nary a handwritten word on it. Neither pen ink nor pencil lead had befouled this card. Not that I'm complaining, though. Because of its pristine condition I plan to write an appropriate message on it next year and send it to another friend, preferably one who hasn't seen my family for awhile and is unfamiliar with the Williamses. I'll explain away the fourth kid by claiming one of my own children wanted a friend in the photo.

A unique card arrived last week from the company that delivers my heating oil. It said, "Happy Holidays and WARM WISHES FOR 2019." There was also a bill for $467.24 enclosed, along with an offer to let me off for a mere $451.66 if I paid within ten days. (My Hispanic friends refer to that as "cojones grandes.") My children weren't thrilled when they saw it either, knowing it means Dad's not going to be heating the house to a toasty 62 degrees anymore.

In order to pay that oil bill I won't be mailing any holiday greetings this year. But I shouldn't complain; I'll still spread good cheer in my own special way.

Season's greetings, everyone.

And by the way: this essay is your Christmas card! ●

Trying to Accurately Count Blessings

November 7, 2018

Years ago I attempted to write an 800-word Thanksgiving-themed essay listing *everything* I was grateful for. I failed.

But I *know* I can do it now!

First and foremost, I'm thankful for my family's continued good health.

I'm thankful for friendly, kind, and respectful neighbors.

I'm thankful for the prospect of seeing the first of my three children graduate from high school, a privilege which, due to his premature demise, my own father never received.

I'm thankful Maine has an honest, pragmatic, and independent United States Senator, and that in two years we can vote to replace the other one.

I'm thankful I can read the thoughtful, perceptive, and fearless wisdom of two great *Miami Herald* columnists, Carl Hiaasen and Leonard Pitts, without actually having to live in Florida to do so.

I'm thankful for having had the opportunity to bike over 1600 miles this year, and for sustaining only two flat tires in the process.

I am thankful for every teacher, coach, school administrator, and guidance counselor who has positively impacted the lives of my children. I'm also indebted to the friends my kids have chosen. Or maybe for the people who've chosen my children for friends. Either way, I'm much obliged.

I'm thankful for the tolerance my own teachers showed me, even though I didn't always merit it.

I'm thankful I was born a human being and not a tapeworm, a mosquito, or a cockroach.

I'm thankful I live so close to the Canadian border, and so far from the Saudi border.

I'm thankful to my late parents and grandparents for demonstrating the value of hard work, generosity, and integrity. Oh, and also for teaching me how to play cribbage.

I'm thankful for technology that allows me to listen to the Smothers Brothers, the Spinners, Dolly Parton, Kool & the Gang, Tina Turner, Chris Rock, George Carlin, or radio broadcasts of the 1962 Mets while I do the dishes at night.

I'm thankful for having learned that nothing happens after eight o'clock on a weeknight that I can't wait until four o'clock the following morning to find out about.

I'm thankful for siblings who are always there for me, even though they live five hours (sister) and twelve time zones (brother) away.

I'm so thankful for random smiles (from friends *or* from strangers) that I always instantly return them.

I'm thankful for cousins, nieces, nephews, uncles, and in-laws who make it practically impossible to differentiate between "family" and "friends."

I'm thankful for used book sales.

I'm thankful for Trader Joe's, Market Basket, Hannaford, and occasionally Shaw's.

I'm thankful every time someone thanks me for officiating their child's (or grandchild's) baseball or soccer game.

I'm thankful every time someone says something nice about one of my children.

I'm thankful for the opportunity being a teacher gives me to impact the lives of young people.

I'm thankful for the young people who are impacting *my* life.

I'm thankful to the parents and/or guardians who entrust me with a small portion of their children's education.

I'm thankful for collaborative colleagues who value and celebrate my strengths, while never disparaging or resenting me for assets or skills I don't currently possess.

I'm thankful for egg rolls from the Lucky Inn Wok in Waterford, Connecticut.

I'm thankful for canned stewed tomatoes. Really.

I'm thankful for actual beets. But not the kind that come out of a jar or a can. They don't count.

I'm thankful for generic breakfast cereals that taste just like the name brand ones.

I'm thankful every friend I've got is real, and not one is virtual.

I'm exceptionally thankful for what I *don't* have, including addictions to scourges like alcohol, tobacco, gambling, or social media. I have no bullying bosses, petty co-workers, mean-spirited neighbors, or spiteful family members, and as far as I know no one has ever tried to mail me an explosive device.

I'm thankful for the presence of Melissa, Noah, Lisa, Liisa, Nate, Sallie, Michele, Tom, Tracy, Elliott, Lori, Kathleen, Aili, Caroline, Paige, Margaux, Stephanie, Molly, Jeremie, Terri, Marnie, Brendan, Lindsay, Paige, Diann, Bud, Charlotte, Brooke, Frank, Marlene, Aleta, Fran, Jason, Marsha, Sean, Carol, Russ, Shawn, Jackie, Jacqui, Jaqi, Brian, Darrell, Pete, Glenn, Paul, Alvaro, Meg, Renee, Beth, Joe, Mary, Kim, Jean, Jeanne, Eric, Cindy, Scott, Julie, Bonnie, Josh, Candace, Rob, Shannon, Val, Rick, Elaine, Dorcas, Danny, Kristen, Maggie, Keith, Janice, Rich, Fawna, Faith, Jenna, Jill, Karen, Madlyn, Rita, Jon, John, Sarah, Greg, Kathryn, Lyn, Phil, Nancy, Ron, Shirley, Max, Kevin, Dean, Margot, Kelly, Linda, Chase, Arlene, Fred, Dana, Aaron, Rose, Judy, Jesse, Anita, Terry, Jeff, Tony, Erin, Ben, Eliza, Carl, Jim, Amy, Susan, Sharon, Lynne, Emma, Andrew, Laurie, Will, Pam, Mary Pat, Bruce, Mike, Ed, Dave, Jane, Steve, Don, Mark, Betsy, Laura, Troy, Anne, Andy, Tim, Maria, Pat, Aimee, Cathy, Emily, Noel, Chris, Margaret, Polly, Miles, Ang, and Jenny (among others) in my life.

I'm grateful for…drat!

This is tougher than I thought. When it comes to counting my abundant blessings, eight hundred words *still* aren't enough! ●

SECTION 12

Summing It Up

The Breaks Really *Do* Even Up

June 4, 2019

Last month I attended a trio of funerals, each of which honored an extraordinary person who, if life span were based on kindness or merit, would have been granted significantly more earthly time.

But their departures provided further verification that bad things do indeed come in threes. That well-known theorem has been accepted as fact ever since it was first uttered publicly by Confucius, Nostradamus, Ben Franklin, Will Rogers, Dorothy Parker, the person who patented Murphy's Law, or whichever sage, wag, or scoundrel it was who thought to jot it down for posterity.

But that axiom's converse is equally legitimate; *favorable* occurrences often come in threes as well. People just don't notice or appreciate good fortune as much as they bemoan hardship, which is a shame.

The "bad things come in threes" truism helped me get through a series of misfortunes recently.

Until it didn't.

When some dental work set me back a considerable sum (and when I was subsequently informed that I'd be needing five similar such procedures, each at the same exorbitant price as the one I'd just undergone), I winced, but shrugged it off as merely part of the price of continued existence, noting ruefully that the families of my three recently-departed friends would gladly have chosen paying for functional choppers over arranging a memorial service. I also braced myself for whatever was coming next.

I didn't have to wait long. When the furnace man who came by for routine maintenance reported a little extra work would be required, I sighed, just hoping the damage would come to fewer than four figures on the left side of the decimal point. (It did, but just barely.) The third inconvenience in the series befell me the very same day, when a gentleman I had engaged to fix a couple of long-standing electrical issues with my house did so, albeit at considerable cost (though not nearly as much as the furnace or ongoing dental work). But as I wrote out the check to the electrician I felt an immense weight lift from my shoulders, since I knew for a fact my troubles, at least for the foreseeable future, were over.

Until the cable on the garage door snapped. The timing of that unfortunate and costly event not only directly violated the "Rule of Three," it shook my long-held conviction about the existence of karma. Or, more specifically, that sooner or later good things happen to good people, just as adversity, setbacks, and eventually cataclysm inevitably befall devious, hard-hearted, selfish miscreants whose misdeeds entitle them to every disadvantage, disappointment, and discomfort that befalls them. And while I myself have been guilty of a few *minor* transgressions (full disclosure: I removed more pennies from the loose change tray at the grocery store than I contributed in fiscal 2018), a thorough soul-searching revealed no tangible reason why I had been beset by such undeserved hardship.

I should never have doubted fate.

Two rainy afternoons later, a young man who had taken a course I taught two years ago stopped by my classroom shortly after the school day had ended and presented me with a hand-written note. It was entirely in Spanish, but roughly translated it expressed his appreciation of my efforts on his and his peers' behalf. That and his smile were more than enough to make me forget all about the garage door, and whatever those other trifles I had been worrying about were.

But it gets better. Five minutes later another young fellow, one I didn't know, introduced himself, then explained he had been authorized by the senior class to ask if I would consider being the faculty speaker at this year's commencement ceremonies. Quickly checking the calendar to make sure it wasn't April 1st, I told him I'd be honored to do so, provided I didn't have to pay too much for the privilege.

So now I have to come up with some suitable thoughts for the occasion, which means articulating ideas that are meaningful, memorable and useful to not only our school's 172 prospective graduates, but to several hundred other attendees as well. Oh, and my words mustn't offend anyone, and their delivery can't take more than ten minutes.

As the graduation approaches, I'm looking forward to meeting this daunting challenge *nearly* as much as I'm eagerly anticipating that third bit of utterly random good fortune, which I'm convinced is waiting around some nearby corner for me! ●

Note: the invitation to speak at Kennebunk High School's graduation couldn't have been timelier. In fact, it prevented the necessity of publishing the essay that follows this one!

Holding a Grudge

Late May 2019

Life just isn't fair. How do I know this? Because I just got snubbed. Again.

It seems my alma mater, Joel Barlow High School, has **yet again** chosen someone *other than me* to be the speaker at their graduation ceremony next month.

This is patently unfair. I know this because I just looked up "patently," a word which can mean "evidently," "clearly," "markedly," or "apparently." And the annual miscarriage of justice which is *evidently* victimizing me yet again is *clearly* wrongful, *markedly* unjust, and quite *apparently* shameful.

How the powers that be in the Connecticut backwaters comprising Region Nine, the school district that funnels residents of Easton (my old home town) and Redding (where the high school is physically located) into Joel Barlow High School, haven't recognized my qualifications would make a good subject for the latest incarnation of "Unsolved Mysteries," assuming that TV show is still being aired.

Ordinarily I prefer not to blow my own horn, but my class rank was in the *top half* of the 180 souls who graduated from JBHS in 1975. And it wasn't like I snuck in there at number 90; no, I made it *resoundingly*, at number 88. It took a lot to accomplish that, but I was able to find the necessary time by not taking any honors-level courses, not playing any high school sports, not appearing in any high school plays, not being in the high school band, and not participating in any school-related extracurricular activities whatsoever. You would think someone might have picked up on that record of self-sacrifice by now, but apparently that isn't the case.

And it's not like my record of academic and personal achievement stopped after high school. After successfully evading academic probation for all 12 semesters I spent attending a fully accredited university, I not only obtained a degree, I compiled a grade point average of nearly 2.4—which, for the non-mathematicians reading this, is significantly more than half of a perfect 4.0!

Oh, and my post-high-school successes haven't been limited to just academics. When I worked as a laborer at Aspetuck Valley Orchards, my supervisors were so impressed by my tireless efforts digging irrigation ditches that they raised my $1.85 hourly wage 8.1%! (That they did so the same week the federal minimum wage for agricultural workers went up to two dollars an hour was just an odd coincidence.)

According to reasonably plausible data I sort of estimated (okay; made up), I currently earn more money than *9%* of my living high school classmates, and nearly *all* of the dead ones. And thanks to the prudent saving and investing I learned while taking beginning accounting as a JBHS senior I won't have to work a full-time job after I turn 80. Probably.

If it's character those snobs want in a commencement speaker, well, I've got that *in spades*. I've never been convicted of producing, selling or purchasing illegal drugs *or* pornography. I've never stolen anything from a store, and I've never been arrested for any violent crimes, either. In fact, I've never spent a single night in jail, or in a prison (domestic *or* foreign!).

And it's not like they haven't heard me speak before. In fact, just last November I served as master of ceremonies at the school's Athletic Hall of Fame banquet, and since none of those tomatoes actually hit me *and* I wasn't booed off the stage I'm assuming I was a huge hit.

Maybe the people in charge were put off by the demands I made afterward, when they enthusiastically asked if I'd do it again for them next year. I pointed out I had handled the hosting duties for free, but driving down there involved a lot of time and expense. Uncharacteristically playing hardball, I insisted they double my pay if they wanted me back in 2020.

I still haven't heard back from them.

Sure, my old hometown is 250 miles from here, I haven't resided there in over 30 years, and no one currently living there knows I exist, but still: *how* can they overlook a proven success story for the *44th consecutive year*?

Some of my so-called "pals" tell me to let all this go, but that's easy for them to say. Unlike me and Charlie Brown, they've never had a figurative football pulled away from them again and again and again right before they're about to boot the game-winning field goal.

When Joel Barlow High School's administrators finally come to their senses (and they will), it's gonna cost them. They'll apologize, then ask me to host their banquet and, oh by the way, be the guest speaker at the school's 2020 graduation. But when they grudgingly agree to double my pay from last year, I'll have two words for them: "*Triple* it!" ●

Graduation Speech, June 9, 2019

Thank you, Class of 2019, for granting me the privilege of addressing you here today.

Being an English teacher, this seems like the perfect opportunity to demonstrate the real-life relevance of an important literary device: **irony**.

About a month ago, KHS science teacher Melissa Luetje, my longtime carpooling partner, "innocently" asked me if I knew the identity of this year's graduation speaker. I didn't, but I told her I felt sorry for whoever it was, since *no one* would be able to replicate her moving, genuine and inspiring remarks at last year's ceremony.

Ironically, the very next day *I* was asked to speak at this year's commencement! And, after getting notarized written assurance I wouldn't have to pay to do so, I accepted the invitation. So…

Good going, Class of 2019! You've all earned your high school diploma, and thus proven you're capable of finishing what you've started when you put your mind to it. That's important, because from time to time life will present you with daunting challenges or adversities that will tempt you to give up. That's when you need to remember "I can do this!" Because now you know for a fact that you can!

Always believe in yourself. But don't forget to acknowledge the family members, friends, teachers and school staff, neighbors, employers, and (for a select few of you) law enforcement officers who helped you get here. They believed in you EVEN WHEN you didn't give them any rational reason to do so…*or* when you gave them a reason or two to abandon their faith in you entirely! Thank them, not only with words, but by being and doing your best, at *everything* you undertake, from *this day forward*.

To those of you who've earned lofty grades, done hundreds of hours of community service, represented the school (and by extension its communities) through interscholastic sports or the performing arts, THANK YOU.

And for those of you who did *just enough* to get here, well, congratulations to you as well. I've been where you are. But please understand: what you'll get out of life will be *directly proportional* to the amount of effort you put into it. **Ironically,** I "earned" my high school diploma by maintaining a pulse and getting eight semesters' worth of straight A's in phys ed. But that piece of paper was absolutely worthless—*until* I began challenging myself to do my best *all the time,* and not just when I thought other people might be watching me.

To strivers and slackers alike: you will go far in life if you possess four essential things: effort, determination, kindness, and…dumb luck. But **ironically,** you have absolutely no control over the last of those factors, so it's *vital* you maintain the *highest possible level of focus* on the other three.

So. You want some valuable advice that'll help you succeed in life? Well, you already *know* the basics: don't smoke, don't abuse alcohol, don't electronically transmit potentially embarrassing photos of yourself, and don't count on winning the lottery… duh! And I can't add any academic content to what you've already acquired, since your Kennebunk High School diploma *certifies* you already *know* the quadratic formula, the difference between simile and metaphor, the atomic mass of every element on the periodic table, *and* the year the War of 1812 started.

I'll start with a recommendation from my friend and role model, former KHS guidance counselor Mike Laverriere. He'd tell you to find something you love doing *so much* you'd do it for nothing, and THEN figure out a way to get paid for it!

And you know what? It works! Look at me: I get to interact with young adults who are finding their individual and collective voices *every day*!!! The pay I get for doing it is just icing on the cake!

Here's another suggestion: show *sincere* appreciation for every*one* and every*thing* around you. The ability to recognize and *consciously enjoy* your *many* everyday blessings is the *single most important* factor in enabling you to make a positive impact on the world around you. Maintain an "attitude of gratitude" and you'll *never* have an unfulfilling day.

And…never take even a *single* day for granted. Treasure *every one* of them.

Why? Well…last Sunday I attended the graduation of the oldest of my three children from Greely High School in Cumberland, where we live. An ordinary life event? Maybe, but one I appreciated more than most.

You see, while I was there I couldn't help thinking about my own father, a World War II vet who saved *every* spare cent he earned so *his* three children could get the opportunity to attend college after high school, which no one on *either side* of our family had ever done. But when his oldest child—me—was 16 years old, my dad learned the abdominal pain he had been experiencing wasn't indigestion; it was being caused by pancreatic cancer. **Ironically,** he never smoked, he never drank, and he didn't weigh any more than he had in the army…but *he* didn't live to see *any* of his kids finish high school. Be grateful for *every day*, because tomorrow is *never* guaranteed.

That's the big stuff. But my specialty is <u>small</u> stuff, so here are ten "Life Tips" you are free to use (or ignore) as you see fit.

1. Step outside your comfort zone. Donate blood, even if you're petrified of needles. Read a book every month. Climb a mountain. Move to another place for a while, too. You'll never fully appreciate your own hometown (for better *or* for worse) until you've actually *lived* somewhere else.
2. Learn to prepare your own food. That way you'll know *exactly* what you're eating, and *you'll* decide what's on the menu!
3. Think independently. Spend less time on social media. If you *really* want to socialize, interact regularly with other live human beings *face-to-face*! Try this: challenge yourself to avoid all electronic stimulus for the first hour of your day, and for the *last* one before you go to bed at night. If you can't do that, you need to re-order your priorities. Now.
4. Don't make promises you can't keep, because when you give your word, you've *got* to deliver on it. Your integrity is one of your most valuable assets, but **ironically,** *you can't buy it back.*
5. Do something nice for somebody else every day. Buy someone lunch. Pick up litter. Give a compliment. Volunteer.
6. Always have someone in your life who is under five years of age, and someone who is over 80 years old. Both can teach you things far more valuable than you've ever learned (or *will* ever learn) in a classroom.
7. If you see a face-up penny, pick it up. It's good luck. And if you see a face-down penny, pick *it* up, too. Find four more (face up *or* face down) and you can go get a nickel with 'em!
8. *Never* start a sentence with the phrase, "To be honest…" Because it will make people wonder—justifiably—just how genuine and sincere you've been with them the rest of the time.
9. **Ironically**, I don't *have* ten "Life Tips." I don't even have *nine* of 'em. To be honest…I don't have any more advice at all. You're going to have to learn the rest of life's secrets by trial and error. Which is, **ironically,** just what the rest of us are doing.

Oh, and here's how that "Attitude of Gratitude" works.

I'd like to express my *sincere* appreciation to *all* of you for coming here today, and for patiently listening to me. To the entire RSU 21 community, thanks for the everyday kindnesses you've treated me to over the past 17 years, and for the daily affirmations you and your children have been giving me throughout that time.

And here's today's final bit of **irony**, Class of 2019: if you've learned half the amount from the people who've raised and educated you (to this point) that we've learned from you, well, I'd say we've *all* done a pretty good job!

Congratulations to each one of you on reaching the first of what I expect will be many great achievements in your lives. Savor this day…*and* all the ones that follow.

Thank you. Mary - for reading this far!

:)

Acknowledgements

To acknowledge everyone who had something to do with this book becoming a reality would require a book of equal or greater length than this one. That said, the following people provided vital assistance; without them there would be no *Works in Progress.**

Carol Young meticulously proofread nearly every word, and she suggested needed changes clearly, completely, and with as much kindness as possible.

I could not ask for better friends, colleagues, role models, and supporters than **Josh Viola**, **Melissa Luetje**, and **Michael Laverriere**. And the same goes for my English Department colleagues and the entire staff at Kennebunk High School. Even the ones who had the nerve to be born after I graduated from college.

Were it not for the patience, creativity, encouragement and technological skills of **Jean Jackson** and **Lori Harley**, this book would not exist. Period.

Without **Mary Greely**, **Joseph Foster**, and **Susan Cressey**, I don't know where I'd be today. But it wouldn't be in Kennebunk, Maine, writing and encouraging others to do likewise.

Mary Couturier's drawings make this book better, and her existence makes the world better. She is the embodiment of why I'm optimistic about our planet's future.

The students of Kennebunk High School energize me every day I'm there. Anyone who's ever taken a class I've taught has added something to my life, so it's hard to single out just one person. However, since there's a specific name in each of the paragraphs above this one, I'll recognize **Alvaro Coto**. *El es el polo opuesto de un jackanapes.*

***Note:** the people (and groups of people) above are listed not in order of significance, but in inverse alphabetical order. And if you'd spent half your life waiting in literal or figurative lines waiting to be recognized because your last name comes near the end of the alphabet, you'd understand why.

•

Oh, and one very last thing to leave with you: I was once told that every human being dies twice. The first time is when their body's biological functions cease; the second (and final) death occurs the very last time someone mentions their name.

If that's true, Ed Sundt, Sally Reid-Haraske, David McConnell, Jean Maday, Will Fulford, Irene Danowski, Ted Damon, Rick Bruhn, and Mike Beveridge will live forever. Even though each of these incredibly kind and generous individuals is gone physically, I feel their positive influence every day. And as all nine of them would undoubtedly want, I do my best to share it liberally with others.

For the past twenty years **Andy Young**, a former picker of fruit, digger of irrigation ditches, landscaper (scaper of land?) radio announcer, dishwasher, shoe salesman, gutter cleaner, algebra tutor, and playground director, has been teaching English at Kennebunk High School. In his spare time he's been turning out essays for several different publications in Maine, a couple of which are, at this writing, still extant. He rises before dawn 360 days per calendar year, and on each of those mornings is consciously grateful for having the ability to do so. He and his three children reside in Cumberland, Maine.

Mary Couturier, creator of the illustrations found in *Works in Progress*, currently resides in Boston, Massachusetts. She is in her senior year undergrad at Suffolk University studying Brand Marketing. She spends her free time studying and playing around with new art techniques. Mary is a first generation college student and recipient of the Coca-Cola Northeast Scholarship Program. She has sent her last essay into the program. She hopes to continue with art, and with using her sense of creativity in her professional career. She is honored to be a part of this book, as Andy Young is one of her greatest role models in life.